HE MELE INOA NO AIKANAKA

A Name Chant in Honor of Aikanaka

E aua ia e Kama, e Kona Moku

Oh Kama, look, and observe thy lands,

Kona moku e Kama e aua ia

Oh thy lands oh, Kama, oh, retain them

Composed by Keaulumoku

Translated by Lili'uokalani

O ke Kama, Kama, Kama, i ka huli nuu

Thou child, child, child of the highest grade

O ke Kama, Kama, Kama, i ka Huliau

Thou child, child, child of the turning tide,

Hulihia ke au ka Papahonua o ka Moku

Overthrown are the foundations of the land

Hulihia Papio e ia ilalo ke alo

Overthrown, and with its face downward

E Uli—e, Aui—ia, Hulihia i Munaake—le

Oh! thou Uli, look, and observe—overthrown is Manuakele

Hulihia i ka Uunukaokoa, a Ku

Overturned on the coral rocks of Ku

Ka maka o Ku, ka Aha o Makiilohelohe

For the eyes of Ku, and the cord of Makiilohelohe

Ka Aha nana i hiki o Hulahula

There the cords that bound Hulahula

Ua kalakala ia Ua wekewekea

Are loosened and opened

Ua hemo ku la ka piko o ka aina

Thus will the centre of the land be moved

Ua kala Kaalihi Pohakuku

For the stone weights of the Bonito nets

Me ka upena Aku Oihuaniani

And the Bonito net of Ihuaniani

Me ka Ulu Oini, Olaa, O Keawe

With the stick of Uini, and Laa and Keawe

O ka Manu Aiakualaahia

And the bird that ate the sacred Bonito

Keiki ehu Kama ehu a Kanaloa.

The golden-haired child of Kama [Maui] from Kanaloa.

Nā Mamo

HAWAIIAN PEOPLE TODAY

⊚

Jay Hartwell

Photographs by Anne K. Landgraf

'Ai Pōhaku Press
Honolulu

*Page iv: Newborn kalo leaves quiver
in a cooling breeze in Hanalei, the
Kaua'i district where most of the
kalo in Hawai'i is grown.*

Published by 'Ai Pōhaku Press
For information on how to obtain
copies of this book, please contact:
  'Ai Pōhaku Press
  c/o Native Books
  P.O. Box 37095
  Honolulu, Hawai'i 96837-0095
  808-845-8949 or 1-800-887-7751

ISBN 1-883528-04-6
Library of Congress Catalog
Card No. 95-083320
Printed in the United States of America

*Designed and produced by
Barbara Pope Book Design*

Contents

FOR HAWAI'I

In memory of
Pierre L. Bowman
Alvin 'Ainoa Kaiaokamalie
Louis Adam Lopez, Jr.

Introduction

F or fifteen hundred years the Hawaiian people perpetuated life, with help from the land, sea, and sky. Even after the first European explorers arrived in the Islands, in 1778, introducing diseases and customs that began to unravel the Hawaiian culture, most islanders saw no reason to heed the words of the prophet Keaulumoku, who forewarned that his people would be overwhelmed by foreigners. In his chant "He Mele Inoa No Aikanaka," Keaulumoku urged the newborn chief Aikanaka to hold on to his lands and culture during the coming apocalypse.

Little more than a century after the explorers' arrival, the fears of Keaulumoku were realized. Foreign diseases had killed most of the Hawaiian population in the archipelago; foreign ideas had gutted the Hawaiian religious and political systems; and foreign commerce had transformed abundant, small farms into vast sugar and pineapple plantations owned by Caucasians. In 1893, a few foreign men used the threat of armed force to overthrow the Hawaiian monarchy, creating an oligarchy and eventually gaining U.S. annexation. In the following decades, newcomers helped commercialize the remains of the Hawaiian culture and landscape, resulting in millions of tourists and thousands of new residents being lured to the Islands each year.

Similar histories can be heard around the globe, in country after country where cultures have been absorbed as a result of changes wrought by newcomers. In modern Hawai'i, few visitors or residents think about what the Hawaiians have lost and why so many of them are so angry. Nor do they understand the pride of many Hawaiian people—pride in the roots of their culture, which goes deeper than the orchid lei tossed around a vacationer's neck.

Joe Chang, a Hawaiian professor of English, described the situation in an essay for *Ke Kia'i: The Guardian,* a publication of the Native Hawaiian Advisory Council:

There is so much Hawaiian decor and treatment [in the Islands] that few people will stop to think that they really don't know very many Hawaiians. Those they know, they know in the most superficial of ways, or they only know those who have passed over into the mainstream culture, having left behind that which was truly Hawaiian. I have a hunch that most local people care in an abstract way about preserving Hawai'i and its ancient culture. But because they really don't know Hawaiian people as Hawaiians, they don't appreciate the depths of pain and anger that this generation of Hawaiians is experiencing. Because they themselves are fairly comfortable with the status quo, and because they think of themselves as kama'āina [Hawai'i born], they can't understand the Hawaiian movement—the restlessness of the Hawaiian spirit.

At places unknown to visitors and many residents—Kē'ē, Hālawa, Kā'ana, Hakioawa, Honokahua, Pu'u Koholā, Wao Kele o Puna—Hawaiians from time to time gather to chant, dance, and sing. Elsewhere, they plead, protest, and sue with the hope of persuading bureaucrats, politicians, and developers to acknowledge their culture and their claim on the land.

Claims for recognition persist one hundred years after the armed usurpation of the Hawaiian Kingdom, which was followed in five years by American annexation. Hawaiian expressions of anger, pride, or cultural awareness surprise many tourists and disturb non-Hawaiian residents accustomed to silence or smiles from the native population. When indignation and anger stand alongside aloha and humility, sympathies disappear. Alienation will increase unless more people understand the past and the barriers between the kānaka maoli (native Hawaiians) of today and the traditions that nourished their ancestors for generations.

In an interview published in *MidWeek,* an O'ahu newspaper, hula master Frank Kawaikapuokalani Hewett called on all non-Hawaiians to support native Hawaiians as they seek justice and the preservation of their heritage. "We're not angry at non-Hawaiians," he said. "We're angry at the injustice that was done [to us]. . . . If you are not aware of the way in which the United States acquired Hawai'i, go out and educate yourself."

For me, that education came late in life. I went to high school in Kailua, but I did not become curious about my island home until I returned to O'ahu after college and graduate studies. As a reporter for Honolulu's morning newspaper, I had opportunities to meet Hawaiians and report on their efforts to perpetuate their culture. Those stories led to encounters with other Hawaiians, people whose lives might be easier if they used their energy and intelligence to become "successful" in the modern American understanding of the word. Instead, many choose a lifestyle that combines the foreign and native cultures—paying off the mortgages owed to one as they strengthen the foundations of the other.

These ambitious people have established schools where they are reviving the Hawaiian language; they train navigators, build canoes modeled on ancient designs, and embark on voyages to confirm the old stories about Polynesians who traversed the Pacific generations ago using only their knowledge of sea, wind, and stars; and they have lobbied successfully for millions in federal and state funding for programs to promote Hawaiian health, education, arts, self-sufficiency, and nationhood.

I left my job at the newspaper to share some of their stories in this book, a collection of profiles about Hawaiian people holding on to their heritage today. During my research, I encountered some Hawaiians who believe their stories should not be shared and a few who do not want to be written about in "another haole's book." Outsiders often exploit and misrepresent Hawaiians and their culture to make money or reputations for themselves; that is not my intent.

My newspaper work opened doors to modern Hawaiian life, and I want to open some of those doors for others. These glimpses of contemporary Hawaiians may help readers understand how the native culture is being perpetuated. Perhaps after reading them, you will be inspired to learn more.

From the start, I intended to have Hawaiians participate in this project—it would not be solely from the perspective of an outsider looking in. Anne Kapulani Landgraf provided the photographs, and other Hawaiians contributed songs and chants. All the people I interviewed read their respective sections before publication and made changes to ensure accuracy and privacy. This is their work as much as mine, and any profits from it will be shared with them.

Although many of them live on Oʻahu, the most urbanized of the Hawaiian Islands, I intentionally chose these Hawaiians because their dedication to living the culture is noteworthy. They are optimistic, independent, hard-working people—role models for all of us. In sharing their stories and their history, I have tried to follow the advice of Mary Kawena Pukui, whose contributions to modern Hawaiian scholarship are unmatched. Mrs. Pukui used to say, "Do not look back on the past with scorn and criticism, look back with understanding and appreciation."

This is a book about modern Hawaiians—their roots and their evolving culture. I hope these portraits will draw you into the true life of Hawaiʻi.

WAILUPE, OʻAHU
1996

KUMULIPO *Ka Wa Akahi*

Origin   The First Age

O ke au i kahuli wela ka honua

When space turned around, the earth heated

O ke au i kahuli lole ka lani

When space turned over, the sky reversed

O ke au i kuka'iaka ka la

When the sun appeared standing in shadows

E ho'omalamalama i ka malama

To cause light to make bright the moon

O ke au o Makali'i ka po

When the Pleiades are small eyes in the night

O ka walewale ho'okumu honua ia

From the source in the slime was the earth formed

O ke kumu o ka lipo, i lipo ai

From the source in the dark was darkness formed

O ke kumu o ka Po, i po ai

From the source in the night was night formed

O ka lipolipo, o ka lipolipo

From the depths of the darkness, darkness so deep

O ka lipo o ka la, o ka lipo o ka po

Darkness of day, darkness of night

Po wale ho'i

Of night alone

Hanau ka po

Did night give birth

Hanau Kumulipo i ka po, he kane

Born was Kumulipo in the night, a male

Hanau Po'ele i ka po, he wahine

Born was Pō'ele in the night, a female

*Translated by
Rubellite Kawena
Kinney Johnson*

1 CLARENCE ELI KAONA

Mahi'ai & Farming

Ten days from harvest, Clarence's kalo corms will be in Honolulu, transformed into poi.

Preceding page: Nāmolokama Mountain catches rain that flows down to water five acres of terraces where Clarence Kaona carries on his family's kalo farming traditions. The skiff holds buckets of harvested kalo and the huli, cut-off stalks, that Clarence will replant.

S pace was dark when the cosmos first rubbed against Earth and warmed the planet. When the ocean floor became hot enough to ignite life, silent waters carried the procreative force of Kumulipo, the first male, and Pō'ele, the first female. Coral was born, then the grub that digs through land, then starfish, sea urchins, limpets, and their children. These were followed by the creation of fish and forests, insects, birds, and pigs. Much later, the great-grandparents of the human race came forth: Sky-Father Wākea and Earth-Mother Papa.

Wākea and Papa created a heavenly daughter, Ho'ohōkūkalani, whose beauty aroused her father's passion. One night, father and daughter became one. Ho'ohōkūkalani delivered a stillborn baby, and from the infant's grave a kalo (taro) plant sprouted. Wākea called the plant Hāloa-naka, for its long, quivering leaves. Later, father and daughter produced a boy, naming him Hāloa in honor of the starch, the kalo, that nourished him as he grew into a man.

In the following centuries, Hawaiians cultivated kalo in gardens large and small; the kalo, in turn, sustained their families. They knew kalo as their ancestor Hāloa, his heart-shaped leaves and genealogy entwined with their cosmos, their land, their gods, their chiefs, and themselves.

Today, as the evening sky deepens into twilight across the Hawaiian Islands, thousands of visitors sit down to sample a "Hawaiian" lū'au. They heap pork, chicken, and pineapple onto their plates, but they cringe at the thimble-sized cups of steamed, mashed kalo, called poi, likening it to wallpaper paste. Entertainers and waiters joke about the taste of poi, and diners by the hundreds toss it into the trash, missing out on the fundamental pleasure of eating poi with traditional Hawaiian foods such as smoked fish and steamed pig.

The purple-gray starch was once the staple food of Hawai'i, but these days only a few plastic bags of poi can be found in grocery stores here and there. The scanty supply dwindles even more in late spring and summer, just when traditional reunion, graduation, and wedding celebrations place it in high demand. And poi is expensive for most Hawaiians—a pound of poi costs the same as five pounds of imported potatoes.

Sixty percent of all island poi kalo is grown in the irrigated terraces, or lo'i, of Hanalei, Kaua'i. Six days a week, kalo farmer Clarence Eli Kaona wades through his muddy lo'i, caring for the kalo by hand, knee-deep in waters flowing down from the green mountain behind him. The scene defines a timeless tranquility, withstanding even the helicopters buzzing overhead on their way to show tourists the Nāpali coast.

Watching Clarence at work, it is difficult to imagine a time when he, kalo, and Hanalei were ever separated. But the peacefulness of Hanalei, like that of all Hawai'i, has repeatedly been disrupted. Events long past dislodged most native Hawaiians from their kalo patches in Hanalei, and only a few ever returned. Clarence Eli Kaona is one of them.

Clarence was seven years old when his family settled in Hanalei, driven from their house at nearby 'Anini by devastating tidal waves in 1946. The tsunami inundated the Kaona property, and as the wave receded, it carried away the family's chickens, pigs, and ducks. The family bolted to safety just ahead of a second wave, which destroyed their house and a quarter-acre kalo garden. The family gave up their lease on the narrow coastal strip in 'Anini and moved to Hanalei, where Clarence's father, David, could afford to buy a plot of land. Red Cross relief funds provided lumber for him to build a house.

Before the family moved, Clarence's grandfather had raised kalo in the back of Hanalei Valley. Clarence's father began growing kalo there during his free time from work at the county fire station. Later, David moved to patches closer to town, behind the Wai'oli Hui'ia Church and Mission House. He did not use machines, pesticides, or fertilizer on his kalo crop, and it grew to be the largest in Wai'oli. Honolulu Poi Company bought much of the harvest, and the proceeds helped feed his family and send most of the children to college. David's best kalo went into burlap sacks for shipment to Honolulu; he kept the rest for family and friends.

David Kaona at first made poi the traditional way—he boiled the kalo tubers and mashed them by hand into thick globs of poi, using a stone poi pounder and mango-wood plank. But after the tidal wave carried away the family's pounding board, David and his father mechanized the grinding process with a modified Model A engine and transmission. After school and on Saturdays, while other kids sneaked smokes or played ball, David's children helped plant and harvest kalo.

Clarence, a burly teenager, graduated from Kapa'a High School in 1956, but he wasn't ready to settle down in Hanalei. "I figured I might as well venture out a little bit. . . . I wanted to get away for a while." He did a two-year stint in the Navy, then attended Church College (now Brigham Young

University–Hawai'i) on O'ahu for two years. After a three-year Mormon mission to Taiwan, he once again returned to Hawai'i, and married a local girl in 1963. They moved to San Francisco, and in the space of a few years Clarence fathered two children, became a $40,000-a-year warehouse foreman, and bought a house. Eventually, his marriage ended and he remarried.

At home in Hanalei, Clarence's father retired from the Fire Department in 1959 and thereafter spent his days in the kalo patches. He grew old tending the kalo year after year. A son-in-law helped him, but David's own children had other interests. Whenever Clarence went home for vacations, he worked side by side in the muddy kalo patches with his father. "I liked to work, and helping him was something that I wanted to do." After a day's work, father and son would rest beside the lo'i, watching the big kalo leaves nod and quiver in the breeze. Sometimes, after a long silence, David would ask his son, "Can you hear the taro growing?" Even though he couldn't, Clarence promised his father that he would care for the kalo after David passed away.

David Kaona died in 1985, and Clarence knew it was time to leave the mainland and return home. "If I had not made that promise, I don't think I would have come back real soon. But when you love your dad, you do anything." His father's death coincided with the collapse of Clarence's second marriage. He sold his house, took early retirement, and moved back to Hanalei with one teenage son and a new wife, Dawn.

Clarence kept his promise to his father and began reviving the family kalo patches. He and Dawn planned to live off the income from kalo, and his weekends would be free for him to take his 30/30 carbine into the mountain forest to hunt wild pigs. Clarence set to work clearing weeds that had sprung up throughout the family's eleven kalo patches. Altogether, the patches covered about five acres of land, either leased or owned with other families. Clarence's brother-in-law didn't have time for kalo any more; he worked as a fire fighter and grew flowers for his wife's floral shop. When Dawn gave birth to twins, Clarence began driving school buses to bring in some extra money, which still left the middle of the day free for farming.

At 6:00 A.M., hours before the tourist rental cars started to clog the main road in Hanalei, Clarence sat behind the wheel of a Chevrolet Blue Bird school bus, negotiating the narrow, dark road that strings together the villages along the north shore of Kaua'i—Hanalei, Wainiha, and Hā'ena. The noisy energy of the children ricocheted inside the bus as it rolled along the winding back roads.

"Your mom's a hippie," one child yelled.

"No she's not!" another shouted back.

Hāʻena, a village dating from the remote past, sits at the end of the coastal highway beneath the plunging Nāpali cliffs; it became a magnet for hippies in the late 1960s. They built tree houses and communes and became squatters on the beaches until the state forced most of them out in the mid-1970s. Some of them stayed on, paid rent, and started families. Their businesses gave them real property and a claim to Hanalei's future. As more outsiders moved in, Hanalei and the rest of the north shore evolved from a predominantly agricultural community to one that mixed locals with retirees, surfers, urban escapees, and tourism-oriented entrepreneurs.

Like the traders, whalers, and missionaries who had come to Hawaiʻi generations earlier, these newcomers, too, chipped away at established Hawaiian customs. Their notion of private property, for example, clashed with the communal orientation of longtime residents. During summer vacation, when Clarence worked transporting tourists, some of the new arrivals complained when he backed his bus into their driveways to turn around, and he was forced to alter his route.

"Hawaiians used to invite you into their house," Clarence said, "but now people say 'Don't back in.' Only people complaining are the haoles. I'm not saying all of them. But the idea I get is wherever they buy land, they don't want you to cross their land. That's where we played when I was a kid. That was our ʻāina. Makes your blood boil once in a while."

The water irrigating Clarence's kalo cools his temper as it flows through the patches at Waiʻoli. He steps into the water barefoot, wearing shorts, a loose T-shirt over his barrel chest, and a jacket in case the clouds drop rain—as they often do in Hanalei. His mother, Miriam, sometimes joins him during the weekly harvest. She is originally from Niʻihau, a small, privately owned island fifteen miles from Kauaʻi, and like the native people who live there, she speaks Hawaiian fluently. She wears gloves, a hat, cutoff shorts, a long-sleeved shirt, and Japanese sock-shoes known as tabi—unassuming work clothes that mask an endurance and strength remarkable for a woman in her seventies.

Each harvested kalo plant provides the stalk to generate a new plant, so kalo planting is preceded by kalo harvesting. Clarence's harvesting technique differs from terrace to terrace, depending on the water level. Usually, he pulls an aluminum skiff loaded with plastic buckets and tubs behind him across the water. Using a long galvanized pipe, he prepares a six-foot-wide swath in the loʻi to be harvested. First, he shoves the pipe through the water and into the mud to loosen the precious kalo tubers, or corms, which usually grow to soft-ball size or bigger. Then he leans over and pulls up each plant, shakes the mud off the corm, and stacks them in the water behind him.

His mother follows with a knife, trimming off the floppy leaf tops and slic-ing off the stalk one-half inch below the top of the corm. She puts the stalks, called huli, in the skiff for replanting later and drops the trimmed kalo corms into the buckets. After harvesting a section, Clarence gathers the floating weeds and debris and tosses the pile into a plastic tub for stacking on the banks. Once he and his mother have filled all the buckets with kalo corms, Clarence pushes the loaded skiff back to the bank, where the kalo is packed into burlap sacks, which will each weigh eighty pounds when full. In 1996, a bag was worth about $36, or forty-five cents a pound.

Clarence gets his kalo to market by trucking the bulging kalo sacks in a trail-er from the loʻi to a nearby Honolulu Poi Company warehouse in Hanalei. At the warehouse, he piles the sacks onto pallets for twice-a-week deliveries to Nāwiliwili Harbor, on the southeast coast of Kauaʻi. There the island's kalo harvest is loaded onto barges and towed to Honolulu. It will arrive in the cap-ital a week to ten days after leaving the loʻi.

The Honolulu Poi Company factory on Oʻahu pressure-cooks the kalo. After boiling it, workers peel the skin off by hand. Then a machine grinds the cooked purple corms and strains the mash into poi. Packed into polyethylene bags, the poi will be in Honolulu markets the next morning: $2.99 a pound.

Clarence and his mother normally harvest fifteen bags of kalo in a morning. They work in simple rhythms—a human counterpoint to the neat rows of heart-shaped leaves undulating in the breeze. Mud sucks at their legs as they move through the rippling water; the sun warms their muscles, which are kept strong with each push into the earth and every pull from it. Try to duplicate their bent aspect, the nonstop work pace—any romantic farmer-in-the-land-scape notion is quickly dispelled. Clarence and Miriam crouch in a posture doing a task that the world's best agronomists have been unable to duplicate with machines. For hours they press, yank, stack, weed, and shove, without wasted motion.

"All the time, aches and pains," Clarence said later. "Sometimes you don't do it right, your back hurts, your legs, your arms. . . . Taro farming is a very hard job, but I enjoy doing it. It's a challenge every year to see what kind of crop you gonna get, and I'm my own boss. I can work when I want, and when I don't want to work, I don't.

"But if you don't work, you can't produce. Right now I got my hands pret-ty full with five acres. That's about as much as I can handle. I'm doing mostly all the work. When it's time to harvest, then I have my mom, and sometimes my brother comes over and helps me. . . . I don't know—in twenty years you might not see any more Hawaiian taro farmers."

The following day, Clarence plants the shorn huli stalks. To keep the newly planted huli from floating away, he first levels and compacts the mud with a weighted plastic pipe fifteen feet long and six inches wide. After dragging the pipe across the patch, he pushes each huli into the firm mud. Soon the newly planted patch will bristle with the next generation of kalo, lined up in neat rows. During the next ten to fifteen months, while the kalo is growing, Clarence will drain the patch four different times, fertilize it, and flood it again. A month before harvest he will drain it one more time to kill the roots, making the corms easier to pull. When necessary, he sprays the soft banks with Roundup herbicide to control invading grass, and he regularly mows the firmer banks that divide the lo'i into green-edged pools.

Abundant rain and a protected bay made the windward district of Hanalei ideal for the first Hawaiian fishermen and kalo farmers. Their families probably moved to the area in the seventh century, and archaeologists believe Hanalei at one time supported tens of thousands of Hawaiians. These people worked together to engineer and maintain intricate networks of ditches for irrigating several hundred acres of lo'i kalo. The concept behind the Hawaiian system was simple—diverted stream water flowed down from one terrace to another and on to another, before rejoining the stream below. At the time, the engineering made this the most productive agricultural method developed anywhere in the Pacific.

To prepare a new lo'i for kalo, the farmer of old invited his neighbors to a party where together they helped compact the mud. Villagers stomped on the mud until it was firm enough for planting. Then they celebrated with a feast. Historians also say the lo'i were more than garden terraces to those Hawaiians. Their health and that of the kalo depended on how well they balanced the elements in their lives, both natural and fabricated, including those in and around the lo'i. The farmer made sure the water flowed uninterrupted through his patches and on to his neighbor's. He planted the banks of his terraces with more food, including banana and sugarcane. He grew ti there as well, to ensure a supply of leaves for making rain capes, thatch, sandals, wrappings for cooking, and whistles for children. Inside the flooded terraces, he raised fish, which fertilized the kalo as they grew.

The Hawaiians' intimate relationship with the land began to deteriorate soon after the arrival of British explorer Captain James Cook, who first landed at Waimea, Kaua'i, in January 1778. Foreigners introduced venereal diseases to the native population—then tuberculosis, whooping cough, and smallpox—and Hawaiians died by the thousands. The haole also introduced guns, liquor, tobacco, and, equally threatening, new ideas. Hawaiians watched as the haole violated the strict prohibitions (kapu) that had controlled their society for generations; native people began to question and then to ignore the laws.

Newcomers affected the landscape, too. The Chinese prized 'iliahi, sandalwood, and the abundant stands of it in Hawaiian forests quickly succumbed to the demands of traders who wanted the fragrant wood as barter for Asian silks and porcelains. Hawai'i ali'i (chiefs) capitalized on the demand, ordering commoners into the mountains to cut 'iliahi. Kalo terraces were neglected, and villagers converted more and more kalo patches to cultivation of other crops when chiefs demanded foods they could sell to visiting ships. The ship captains did not want kalo; it spoiled too quickly.

Hanalei Valley, isolated on the remote north coast of Kaua'i, was spared much of this turbulence. Still, roughly fifty ships a year stopped at Kaua'i between 1830 and 1850, and inevitably, some foreigners decided to stay on the island. As early as 1831, the island's governor approved a lease for an upland cattle ranch in Hanalei. Haole immigrants were soon using Hawaiian labor to establish sugar, silk, and coffee plantations in the nutrient-rich lowlands along the Hanalei River. The plantation owners diverted native shares of water for their own use and evicted Hawaiian kalo farmers to make room for other crops.

Over time, the plantations were responsible for consuming tremendous amounts of water. There is no documentation of the exact number of streams that had dried up by the early twentieth century or the number of Hawaiian kalo farmers who had lost their water. Many Hawaiian farmers had moved their families from rural areas to what they hoped would be an easier life in the towns. The elaborate system of water ditches and lo'i, abandoned and neglected, fell into decay, and the towns became ghettos for impoverished, landless natives.

Earlier dispossession of many kalo farmers came about in 1848 when, on the advice of his haole advisors, King Kamehameha III established the first private property ownership through a land-tenure reform act called the Māhele. The Māhele gave commoners the chance to register their farms and homelands, but few of them understood the importance of registration, nor did most of them have money to pay the surveying fee and annual tax. Commoners recorded fewer than thirty thousand acres; non-Hawaiians took more than a million.

By 1850, disease had reduced the Hawaiian population by at least two-thirds to 84,000, and expanding urban economies were hiring away many of the rural survivors. The plantations began to look overseas for cheap labor. Landowners imported thousands of Chinese contract laborers, then tens of thousands of Japanese. The staple food of the Asians was rice, and soon the kalo terraces of Hanalei were transformed into rice paddies that produced so much grain there was a surplus to export to California. With a generosity that would come back to haunt them, in the 1930s farmers in Hanalei shared their rice seeds with California farmers. A decade later, California was growing far more rice than Hanalei, and the farmers of Kaua'i, unable to compete, once again planted kalo.

When Clarence Kaona returned to Hawai'i with his wife and teenage son, most of the kalo farmers in Hanalei were Japanese. Today, like Clarence, they wonder who will take over when they are gone. Many of them are in their seventies, and although the price of kalo has risen due to demand, most of their children do not want to get their hands muddy. Clarence's oldest son was raised on the mainland; he tried kalo farming and stuck with it for two months. When the farmers share stories, they remember the Hawaiian farmers of old and their prowess in the kalo patch. And they, too, lament how Hanalei has changed.

"John Ho'okano of Kalalau used to grow such a big taro, he could only carry out four at a time," recalled one Hanalei old-timer, whose years of kalo labor have kept his body trim and strong. "Never used to fertilize. All weeds were stuck in mud. All leaves and tops used as fertilizer. . . . Doesn't spoil as fast as fertilized taro. Today's farmer looking for dollars, so fertilize to get big taro, but doesn't necessarily mean good poi.

"Farmers get too much hassle from people; it's not funny. Can't even let water back into the river from the patch. People complain fertilizer washing back into river. Pretty soon we have to quit. Why? Too much hassle. EPA jumps on us for herbicide; how spray; how drift. Gotta wear hat, glove, mask, breather, pants, boots. Have to wear protective clothing to protect yourself from mist and spray. You try wear all that clothing and do it."

These Hanalei farmers have spent their lives in the kalo patches and know the exhaustion that comes with their chosen lifestyle. But as much as the old-timers grouse about their work, there is genuine melancholy in their voices when they consider the future.

"We're losing land 'cause it getting swamp," one said, "'cause farmers won't cooperate to clear drainage ditches. Old days, thirty to forty in a group would spend one day each month cleaning ditch. If don't go up every month, pebbles fill up ditch. Gets hard like concrete. Irrigation system all screwed up.

"Farmers get the short end no matter how you look at it. Middleman making all the money and no hassle. You don't find too many rich farmers. . . . My land more valuable for building homes than taro field. Everybody look for land. They don't care price. If I sell my land, I don't have to work hard."

Clarence Kaona's five acres were part of the 310 kalo-producing acres statewide that yielded about four million pounds of poi kalo in 1994. Another 180 acres yielded about two million pounds of "Chinese" dryland kalo, which is boiled like potatoes or sliced and fried into snack chips. When David Kaona moved his family to Hanalei in 1946, kalo farmers across the state cultivated a thousand acres, and Hawai'i didn't import any kalo. Fifty years later, the state imports about 700,000 pounds of fresh kalo a year from American and Western Samoa, Fiji, and the Cook Islands.

Ancient Hawaiians had 150 names for eighty different varieties of kalo. Today, farmers and poi processors favor the lehua variety, which has the consistent quality, color, and taste expected by consumers. But the lehua variety

Clarence and his mother, Miriam, begin a new kalo crop by planting stalks cut from the previous day's harvest. They push the huli into compacted mud, guided by strings stretched from bank to bank. After two thousand years, kalo farming is still mainly back-bent-over labor.

requires lots of cold water to grow, and the root must be harvested in mud, a manual labor no one has figured out how to mechanize. Some wetland farmers switch to growing dryland kalo because it is easier to handle and commands high prices on the U.S. mainland.

"Taro was the staple for the Hawaiians, but the modern age hasn't rediscovered it," said Ernest Tottori, president of Honolulu Poi Company and grandson of the firm's founder. "I'm hoping and praying that one day poi will be rediscovered. Lot of people know about it, but supply has been the biggest problem. There is a different type of generation [now], more educated, and if we can educate them with this product, there's a big future market for it. The new generation has a chance."

Tottori is not alone with this dream. Jim Hollyer, with red hair and sunburned skin that looks out of place in the kalo fields, sees real potential for kalo. A former Peace Corps worker, Hollyer is the point man for kalo at the Department of Agricultural and Resource Economics at the University of Hawai'i. He and his colleagues want to expand the statewide crop beyond the six million pounds of dry and wet varieties marketed in 1995.

Hollyer believes Hawai'i is capable of producing enough kalo to satisfy demand for the entire United States. He has discovered that the potential market for all varieties of Hawai'i kalo exceeds the forty-seven million pounds that the United States imports annually, mostly from the Dominican Republic, Costa Rica, Jamaica, and Western Samoa. He is trying to develop ways to help farmers manage their businesses and promote the crop. And he envisions new uses for kalo, particularly marketing it nationally as a nutritious, hypoallergenic food with more iron, calories, and vitamins B and C than rice.

Millions of people in the United States suffer from food allergies, and Hollyer persuaded a Hawai'i company, C. Brewer, to try growing a white variety of kalo that could be processed into flour and used in allergen-free foods. If the five-acre experiment succeeds, C. Brewer has the capability to expand to meet the market, Hollyer reasoned, because the company already manages large agricultural plantations and knows how to keep costs down. "We are not messing with the existing poi industry. We are trying to create a whole new product line based on a variety of taro that hasn't been grown commercially."

The few Hawaiians willing to follow in their ancestors' muddy footsteps find they can hardly afford to try it. More than a decade ago, experts estimated a full-time kalo farmer needed twelve acres to produce a livable income, along with capitalization of about $35,000 for startup costs and equipment. And this did not include the cost of land, which has skyrocketed in recent

With muck between his toes and under his nails, Clarence pulls up a kalo corm loosened from the mud by an ʻōʻō, a Hawaiian digging stick. After he tears off the corm's hair-like roots, Clarence sorts the kalo by size. Then he weeds the loʻi section, tossing the debris onto the banks to decompose.

years, or housing and food. There would be no income for two years, but after four good years, the experts predicted, a farmer and his family could live off the income—provided there were no problems with water supply, aphid infestations, plagues of corm-eating snails, or the people who steal kalo leaves for lūʻau.

Water supply is a major frustration for kalo farmers. For generations, owners of the large plantations used water as if it were their own, siphoning public streams to irrigate their pineapple and sugarcane fields. In the 1920s, Lihue Plantation tunneled one mile through the Makaleha Mountains and began diverting as much as thirty million gallons of water a day from the Hanalei watershed to irrigate sugarcane fields in Wailua on the east side of Kauaʻi. On the other Hawaiian Islands, housing, resorts, and golf courses have claimed much of the water.

"Some Hawaiians living in Hāna, on Maui, commute four to five hours a day to jobs at hotels in Kapalua and Lahaina," observed island attorney Williamson B. C. Chang. "If taro cultivation and diversified farming were commercially feasible, many would rather be farming their own lands and living near their families."

In a memo to U.S. congressional staff members investigating Hawaiian water rights, Chang wrote:

> *Without water, land is valueless. If Hawaiians do not claim their rightful share of water, others—developers, cities, golf course owners—will claim and use these waters. State and county planners have little inclination to support a rural Hawaiian life-style in their plans. The waters that are at stake in these legal contests will either support taro farms or resort developments. Given the vast difference in the money at stake for interested parties, no one in the private sector is encouraging or assisting Hawaiians in asserting their valid claims to water. . . . Hawaiians are simply not aware of their rights, nor adequately represented.*

In 1973, the Hawai'i Supreme Court took a major step when it ruled that the state owned all waters as trustee for the people, and kalo farmers had legal rights to water in streams next to their terraces. State legislators later adopted a code allowing water users to register their water use and protect themselves.

Clarence drags a weighted plastic pipe across the lo'i to smooth out small craters left in the mud after harvesting. Weeds accumulated from previous harvests gradually build up the surrounding banks. A small gate in the bank allows water to drain into an adjacent lo'i.

Anxious that the state's registration effort would overlook small-quantity water users, Chang and fellow Hawaiian attorney Elizabeth Pa Martin formed the Native Hawaiian Advisory Council to help register kalo growers like Clarence Kaona. Law students volunteered to visit Clarence and other farmers to inform them of the new code. Without such outreach, Martin and Chang feared a double loss—Hawaiians with existing farms might lose the water they already depended on, and farmers who wanted to establish new loʻi or restore old ones might not have water made available to them.

Close to Clarence Kaona's farm, at Waipā, the Hawaiian Farmers of Hanalei group is trying to revive a complex of abandoned kalo terraces. Even more rain falls in Waipā than in Hanalei, and over the years the neglected Waipā terraces had turned into bogs. After four years of negotiations with the landowner, Bishop Estate, the group secured a lease for a 1,600-acre property extending from the mountains all the way down to Hanalei Bay. Hawaiians call this kind of district an ahupuaʻa. Before Western contact, ahupuaʻa provided complete sustenance for the Hawaiian people, from kalo and other upland crops to fish and seaweed from the ocean.

The Hawaiians at Waipā envision the ancient ahupuaʻa restored. They grow kalo and native medicinal plants, and fish Hanalei Bay with canoes. The group hopes that one day the federal and state governments will return lands taken from the Kingdom of Hawaiʻi, and people will be able to see at Waipā a Hawaiian model for developing a subsistence-style economy.

To survive, the Waipā farmers have to rely on hard work and ingenuity. They established a tropical plant nursery to qualify for a government agricultural loan. The loan allowed them to purchase equipment to grow and harvest poi kalo and exotic flower crops such as torch ginger and bird of paradise. Profits from the exotics also help subsidize seminars, including a six-week kalo production course developed with Kauaʻi Community College. It teaches students every aspect of kalo production—how to prepare the land and then how to plant, fertilize, cultivate, and harvest.

But the Hawaiian farmers at Waipā, and those who established a kalo growers association for West Maui and Molokaʻi, encounter the same problems that confront Clarence Kaona and other Hanalei farmers. Many people dream about farming kalo, but only a handful have the discipline and strength to continue the hard work day after day; the knowledge to cope with buyers, competitive crops, fluctuations in the kalo market, and the labyrinth of federal grants; the willingness to cooperate with other farmers, landowners, or wholesalers, whom they may distrust or not like; and the patience to rebuild after bugs, floods, mistakes, or hurricanes damage their crops.

When Hurricane ʻIniki ripped up Kauaʻi in 1992, it destroyed Clarence's house and his mother's. Wind and rain stunted the kalo crop, and Clarence, like other Kauaʻi farmers, had to harvest prematurely. The housing shortage forced the Kaonas into an expensive Princeville condominium, and after several weeks their federal assistance ran out. "ʻIniki made it a little bit rough for us because we don't have a place [of our own] to stay. We just got to hang on and hope there is something better."

For Clarence, hope, hard work, and hanging on are the prerequisites to surviving as a kalo farmer. "It's a good thing that they are doing, trying to get the Hawaiians back into farming taro. But if you weren't raised with your parents in the taro field, it's not very easy to do it. It's hard work. From my experience, you have to be raised in the taro field to like taro farming."

In Hanalei, Miriam Kaona washes the small, leftover kalo in an irrigation ditch that flows beside a crumbling shack—the family's kalo-processing headquarters. Patiently, she pours water and the cleaned kalo into a 55-gallon drum that rests on two I-beams straddling a pit beneath the eaves of the shack. She stuffs burlap sacks on top of the kalo and covers the drum with a sheet of corrugated steel. Underneath the drum she builds a fire with scraps of tar paper and salvaged lumber. An oil-soaked newspaper ignites the fire, and the kalo is left to boil for two hours. Periodically, Miriam checks the fire, then steps back to escape the smoke. "I don't know who's going to do this after I'm gone," she said.

Later, Miriam peels the kalo and grinds it twice with the Model A contraption fashioned by her husband fifty years ago. On the third and final grind, she adds fresh water from home to thin the poi. "Our friends always say we make the best poi," Clarence said. "They know the difference between the poi we make and the poi you get in the store."

While Miriam drips water into the Model A grinder, Clarence finishes mowing the banks of his loʻi. Behind him, the green mountain glistens after an evening rain. "Sometimes I come out here just to wind down," he said, after parking the mower. "I bring my two kids up here and they run around. I hope one of them will take over, but I don't know. Wife says she'll probably move back to the mainland after I die. Her family all living up there. Like I told you, taro patch is kind of hard life."

KĀHEA O KEALE

The Call of the Surf

E hoʻolohe, e ka poʻe ala,

Listen, all you who are awake,

ʻAʻohe wau i hiamoe,

For I do not sleep,

Akā, ua hiamoe ka nui lehulehu,

Though the multitude sleep,

ʻAipaha, ua ala au,

Yet, I am awake,

E hoʻolohe, ua pīhoihoi au,

Listen, for I am restless,

Hōʻūna koʻu leo i ka hoʻolaha,

I send my voice to all,

I ka poʻe i lohe,

Those who may hear,

E hele mai, ke hea aku nei au,

Come, for I am calling,

E hele mai, ke hea aku nei au.

Come, for I am calling.

*Composed by
Louis Robert
"Moon"
Kauakahi*

E hoʻolei ka ʻupena ma ka ʻapapapa,

Set your nets upon my reefs,

Malaila, loaʻa he nui lehulehu,

That you may reap abundantly,

Ma ka mālie o ke kakahiaka,

In the stillness of the morning,

E hoʻolohe mai, ke hea aku nei au,

Listen, for I am calling,

Ma ke kuahiwi e hea aku ana,

In the mountains, I echo,

Hōʻūna nei i kaʻu mele,

Sending my song throughout,

E hele mai, o wau hoʻi ke kahakai,

Come, for I am the sea,

E hele mai, e haʻawi wale aku au i kaʻu,

Come, and freely I give of me,

E hele mai, e haʻawi wale aku au i kaʻu.

Come, and freely I give of me.

2   LOUIS ROBERT "MOON" KAUAKAHI

Mele   &   Music

When Moon Kauakahi recorded the Mākaha Sons' tenth album, in 1991, the group was a quartet. They had begun singing together fifteen years earlier, gathering in a friend's backyard. Today, the Sons are a trio, featuring (from left) Jerome K. Koko, Moon Kauakahi, and John K. Koko. Israel K. Kamakawiwo'ole (seated) left the group in 1993 to pursue a solo career.

The sound rolled through the still night air and into the house where Louis slept. Stirred from a dream, he gradually surfaced and identified the boom and roar: Enormous swells at nearby Mākaha Beach were pounding the reef. As he listened, he heard another sound whispering through the din. He concentrated, trying to identify the ghostly voice. It was the echo of the pounding waves reverberating off the cliffs above his house. Louis could not understand why, at three o'clock in the morning, the ocean seemed to be calling to him, but he grabbed a pencil and began to write down its words. Later, he translated the words into Hawaiian and composed a melody to convey the haunting quality of his early morning encounter, and the ballad "Kāhea o Keale" was born.

When Louis joins his voice to others and adds instrumentation, he breathes life into "Kāhea" and recreates a power that can change a listener's mood and transport an audience beyond the walls of a smoky club, perhaps to the cliffs near Mākaha, where the ocean sings to them. A songwriter, like any artist, can only hope the words and music will continue to come, so the transformation will take place again and again. But a musician's life, especially in Hawai'i, has challenges that go far beyond realizing artistic dreams. The high cost of island living can make one or two, even three jobs a necessity, with little time left over to keep a musician's own life in tune, much less the life of a musical group and the songs it sings.

At the time he wrote "Kāhea," Louis Robert Kauakahi had his life under control. He could support himself, his immediate family, and his guitars. The musical group? Well, Louis played with a quartet called the Mākaha Sons of Ni'ihau, which would become one of the most successful and influential of all Hawaiian music groups. But their eighteen-year journey to award-winning albums and sellout concerts would not come easily. Along the way, the members would struggle with poverty, illness, drug abuse, embezzlement, and death. Changes in popular taste would challenge them as interest in Hawaiian songs faded and the "Jawaiian" craze took hold. Eventually, after the group became widely known for its sweet musical harmonies, even Louis would no longer be able to hold the quartet together.

Among Hawaiian entertainers, Louis has a reputation as a shy, private person. He lets others in the group enjoy the spotlight, preferring to concentrate on musical arrangements, Hawaiian pronunciation, and filling in harmony when the Sons perform. In conversation, Louis, who is forty years old, guards his past and present with the same discipline he uses to manage all the demands of his life—Hawaiian language classes, concerts, family, league volleyball, and a full-time job with the National Guard. He squeezes in interviews over the phone, between rehearsals at the union hall, on the grass after a weekend drill or class, or during breaks at the recording studio—never at home or at work. And on most subjects, his replies are as lean as his build and military haircut, and they become cryptic when the issues get too personal.

Louis's story as a Hawaiian musician begins in the 1970s, when he was a student at Nānākuli High School on the leeward coast of Oʻahu. Nānākuli is an hour's commute from downtown Honolulu, and the isolation before the highway was built, along with the hot, dry weather, discouraged developers and realtors from undertaking there the transformation that was going on in other areas on Oʻahu. The predominately Hawaiian residents enjoyed serenity, the ocean, open farmlands, low-cost housing, wide-open beaches, and a strong sense of community among neighbors. In their backyards, beneath mango and plumeria trees, families such as the Kauakahis gathered on weekends to play Hawaiian music and eat poi and fish freshly caught from the sea.

Louis's father, Robert, was a professional musician on Kauaʻi until he moved to Honolulu in 1940. He started a family and worked as a stevedore at the Navy ammunition depot and for Standard Oil. He could fix cars and trucks, make his own nets, and fish the reef for dinner. But when he played music, when he spoke Hawaiian with older family members, the outside world disappeared.

His son Louis watched him, thinking, "Someday, when I get old, I'm going to play music and talk Hawaiian, too." Louis was the oldest surviving son of thirteen children, of whom only seven lived to see adulthood. Louis's father, who did not finish high school, emphasized the importance of education, and his urgency fell upon Louis. "It was through me my father would exert his authority."

Louis developed into a scrawny teenager trying to plan and control his own future while coping with the stress of having to be the responsible one among siblings who did not care about school. "Nobody else in my family was thinking the way I was thinking. At the time it frustrated me. I felt I had to go to school because nobody else took an interest in it."

It was not easy being the only member of his family who graduated from high school. In retrospect, Louis smiles quietly, perhaps in gratitude for a process that forged the discipline and convictions he could call on later to help him overcome great obstacles.

During high school, Louis handled pressure by keeping busy. He left home and moved in with an aunty so he could concentrate on studies and his involvement in student government, the Interact Club, the school band (where he learned how to read music and play the French horn and trumpet), two part-time jobs, and Hawai'i Upward Bound—a series of summer classes for gifted, underprivileged students.

During the 1972 Upward Bound program, Louis heard two students playing guitar and 'ukulele. "I liked what I was hearing, not knowing it was a Hawaiian song. I stood there and I listened and I listened, and I thought it was a rock thing that I felt that I could learn."

The song was "Kāwika." A young Hawai'i trio, a new group called Sunday Mānoa, had used rock-and-roll guitar licks to transform a traditional Hawaiian chant honoring King Kalākaua into a contemporary tune. Islanders loved the first Sunday Mānoa album, *Guava Jam*. It was a landmark album at the peak of the Hawaiian Renaissance, which began in the late sixties as a result of young Hawaiians watching the civil rights struggles on the U.S. mainland and witnessing the empowerment that came from the African American community's new-found pride. They began to search for their own identity and discovered they could play native music and attract hundreds, sometimes thousands, of paying people, Hawaiians and non-Hawaiians alike. They resurrected the Hawaiian language, traditional hula, Hawaiian seafaring arts, healing arts, and the conceptual underpinnings of the Hawaiian mind. They began teaching the history of Hawaiian disenfranchisement, Hawaiian displacement. Cultural survival became the imperative in a state that was becoming increasingly—some would say devastatingly—American.

"Kāwika" snared Louis. By himself, he learned two songs off the *Guava Jam* album, and he formed a high school combo that memorized and played the rest. His friends called him "Moon" because he tried so hard to imitate Peter Moon, Sunday Mānoa's leader. The nickname stuck—permanently.

While most graduating seniors as smart as Moon went on to college, Nānākuli students rarely considered it seriously. They were eager, Moon said, but lacked money and direction. "I guess it was the right time when the National Guard recruiter came over."

Before graduation, in 1973, Moon took the military entrance exam and scored high enough for officer's training, but he joined the National Guard as an enlisted man. "If I didn't know how to work as an Indian, I had no business being a chief. So I decided to start off at the bottom and slowly work my way up."

Moon and his friend and classmate Jerome Koko, known as Jerry, packed their 'ukulele with them when they headed off to basic training in Louisiana and then to advanced training in Oklahoma. The trip, Moon's first time away from Hawai'i, gave him a new perspective on his home and his culture. "I needed a period away from the Islands to actually appreciate the Islands."

When the two friends returned to Nānākuli in 1974, they began studying Hawaiian culture at a community college near Wai'anae. Their interest in contemporary native music was ignited after Jerry happened to meet someone at the beach who was jamming on an 'ukulele. It was Israel Kamakawiwo'ole.

Like many Hawaiians, Israel had grown up hearing music at home and at church, but his family could not afford voice coaches or piano teachers, so he and his brother Henry, nicknamed "Skippy," learned to sing and play by ear. At Wai'anae High, Israel and his friends regularly cut class and set up in the bathroom to practice. "We had pianos, upright bass, harmonicas, harps, everything. Sneak 'em out of the band room and push 'em into the bathroom, brah," Israel said. "It was unreal. Fourth period. Bass and all. Four-part harmony. Everybody stay in class and trip out. Then [during recess] they come inside the bathroom, chicks and all. We used to pound."

Israel invited Jerry Koko to stop by his house and play music. A few nights later Jerry, Moon, and their friend Sam Gray heard music coming from the Kamakawiwo'ole home. They played through the night with the brothers. "We all got together, about six or seven of us . . . and we just started playing music," Moon said. "It was like, we play a song, they follow. They play a song, then we follow. . . . Right about then, we felt we had something. And if we just maybe rehearsed more, practiced a little bit, we probably could get something together. . . . Of course, our inspiration came when Gabby heard us play."

During Louis's teens, Gabby Pahinui was a hero, a humble, slack-key guitar player who inspired many young Hawaiians. Gabby had the talent to become a star, but he was not going to change to match some promoter's definition of success. Even after he became popular, he kept his job working for the county road crew. He became the father of thirteen children, enjoyed his beer and his model trains, and to paraphrase the late Hawaiian journalist Pierre Bowman, over the years Gabby's music remained in tune with the cliffs rising behind his trim Waimānalo home, with the wind blowing briskly from the nearby sea, with a world that can sing even as it mourns.

"Pops" Pahinui was already there, passed out on a table, when Moon and his music buddies arrived for their gig at a graduation party. When the boys started singing, Gabby woke up. "Skippy! Skippy! Sing Pops a song. Skippy, please sing Pops a song," he pleaded. Amazed that Gabby Pahinui knew Skippy's name, they pulled themselves together and dedicated their next song to him. Then Gabby got up and sang with them.

"That was neat," remembered Moon. "That was a really, really good experience. And everything from there just grew. That's when we started taking everything a little bit more seriously. Not real serious where we got down to formal rehearsals, but a little bit more than just a backyard jam."

They named their group the Mākaha Sons of Ni'ihau, because Israel and Skippy's mother was from Ni'ihau, a small, privately owned island off Kaua'i where two hundred Hawaiians still live and speak the native language. The Sons started getting club dates. Producer Bill Murata heard them at Yoko's in 1976 and asked if he could record them. The session took two days. Before their second album came out, the following year, Jerry Koko dropped out of the group to take care of his ailing younger brother. After the third album, the Sons became a quartet, with Skippy Kamakawiwo'ole on twelve-string guitar, his brother Israel, the lead vocalist, on 'ukulele, their new brother-in-law on rhythm guitar (Moon had married one of their two sisters, Lydia Kamakawiwo'ole), and a cousin, Melvin Amina, on bass.

In those days of weaning from "Tiny Bubbles," island people hungered for the new Hawaiian sound, and critics called the Sons' music "unspoiled," "pure and simple," and "down home." These qualities captivated Hawaiian elders, and at the same time, the new songs drew young people who were grateful for a group willing to sing songs describing the desecration of their native lands. In one set, the Sons might have combined a traditional Hawaiian hymn from their childhood, "E Iesū E Ku'u Kahu," with "Pakalōlō," Israel's tune about the pleasures of smoking marijuana, or "Pule a Ka Haku" (The Lord's Prayer) with "Lai Toodle," whose lyrics express contempt for a Caucasian plantation boss riding a big white horse ("Here comes that son of a bitchin' haole").

By 1979 the group was performing so often that Moon decided to leave the National Guard. Regular dates at clubs such as Hank's Place in Kaimukī had given the group some financial stability, and the freedom to grow. The audience grew, too, though they were not always attentive. Late arrivals at Hank's Place wedged into a small, smoke-filled room, and the noisy crowd often jabbered right through the singing. The audience's idea that the Sons were there to provide background music challenged Moon to arrange harmonies and instrumentation that would woo them to listen, perhaps even move them to hula.

Admirers recognized that these musicians, like their mentor, Gabby Pahinui, were being true to the basic honesty and sensitivity in Hawaiian music. "If we were to want money more than our music, our group would never make it," Skippy told *The Honolulu Advertiser* in 1981. "But you see, we love our music, and we now have a way that one day Mākaha Sons going to show what we got. But it's not to prove anything to anybody. It's to prove something to ourselves—that there is a different way, a different route to success besides a dog-eat-dog style."

Moon's arrangements, the depth of Skippy's convictions, the compelling warmth of Israel's lead vocals, and the group's unique harmonies, made complete by Melvin Amina, attracted more and more fans. On a good night at Hank's Place, the Sons would sing "Kāhea o Keale" and everyone would get "chicken skin"—that rare pleasure when a song transforms your soul; the babbling crowd was stilled at last. But on other nights, nothing special clicked. Sometimes the group showed up late, or minus a member or two, or not at all.

"Back in the early eighties," Moon said, "the attitude of the group was more lean back, kick back, just take what comes, not really serious. After the public started noticing us, and once the group was recognized as a musical attribute to Hawai'i, then I felt we had to do something. Now we are in the public eye, and the public knows of the Mākaha Sons. Everything that we do, both good and bad, will reflect on the group. . . . We just needed to polish our act."

Polishing their act was not easy. Major health problems and financial difficulties hounded the group. Schedules were difficult to make and easy to break. Their manager embezzled a year's worth of earnings and their family savings, $75,000 altogether. The Sons never recovered the money. "Eventually he will get his due," Moon said. Newspapers and television stations eagerly reported a traffic incident involving Israel; he punched a man in Waikīkī, a pastor, and broke his jaw. Both Kamakawiwo'ole brothers suffered from what is technically termed "morbid obesity," and were frequently in the hospital, struggling with their weight and complications from it.

At times when the Sons had some money, the high cost of living on O'ahu required more. "Truthfully, our music just wasn't enough to pay for all the necessities," Moon said about those years. "I told myself, 'I cannot live like this. I know I can do something better,' because I had the ability to do whatever I wanted."

Eighteen months after leaving the National Guard, Moon reenlisted. He began working weekdays (sometimes with weekend drills) and played music Wednesday through Saturday nights. On those nights, he slept at work to avoid the ninety-minute commute home. "I couldn't quit the group, even at

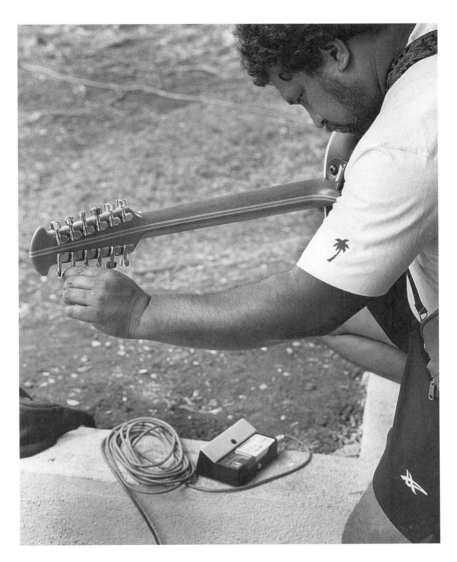

Jerome Koko has played lead guitar for the Mākaha Sons since joining the group in 1982. During the following decade, he worked a day job as foreman for a construction company. In 1995, he began studying business management at Leeward Community College.

John Koko has two upright basses, one black and one white. His brother Jerome taught him how to play music after a heart condition made sports impossible for John. During the day, John works with his partner at their upholstery shop. At night, he and the Sons often perform, sometimes flying to the West Coast or the outer islands for weekend concerts.

times I felt I should. When I first had that interest in Hawaiian music, I told myself that maybe one day I would become a professional musician. And now that I was a professional musician, I committed myself to all the bad, as well as the good. I guess you can say I was married to Hawaiian music. . . .

"It was frustrating as heck at that time. Just when I thought the group was really going somewhere, then something else would come up. Somebody would get sick. Or someone else would get sick. Or somebody else wouldn't show up for performances. Or somebody would be mad at somebody."

In 1982, ill and frustrated with Moon's attempts to manage the unmanageable, Skippy Kamakawiwoʻole decided to leave the Sons. He and Melvin Amina wanted to start another group. Two weeks later, Skippy died from a heart attack. A decade afterward, the memories were still painful for Moon. His throat tightened and he stopped speaking, searching for words to convey a sense of what he and the group had gone through without revealing too much. "The change was drastic in other ways than music. There were a lot of things that happened when Skippy died. The group came to a halt, a screeching halt."

The Sons were down to two performers: Israel and Moon. Looming ahead of them was a six-week engagement—a gig arranged before Skippy died—at the Ranch House, a popular family restaurant featuring Hawaiian music.

"I called Jerry Koko," Moon remembered. "Before, whenever the group had nights off, I would just call Jerry, and if he didn't have anything to do, I'd just jump over to his house and then he'd call his brother John, and then John would bring over his bass, and the music that we played was different from what we as the Mākaha Sons then were playing."

The Koko brothers had full-time day jobs, but they agreed to help out with the Ranch House commitment. Thirty-odd performances later, the Kokos were part of a group that felt comfortable together, but the sound still wasn't quite right. They took eleven months off to learn new songs and rearrange old ones. Moon emerged as the leader; Israel was still the lead vocalist and comic; and with the Kokos, Jerry on twelve-string lead guitar and John on upright bass, they maintained the harmonies that had always been the group's forte.

"The Ranch House was calling for us all through the year. I said, 'We are not ready.' Finally we went back. . . . They couldn't believe that it was the same group. . . . The sound was closer together. The harmonies were tight; very simple instrumentation, capitalizing of course on the vocals. We just went from there," Moon said.

By the mid-1980s, the public was no longer flocking to hear Hawaiian music. Hank's Place had become the Aina Haina Garden Shop. The Territorial Tavern was turned into a furniture store, then a law office. The Hawaiian lounge at the Ala Moana Hotel became a karaoke bar, and the Ranch House was bought by a businessman from Japan whose twenty-three-year-old son gutted the restaurant, redecorated it with trendy postmodern doodads, raised the prices, and called it Rockchild's. He bankrupted the place, and his father tore it down. Other taverns, other venues disappeared as well, made extinct by discos, karaoke, home video, and a campaign against drunk driving.

Hawaiian musical groups had to adapt to survive. For some, like the Mākaha Sons, it was enough to travel more—to the neighbor islands or to the continental United States, where approximately 72,000 Hawaiians, scattered up and down the West Coast, thirsted for the real thing.

Other groups added drums and reggae rhythms from Jamaica to broaden their appeal, just as previous generations of Hawaiian musicians had appropriated country-western, opera, jazz, and rock styles.

Islanders had been dancing to a reggae beat ever since Bob Marley's international triumph in the 1970s, but in 1990, seemingly overnight, a new hybrid Hawaiian-Jamaican sound called "Jawaiian" became the most popular style of music in Hawai'i. One Jawaiian recording sold sixty thousand copies—in a state where ten thousand sales meant a major local hit. Disaffected teenagers, tired of Top Forty music but not urban enough for rap's attitude, craved a new sound and identity.

Jawaiian's success boosted sales and bookings for other Hawai'i musicians, but the reggae-influenced groups drew the headlines and the huge crowds. This trend disturbed island musicians—those who sang in the Hawaiian language—and many serious observers of Hawaiian culture. They believed island performers should have been encouraging young people to experience life in a Hawaiian rather than Jamaican way. Frank Kawaikapuokalani Hewett, a well-known kumu hula, musician, and teacher, told *Honolulu Weekly*, "I have no trouble with reggae. In fact, I like reggae music. It represents a people's emotions, a people's culture. But it is the kuleana [province] of the Jamaican people. . . . The problem is when Hawaiians get lost in someone else's culture. Time and time again we've gotten lost in assimilation, and it's so sad because we have our own rich traditions that take us back to Sky Father and Earth Mother. . . . Our language is our mana [power]. The word is so very important to Hawaiians. Our music is based on our language, not the rhythm and percussion of reggae music."

People associated the Mākaha Sons of Ni'ihau with acoustic, harmonious music in the native language, but the group had always mixed other styles and languages into their repertoire, from the ballads their parents had enjoyed in the 1940s and 1950s to reggae and Tahitian-style songs. The Sons decided to reinforce their traditional identity—they would continue to focus primarily on songs in the Hawaiian language. In 1991, as they completed their tenth album, *Ho'oluana,* Moon insisted on excluding anything Jawaiian and was uncomfortable when the group decided to end the album with two English-language tunes.

"I just want to try to keep an identity," Moon said. "I felt that once we got into Jawaiian, it would be even harder for us to backtrack and stay basically Hawaiian. The public knows the Mākaha Sons as being traditional Hawaiian, at times contemporary Hawaiian. . . . But whatever we do now, with whatever song, it will sound Hawaiian, and I will try to keep it that way. Even if it's a real contemporary song, once we get ahold of it, it will sound like it is Hawaiian."

Moon could not define the "Hawaiian sound" beyond the usual earmarks—Hawaiian language, guitars, upright bass, and 'ukulele. "I cannot explain what it is, but it's something that turns this light bulb in here on. To me, it is basically sticking with the roots, trying to keep that as a basic foundation of what this group started off with."

Moon recognized the irony of the Sons being considered a traditional Hawaiian music group and having only one member who was proficient in speaking and understanding the language—himself. During the recording of *Ho'oluana,* he had to coach the other singers on pronunciation, mindful of listeners who would scold Moon for any mispronunciation.

In the group's earliest days, some Hawaiians drew the Sons aside and told them they should not sing Hawaiian songs until they could speak the language. "You folks have no business singing Hawaiian music," they said.

Moon decided to enroll his daughter in a private preschool where teachers speak only Hawaiian and the children become fluent through the language-immersion technique. He studied the language himself and gradually became comfortable speaking Hawaiian in public. Moon was motivated by an altercation with a man who insisted the group give up Hawaiian-language songs until they could all understand the language. Moon told him, "We feel singing the music will eventually bring us to the language."

"No," the man said, "that's all wrong."

Moon is as picky about pronunciation as he is about the songs he selects for the group to sing. In 1986, Moon decided the Sons should record "Ho'ōla Lāhui Hawai'i," a tune that would become a popular anthem about perpetuating the island race and culture. But as originally written in English, the words to "Ho'ōla" decried the death of Hawaiians. The message changed after the original English-language lyricist, Dr. Hiram Young, gave his song to Jean

Ileialoha Beniamina, a Kaua'i woman and native speaker who was unable to translate into Hawaiian the poignancy of the pain being expressed. She in turn gave it to her mother, Jean Keale, a pure-blooded Hawaiian raised on Ni'ihau. "She looked at all the negative points of what the song had and she turned everything around," Moon said. "She made it positive. She said not what the people are dying of, but what can they do. The song described the Hawaiian people as flowers who will live, who will continue to survive. . . . Although it's true that Hawaiians are dying, she didn't want to bring out the message that way. She said, 'They are not wilted flowers. They are pretty flowers.'

"Communication is one of the most important means of change," Moon said. "If you go inside and rant and rave at somebody, you may not get anything. I wasn't for being outspoken. . . . Instead of trying to say something that would hurt somebody, I would rather not say anything at all and think about what the situation was and then come out and say something after I analyzed what I was going to say. This I had to develop. This I had to learn."

When Moon arranges music written by someone else, he thinks about the words, what they mean, and tries to convey their true meaning in the arrangements. "I try to let the audience understand the meaning of the Hawaiian words by the feeling of the music itself. If the audience can feel what the song is, they have more or less translated the song—into much more than what it literally meant. That is basically what I like to see happen. That's my high.

"My awareness of the language is [also] making the music more exciting. It's making it more challenging. The music takes on a new meaning. The culture takes on a new meaning. I can read into a song and more or less understand what the song is saying. That's how I set the mood. . . . Most of the time it will come out because it has been thought of carefully and then is brought out."

In 1989, when the Sons began recording *Ho'oluana,* it was time to bring together their new work. Their fans had not heard anything new in three years—a dangerous delay. For any artist, a new batch of songs means increased radio air play. Air play in Hawai'i for island musicians means consideration for a Nā Hōkū Hanohano Award (the state's equivalent of the mainland music industry's Grammy), and winning a Hōkū generates publicity that revives interest and creates more listeners, more fans, more influence. The Sons' previous album, *Ho'ōla,* won Hōkū awards for Traditional Hawaiian Album of the Year and Group of the Year.

After playing together for six years, by 1989 the Mākaha Sons were better organized and more rehearsed than ever before, but they also had more distractions. They were in constant demand. Organizers of fund-raisers, summer concerts, hula competitions, and neighbor island shows continually asked them to perform. Israel's health problems confounded scheduling, as did his ongoing use of cocaine, marijuana, and crystal methamphetamines. Jerry's night schooling and promotion to foreman at a concrete casting company were two more complications. John worked full-time at Wayne's Upholstery, and Moon's responsibilities to the National Guard included two weeks of summer drills and other mandatory classes on the mainland. All of them had families and children.

Ho'oluana took more than three years to complete. The Sons worked with a new manager named Kata Maduli, producer Lea Uehara, and engineer Jim Linkner at Dolphin Sound, a small recording studio at a television station in the Honolulu industrial district. First, the Sons went into the studio and recorded their instrumentals, repeating take after take until the sections were perfect. The vocals came next, chorused repeatedly until all the words were pronounced correctly and the harmonies were true. A choir from a hālau hula sang background vocals, and then strings and a harpist from the Honolulu Symphony were added. Jim and Kata tinkered with the sound fragments and brought twenty-four tape tracks together. When the album was released, *Honolulu Star-Bulletin* music critic John Berger said *Ho'oluana* "displays the exquisiteness of their music. . . . Cultural pride and music virtuosity permeate the album from start to finish. . . . This is an album with no low points. . . . All Hawaiian-language albums should be produced and packaged this well."

When the NBC "Today" show visited O'ahu in 1991, they invited the Sons to perform one of the songs in English from *Ho'oluana,* Kui Lee's "I'll Remember You." Roughly three-and-a-half million viewers heard the Sons that morning, but as he played, Moon realized that few of them would ever sit down and listen to the album or truly understand the world the Sons sang about in Hawaiian.

To reach tourists, local musicians need a name, and an act, and a promotional budget that few groups can maintain. Furthermore, they are at the mercy of tour packagers who sell activities to big tour groups, activities that salesmen pitch and book in banquet rooms the mornings after tourists arrive en masse. Do they want a trip to the neighbor islands? Snorkeling at Hanauma Bay? A circle O'ahu tour? A lū'au at Germaine's or Paradise Cove? Maybe the Polynesian Cultural Center, or Tihati's Polynesian Revue?

If a show wants the tourists, it has to pay the tour packager a commission for each person lured to the showroom. The higher the commission, the better the sales pitch. As a result only a few big shows can afford the advertising and commissions to keep people coming. This is no guarantee, however, because the major tour companies also have to like the shows they sell. If one says it does not want a particular song or dance included in a lūʻau performance, the song or dance may have to be removed. So may an individual performer. Without the major travel companies' sales teams, the Polynesian revues would not survive.

These revues employ many island musicians and hula teachers. A few of the shows give viewers a fairly authentic Hawaiian cultural experience, but most of the big revues are a little bit of this and that Polynesia, with the emphasis on hula, Tahitian drum dances, and the mandatory Samoan fire knife dancer. Most tourists, sucking up mai tais or beer, cannot say which dance is Hawaiian and most do not care. The average visitor just wants to be entertained—if not at a lūʻau, then at a club with a disc jockey or a karaoke machine. For those who want more than a sunset serenade by the pool, they have to find the handful of Oʻahu bars, restaurants, and special events that offer the real thing. As a result, only a few Hawaiians playing beyond the lūʻau circuit can subsist solely on their music.

A few minutes away from the hotels, clubs, and revues, the Waikīkī Shell has been a favorite site for Hawaiian musicians for many years. The Shell is an outdoor amphitheater near Diamond Head. It seats only 6,500 people, but the setting enables local entertainers to attract crowds without compromising their program for tourists. In 1980 a popular Hawaiian group could make money performing at the Shell either by itself or perhaps with one other act. But as interest in Hawaiian music declined in the mid-1980s, a successful concert had to offer a mixture of hula, comedy, and song. In 1988 a promoter persuaded the Sons to headline their own "Mākaha Bash" at the Shell. Despite an assortment of nightmares (heart attack strikes bankrupt promoter, threatening Bash until rescue by the Sons' friend), the Bash became an annual Memorial Day weekend success up until 1993—the year Israel Kamakawiwoʻole decided to stop using drugs, start losing weight, and leave the Sons to perform on his own.

People who have followed the group over the years have watched more than once as its heart has missed a beat. After Skippy passed away, in 1982, and the Koko brothers joined the group, Israel's enthusiasm for music helped the Sons not just to survive but to continue perfecting their distinctive harmonies. The Sons' fans always returned, confident that Israel would transform an evening of Hawaiian music into a memorable night and leave them aching from laughter. Israel is a Hawaiian who cares deeply about his land and his people, and he voices his concerns in the introduction and dedication of each song. This underlying sincerity, along with his humorous patter and sweet singing voice, make Israel an exceptional entertainer, but until 1993 his enthusiasm for drugs jeopardized his health and ability to perform.

Whenever Israel missed gigs, Moon empathized both with Israel's pain and with the disappointment of an audience deprived of Israel's entertainment. "He has that gift," Moon said. "If I was given the mic, I would freeze up on stage. He is the show for the audience. . . . When the group is whole, all four performing at our peak, there is nothing more the audience can ask for."

When Israel's health deteriorated again, in 1991, Kata Maduli called on island musicians to join in what he saw as a life-saving effort. He decided to promote Israel as the group's headliner—"Israel Kamakawiwo'ole and the Mākaha Sons of Ni'ihau"—hoping that Israel's fondness for the spotlight would help him take a turn for the better. He also produced Israel's first solo album, which featured songs that went beyond the Sons' traditional Hawaiian music. An enthusiastic outpouring of support buoyed Israel up, and on May 26, 1991, the full complement of Sons hosted their fourth Mākaha Bash at the Waikīkī Shell.

Kata lined up a television crew to videotape the Bash, which featured three hālau hula, two Jawaiian groups, and song stylist (and Hōkū award winner) Teresa Bright. As for the Sons' program, concert promoters usually give the headline group an hour to rush through a scripted selection of predictable songs, songs the audience expects to hear. But for this fifteenth anniversary celebration, Kata invited various friends of the Sons to join the group onstage. They shared duets and conversations about the past, and the concert became a relaxed and spontaneous songfest, moving the audience from one mood and place to another. Israel paid tribute to his parents by singing their favorite ballad, "The Art of Making Love." He honored his Ni'ihau grandfather with Moon's song "Kāhea o Keale." Singer Melveen Leed reminded the crowd that the Sons and the late Gabby Pahinui had been members of a mutual admiration society. Then she asked the group to play one of Gabby's choice songs, "Wai o Ke Aniani." "Very, very slow," she instructed them, "with a lot of mana going through the body."

As she sang the words about water, rain began to fall and continued until the song ended. During the encore, when the crowd demanded another song, Israel asked the Sons to play a song that Skippy had made famous. It was "Hawai'i '78"—Mickey Ioane's English-language lament about how pained the ali'i from times past would feel if they could see Hawai'i today. The angry undercurrent in the song had always disturbed Moon, but he set aside his feelings, as he always had before, and sang as if the song's tears were his own. Rain began to fall again.

In the dark, along the back fence of the amphitheater, groups of young local boys, adolescents too cool to sit among the families and couples on the lawn, stopped talking and sang the words they all knew by heart. A girl sitting near the stage turned to her father and exclaimed, "Skippy's here! That's Skippy's song! The rain means Skippy's here because that's his song!"

The encore pushed the concert beyond 9:30 P.M., the Department of Health's noise curfew for Shell concerts. The guest performers went onstage and held hands in front of the Mākaha Sons. The crowd stood up and linked hands in long strings across the sweeping amphitheater. They closed the evening with "Hawai'i Aloha," composed a hundred years ago by an America-born minister, Reverend Lorenzo Lyons. It is traditionally sung at the conclusion of Hawaiian events, and if not everyone remembers the words to all the verses, few people forget the rejoicing chorus, "'Oli e! 'Oli e!" For the six thousand people at the Shell that night, "Hawai'i Aloha" was more than a parting ritual. As they swayed in time with the solemn, sweet melody and sang out their love for the Islands, everyone in the crowd felt part of a community that was—at that moment—harmonious.

> *E Hawai'i, e ku'u one hānau e,*
> *Ku'u home kulaīwi nei,*
> *'Oli nō au i nā pono lani e,*
> *E Hawai'i, aloha e.*
>
> *E hau'oli e nā 'ōpio o Hawai'i nei*
> *'Oli e! 'Oli e!*
> *Mai nā aheahe makani e pā mai nei*
> *Mau ke aloha, nō Hawai'i.*
>
> *O Hawai'i, O sands of my birth,*
> *My native home,*
> *I rejoice in the blessings of heaven.*
> *O Hawai'i, aloha.*
>
> *Happy youth of Hawai'i*
> *Rejoice! Rejoice!*
> *Gentle breezes blow*
> *Love always for Hawai'i.*

The concert carried the Sons through the rest of a remarkable fifteenth anniversary year. Israel's improved health already had revived the group and he had won Hōkū awards for his solo album. The Bash was a success, both musically and financially, and so was the television program that followed. Critics and fans praised the group's new live concert and studio albums. Throughout the islandwide recession, Kata Maduli continued to book the group, enabling them to support their families, and the "Today" show had given them national exposure. Few Hawai'i musicians would have asked for more. But Moon and Israel did.

Israel wanted to be free of drugs, free of 350 pounds, free of welfare (since his weight made it impossible for him to hold a nine-to-five job), and free of Moon's stylistic limitations so Israel could record music his own way. When Israel finally made the break, in 1993, he felt great, and a critic called his second solo album "exceptional . . . one of the most significant Hawaiian albums of [that] year." But the fallout from Israel's departure, widely publicized by the media, became uglier than most divorces.

Any other group might have disintegrated, but Moon and the Koko brothers had already played numerous gigs without Israel, and Jerry took his turn enjoying the spotlight. They knew they could survive as a trio, now called the Mākaha Sons.

In the liner notes for the reorganized group's 1994 album, *Ke Alaula, The Dawning,* Moon wrote, "When we first formed . . . , we dreamed of someday earning the same respect given [the pioneers of Hawaiian music, including the Sons of Hawai'i, Gabby Pahinui, the Sunday Mānoa, and the Kahauanu Lake Trio, among others].

"The road was an uphill struggle, seemingly with only our ambitions to guide us. At times it was frustrating to the point of wanting to abandon our attempts to continue. Yet, these giants of Hawaiian music served as beacons of hope, giving us musical encouragement and the will to continue. To us, these legends were our sunrise, our original rays of light, our guides to what we hoped would be a promising future for us; just as the prior generations now set below their own horizons had been the models for them.

"In our innocence we too wanted to become legends. But today, with eleven albums . . . we still continue in our quest to perpetuate the music of Hawai'i, both old and new, seeking to expand our horizons, to explore other opportunities, with more sunrises yet to experience.

"'Ke Alaula,' the dawning, is a new horizon, a new sunrise, a new ray of hope in the continuing legacy of the Mākaha Sons. We set forth almost twenty years ago when our flame was first lit and burned brightly. Over the years often the flame did flicker, but like the sun, the promise to shine again was always there. And with every flicker, we were fortunate that a new ray did give us the hope and the promise to continue.

"Wehe 'ia ke alaula no nā hanauna nei, a no nā hanauna e hiki mai ana— thus the dawning of a new era emerges for this generation and for the generations to come."

KĀWIKA

David

Eia no Kāwika
> *Here is David*

Translated by
Mary Kawena Pukui

Ka heke aʻo nā pua.
> *The greatest of descendants.*

Ka uila ma ka hikina
> *Like the lightning in the east*

Mālamalama o Hawaiʻi.
> *Brightening Hawaiʻi.*

Kuʻi e ka lono i Pelekani
> *Report of him reached Great Britain*

A lohe ke kuini o Palani.
> *And was heard of by the Queen of France.*

Nā wai e ka pua i luna
> *Whose offspring is this, so high above?*

Nō Kapaʻakea he makua.
> *Kapaʻakea was the name of his sire.*

Haʻina ʻia mai ka puana
> *This is the conclusion of our praise*

No ka lani Kāwika he inoa.
> *In honor of King David.*

3   MĀPUANA AND KĪHEI DESILVA

Hula & Dance

Kīhei and Māpuana deSilva with their daughters, Kahikina (left) and Kapalaiʻula. Their extended family includes the several hundred girls and women who are members of the deSilva's hula school, Hālau Mōhala ʻIlima.

Preceding page: Koa and ʻōhiʻa trees reach for the sky above Hawaiʻi Volcanoes National Park, where hālau dancers share a hula with family, friends, and the Islands' ancestors.

The first warning came in February, as eighteen hālau hula were preparing for Merrie Monarch, the oldest and most competitive hula festival in Hawai'i. At first, rehearsals seemed to progress as in previous years: Three, four nights a week the kumu hula chanted, and over and over again the dancers' motions conveyed the meaning of the words. But this year, each hālau was required to dance a chant that described Wāwāhonua'aho, the magical gourd belonging to Hina, the goddess mother of Moloka'i.

The chant told the story of Hina's love for the island of Moloka'i and its people, who had become haughty and proud and were neglecting to care for the land. To reprove them, Hina uncovered her gourd just enough to release one of three winds, Ilinahu, the warning wind. Ilinahu blew across Moloka'i with such force that trees snapped with a crack heard all the way across the channel on Maui. The people ignored Hina's warning, so she opened her gourd again, this time halfway, and Uluhewa emerged. Clouds darkened offshore and a gale gathered thunder and rain and hurled itself against the island, flooding houses and farms. In spite of the storm, the people remained obstinate. Hina had no choice but to unleash Lūlūku, and only the humblest survived the hurricane that swept away the rest of life on Moloka'i. The island was clean once more.

Hawaiians have an 'ōlelo no'eau, a proverb, that says, "Aia ke ola i ka waha; aia ka make i ka waha/Life is in the mouth; death is in the mouth." Spoken words can enliven, and they can destroy. Some people feared that with the countless rehearsals around the state—the constant reenactment of Hina's story—women preparing for the Merrie Monarch Festival were chanting and dancing Hina's story to life.

On February 16, a fierce windstorm swept down the slopes of Mauna Kea on the Big Island, where the Merrie Monarch is held every year. Another devastating storm hit the island on Thursday night, April 3, when the Merrie Monarch was under way in Hilo. Wind-driven rain drowned the Hilo, Puna, and Hāmākua districts with up to thirteen inches of water. Police closed the highways, as lightning struck utility poles islandwide, cutting power to most areas for more than six hours. In Hilo, the lights flickered and the hula stadium was dark for a few minutes.

The following night, after nine women's groups had danced the required Wāwāhonua'aho hula, a third storm moved over Hilo, matching Hina's trio of progressively fiercer punishments. The sky unleashed bolts of lightning that were purple—the color of Moloka'i. Thunder boomed through Edith Kanaka-'ole Stadium, silencing the usually boisterous hula crowd. Just before the second half of the competition, a lightning bolt struck a transformer outside the stadium, and the building went completely black. The audience of five thousand people waited in darkness, and the festival's emcee, illuminated by a battery-powered lamp, tried to keep them calm by leading them in singing "Row-Row-Row Your Boat" and "Old MacDonald." Underneath the bleachers, where dancers prepared for going onstage, the twenty-four women of Hālau Mōhala 'Ilima held hands and discussed whether they would dance. After a forty-minute blackout, electricity was restored, but many of the dancers were still shaken.

When the O'ahu hālau was called to perform, kumu hula Māpuana deSilva walked onstage and calmly announced, "Hālau Mōhala 'Ilima will not be performing here tonight. We feel it is not appropriate for us to perform. My first concern is for my dancers and caring for them. Thank you."

The storm abated.

Whether the decision of Mōhala 'Ilima not to perform in 1986 was appropriate depends on whom one asks. Some kumu hula believe the wrathful Moloka'i chant was never intended for performance on the Big Island, and that the withdrawal of Mōhala 'Ilima defused the powerful supernatural forces. Others interpreted the thunder as Hina demonstrating her pleasure with the performances. Still others maintain that as long as hālau believe in the Christian God and dance with clean hearts and minds, no harm will result.

Kīhei deSilva, kumu hula Māpuana deSilva's husband and the scholar-in-residence for Mōhala 'Ilima, told a reporter that the lightning and thunder disturbed many of their dancers, disrupting the serenity that the group normally relies on to "center" before a performance. The members of the hālau unanimously decided not to dance. "Hula teaches sensitivity to what comes from nature," Kīhei said. "If you succeed in being sensitive, and you feel that the elements are telling you something, then you have to listen. How can you tell a good story if everyone feels bad about it?"

The deSilvas do not believe their dancers have the power to start or stop a

Hula dancers may practice drills for twelve months before their hālau perform at Merrie Monarch, the state's most competitive hula event. One year, Mōhala 'Ilima took fifty-two women—an unusually large group—to the festival, where they shared the vitality of hula. During the festival weekend, they rehearsed in Hilo outside the Naniloa Hotel and in costume at the Civic Auditorium.

storm, but they know the women's dance motions convey living stories within the chants and songs. Telling these stories well depends not only on respecting the traditions of their elders and the spirit of places such as Moloka'i and Hilo but also on the ability to shape a diverse group of people into a unified hālau. For the deSilvas, the pursuit of physical and spiritual unity has become more important than a Merrie Monarch trophy, but it wasn't always that way.

The story of Hālau Mōhala 'Ilima begins in the late 1960s, when the Hawaiian Renaissance reached out to Leslie Howell in Forest Grove, Oregon. She was studying physical education at Pacific University, where the Hawaiian Club asked her to teach hula for its annual lū'au. Teaching came easily to Leslie, and for four years she taught dances at Pacific University. She made them up or learned them during semester breaks at her childhood home in Ka'ōhao, a windward O'ahu suburb better known as Lanikai. Unable to find a job in physical education after returning to Hawai'i in 1971, Leslie began working at a travel agency. To avoid confusion with another employee named Leslie, she started going by her middle name, Māpuana.

Māpuana was still dating her high school sweetheart, Kīhei deSilva, who had grown up in Hilo and on O'ahu. Kīhei had attended Pomona College in California, and after four years of English studies and water polo, he returned to Hawai'i. He had a bachelor's degree, long hair, and the desire to become a teacher. Kīhei also had the need to assert a Hawaiian identity that he had ignored during high school at Kamehameha Schools, the private academy for Hawaiian students.

While Māpuana learned the travel business and accounting, Kīhei worked toward his master's degree in English at the University of Hawai'i, which eventually led to a teaching job at Kamehameha. In between, he took part in protests against land development and strengthened his spirit by body surfing. He and Māpuana decided to get married.

In December 1971, Māpuana visited a hula class taught by a woman named Maiki Aiu Lake. More than a hula teacher, Maiki was a kumu hula, dedicated to passing on the legacy of hula. Young Hawaiians were hungry to learn, to absorb this part of their heritage, and by sharing her knowledge with would-be teachers, Maiki would ensure that the tradition would survive long after she was gone. Over the course of fifteen years, her classes graduated more than thirty master teachers.

Maiki's knowledge was old knowledge, passed on to her by Lokalia Montgomery, who in turn had received it from Keaka Kanahele. Keaka was born during the 1860s in the remote Oʻahu village of Lāʻie, where as a child she had been set apart for the study of hula and had learned dances and chants passed down through the centuries. In isolated settlements such as Lāʻie and the nearby village of Kahana, as in the Kaʻū and Puna districts on the Big Island, many old Hawaiian traditions were preserved. People like Keaka, Pua Haʻaheo, Mary Kawena Pukui, and Mary Kanahele were hula masters who passed on their living history to students and family, whose own children and students would become teachers of the old dances and chants.

Cultural traditions survived in these villages because of their remote locations, far away from nineteenth-century commerce and Westernization. Beginning in the mid-1800s, traditional hula started to become more of a commercialized entertainment. Honolulu and Lahaina were flourishing whaling ports, with visiting sailors who had the appetite and money to support hula performances that emphasized the more sensual hula moves. Calvinist missionaries and their converts tried to banish the dance entirely but failed, and public hula in the cities gradually came to emphasize romantic, silly, and naughty hapa-haole (English-Hawaiian) songs sung at pageants and carnivals and for the increasing number of tourists. Entertaining the island visitors with hula-hula turned into a small industry employing musicians, dancers, and hula teachers, including those who held on to the ancient traditions and privately passed them along.

Māpuana watched Maiki and knew that she wanted to study hula with her. "Through the whole time that I was with Aunty Maiki, the feeling that I remember most . . . from watching her teach is how much she loved it and how much she loved hula. . . . It didn't matter what the song was or how many times she had taught it. It didn't matter whether the hula was ʻauana or kahiko. The love she had is the strongest image I have, that I always have when I teach. . . . Hula is Aunty Maiki to me. When she was teaching and when she was dancing, it was like nothing else mattered. That's probably what gave her life—her hula. It was her breath of life."

For a year, Māpuana studied ʻauana, a type of hula generally regarded as any "modern" hula accompanied by Western musical instruments. Its counterpart is called kahiko, the pre–Western-contact style hula usually performed to a chant, sometimes with traditional percussive implements. Then she joined Maiki's third class of kumu hula students, graduating in 1975. A year passed before she found an outlet for her training as a teacher of both ancient and modern hula.

Robert Lokomaikaʻiokalani Snakenberg, a Hawaiian-language teacher, asked Māpuana to choreograph the May Day pageant at his high school for the annual festival of hula and lei-giving also known as Lei Day. Māpuana had doubts about being able to do it, but after many long practice sessions her students were so happy—both during and after their performance—that they did not want the hula to stop. Māpuana was inspired by their enthusiasm and energy. In 1976, she opened her own hālau.

Lokomaikaʻi named Māpuana's school Mōhala ʻIlima, for the unfolding ʻilima blossoms, the same delicate orange flower of Oʻahu that had been the symbol for Māpuana's kumu hula class. Māpuana gave her first lesson on the concrete slab fronting her parents' house in Kaʻōhao. When the rains fell, she and her students went indoors and danced around the living room furniture. "When I started, I really didn't know what direction I was going to take. I just wanted to teach because I loved it, and people kept asking me if I would teach."

Māpuana's students told their friends about her, and her cozy hālau grew. Success at the Merrie Monarch Festival, especially the hālau's first win, in 1981, attracted more students. As classes at the hālau filled, more were added, and new opportunities arose for the deSilvas. They tore down the old Kaʻōhao homestead and built a two-story house for their family of four plus Māpuana's parents and brother. The new building included eight hundred square feet of rehearsal space for the hālau, and an office.

By the 1990s, Hālau Mōhala ʻIlima had become one of the state's largest hula schools, with seven associate kumu trained by Māpuana. Several hundred women and girls are enrolled in a variety of classes, including the Merrie Monarch class, for which Māpuana selects certain dancers each year.

After twelve years at Kamehameha Schools, Kīhei was able to quit his full-time teaching job because of the hālau's success. He loved teaching, but it did not afford him time to follow his passion for research and scholarship, for writing, and for creating new songs and chants. At a party, he overheard an elder recall the words of Hawaiian scholar Mary Kawena Pukui: "The talents that we have are gifts from God. If we choose to ignore those gifts, then they will be taken away from us." He decided it was time to leave the Schools and focus solely on the hālau.

Kīhei often worked in the hālau office, spectacled, barefoot, wearing shorts and his favorite baggy T-shirt from Disneyland, the one with Eeyore's head drooping across the front. The donkey's eyes seemed weary from Kīhei's long hours at the computer as he typed up the results of his research at the State Archives.

"If I could go every day to the Archives, I would go, because there is so much there that needs to be translated and interpreted, revived and brought back into the culture. It's overwhelming how much is there, and it's waiting for people to come in. . . . I'm just a scholar, but I'm married to the kumu hula, and what I research in an academic fashion translates into a performance that we can bring to life next year at Merrie Monarch. That is really an incredible, satisfying high. . . . I love being able to do that."

The hālau grew deliberately, with an ever-widening group of family and friends augmenting the core group of dancers. Husbands, boyfriends, fathers, and mothers became devoted followers, and one group of supportive business people devised the nonprofit Mākālei Foundation to raise funds for special hālau competitions and scholarships.

Similar growth was taking place at other hula schools across Hawai'i, but Māpuana and Kīhei were fostering something unusual. Their hālau did several things at once: It communicated their Hawaiian values to students, friends, and audiences; its success allowed the dancers rare opportunities for travel and growth, such as trips to the mainland and retreats at Kē'ē on Kaua'i, one of hula's most sacred places; and it paid their bills. Most other kumu had only evenings and weekends free to devote to the cultural practice that for Māpuana and Kīhei had become an all-encompassing way of life.

Winning the Merrie Monarch competition in 1981 was a major turning point in the hālau's growing process. "When we heard the results that we had won, everybody just lost control," Kīhei said. "I remember people hugging each other, falling on the floor, knocking over glasses on the table. That night two of the girls disappeared and got drunk and we had to track them down. We ended up having a meeting in the hotel room at two in the morning, going over everything with everybody, asking if this behavior was really what winning was about, if winning is really worth it. It got pretty clear after that that winning is harder to handle than losing. If you can lose with dignity, it should be possible to win with dignity."

In the early 1980s, Hālau Mōhala 'Ilima performed Māpuana's self-invented and award-winning choreography, but as the deSilvas matured through hula, they began to sense that their choreography should follow the simple, graceful motions of Māpuana's teacher, Maiki Aiu Lake, and Maiki's teachers. The women of Mōhala 'Ilima danced back to an older, simpler tradition. Many observers thought it was boring. "Who cares!" Māpuana said. "We like what we're doing. It has meaning for us."

Her remark seems unusually pointed for a woman who is perceived publicly as the epitome of aloha. Beneath Māpuana's grace and humility, her laughter and willingness to share, there are her eyes, which transmit convictions as

Two Mōhala ʻIlima dancers embrace, sharing the love that helped the fifty-two women to dance as one.

strong as the Kaʻiwa ridgeline behind the deSilva house. Her strength guards and cultivates Mōhala ʻIlima. Singleminded dedication drives her to balance the books, oversee the hālau calendar, choreograph new dances, command attention from her students, and memorize hundreds of names, chants, and motions. And if a student needs to remove a ti-leaf stain from a blouse, Māpuana will tell her how to prewash it with Clorox Stain Out.

Māpuana made the "Who cares!" statement a few months after a Merrie Monarch competition, seated with Kīhei on the carpet of their hālau. The husband and wife sipped Diet Pepsi as their daughters, Kahikina and Kapalaiʻula, sprawled nearby, reading and drawing.

"We started out pretty competitive," Kīhei said, "and that competitiveness was driven by a desire to make a name for ourselves, to gain recognition, to be something in the hula community."

Although Māpuana is the kumu, the hālau has gradually become a shared responsibility between her and Kīhei. During conversation, the kumu often defers to her husband. Once the silent partner in Mōhala ʻIlima, Kīhei now enjoys articulating the philosophies that guide them.

"It's so different," he said. "It's still competitive in the sense that we enter competitions, but it's noncompetitive in that we don't have a life-or-death interest in the results. To me, the intensity is just as strong in the depth of our understanding of what we are doing, when the dancers really feel the message and meaning and they have an understanding of it—when they have more to think about than their lines or their feet or their hands.

"Of course, our dancers have to learn those things—the stress on formation and precision—but there's much more to teach and talk about. The dancers are learning to sing because Māpuana wants them to enjoy their dancing—singing while they're dancing! And something else is happening; we're not very strong on drill anymore—more emphasis on meaning. There is a transition taking place in our hula, from hula as a visual presentation to hula as a spiritual and meaningful presentation. In order to convey that, to make that change, we need dancers who are willing to spend a lot of time learning what it is they are dancing."

Kīhei cited the hālau's study of the Hawaiian language as the best evidence that the dancers understand what they are dancing. "It's interesting now how many of the students don't need to be told to smile because they understand so well what they are doing that they don't need the prompt."

Over the years, Kīhei has taken on tasks that challenge the scholar and artist within. He writes his own songs, researches dances and chants, teaches Hawaiian language and culture to the dancers, designs and silkscreens hundreds of

Mōhala 'Ilima T-shirts, and generally helps Māpuana guide and shape the younger dancers—like the teacher he has always been.

During practices, however, it is Māpuana who pushes the Merrie Monarch women toward perfection. The routine is always the same: After the dancers warm up, Māpuana has them repeat basic hula motions—Hula 101. Within fifteen minutes, they are sweaty and out of breath.

"Imitate somebody you like so you don't look like one statue walking down the stage," Māpuana has barked at her women with a drill sergeant's exasperation. "Do you know where you are going? Do you know what box you are heading to? Don't be a statue with words coming out of your mouth. Smile!"

Māpuana stops the tape and rewinds it. As the women wipe away sweat and return to their starting positions, some giggle and laugh enthusiastically, and others shyly mask their feelings of insecurity or distraction. Indeed, this group reflects the range of personalities, races, and physiques that characterize humanity—from subdued to exuberant, from native to newcomer, from spare to abundant. The physical heterogeny of Mōhala 'Ilima is notable, given that competition dancers usually conform to a certain look favored by their kumu.

Mōhala 'Ilima dancers instead display an unusual consistency of grace and kindness—a characteristic encouraged by the hālau. From most students the attitude is genuine, and it is reinforced by Māpuana's insistence on rules, discipline, courtesy, and respect—and by the dancers' awareness that compliance means acceptance by the kumu and the hālau.

Māpuana has always had lots of rules, which some new dancers interpret as aimed at controlling their behavior rather than improving their hula. Like the ones about makeup. From the beginning, the kumu hula has prohibited any makeup for ancient hula and allows only a minimum for a modern performance, partly because she does not like the way dancers look with cosmetics on their faces, but mostly because she wants the dancers' true feelings, not makeup, to convey the spirit of the hula.

When they make 'uli'uli (gourd rattles) to accompany a competition dance, Māpuana cautions her students—both children and adults—not to make a rattle when they are frustrated or angry or in a hurry. "This is your dance companion. This is a living thing made from once living materials, so it has to be made carefully and well. . . . If you don't put care into everything that you do, then somehow the negative energy that you put in will return." The longer the dancers stay on with the hālau, the more they adopt the rules and principles of the hālau for their everyday lives.

"In the beginning they're rules," said Māpuana, "but after a while they just become choices for how the dancers choose to be, not just when they come to hula. . . . The values that we teach them here become the values that they live by every day, whether they are in hula or in school or at work or with their families. That's what Aunty Maiki was trying to teach us—through hula you can learn all good values."

"We've lost some dancers who didn't see it the same way we did," Kīhei said. "But we've got really good people and not a lot of robots. . . . And there's proof that we're doing good—the girls are staying. . . .

"There are people who are looking for the one answer to hula, the magic of hula, the mystery of hula," Kīhei said. "People with that kind of feeling . . . ultimately, they don't get along with us because we find the magic is acquired through experience, through repetition, and once you know it, you can't really pass it on except to say, 'Continue. Continue. Continue. Teach. Struggle. Give.'"

"Only good things have come out of hula for us," Māpuana said. "Along the way, there are some things you want to forget; things that you did wrong. I made mistakes . . . but like I tell my girls, it's not making the mistake that's bad, it's what you do after it; how you pick up the pieces, how you get back into things, whether you learn from that mistake or not. . . . I like where we are now. We're working toward a smaller hālau. I'd like to have more time. I don't want to be sixty years old and still teaching eleven classes a week. I'd like my dancers to be kūpuna dancing with Māpu. That would make me happy."

Each year the Merrie Monarch Festival challenges Mōhala 'Ilima to maintain its values and at the same time do well in the competition. In 1988, Māpuana decided to do what most kumu would have regarded as competitive suicide: She added to the Merrie Monarch competition group the "Wednesday Night Mommies," a group of twenty-six women who had studied with Māpuana for many years.

To these women, Māpuana is their friend, and the hālau is a home away from home where they can learn some dances, socialize with their friends, and help at fund-raisers and competitions. Most Mommies no longer have the stamina or agility to execute the difficult motions and choreography expected by the audience in Hilo. And the Wednesday Night Mommies knew that Māpuana's decision would double the competition group to an almost unworkable troupe of fifty-two dancers.

The choreography logistics alone were mind-boggling: moving the sizable hālau gracefully onto the stage and executing the transitions from two lines of dancers for the entrance chant into six lines for the compulsory chant, then to four lines for the elective chant, to the eight lines required for the exit chant.

Ninety days before Merrie Monarch, three Mommy dancers withdrew because of family-related deaths. Māpuana rearranged the lines and choreography. A month before the festival, the competition dancers asked the three women to rejoin them. Once again, Māpuana changed the lines and arrangement of their entrance. With each change, the fifty-two dancers had to learn new positions on the floor, with new partners at their sides. As usual, the dancers were gracious and adaptable, happy to have their hula sisters back.

Māpuana kept them practicing, smiling, and repeating the motions. She pulled out each line of dancers and had them perform alone in front of the others. She started the chant in the middle of a verse, had the hālau dance the chant backward, then forward, as individuals, all together, again and again. Weekly tests ensured the ladies knew the chants and songs inside out, and if skirts and feather lei were incorrectly made, they were resewn, sometimes more than once.

"You should be able to work hard and enjoy yourself and smile," Māpuana told her dancers sternly, adding, "If you're not, then you should reevaluate why you're coming. If you're enjoying it and you're not smiling, then you're on a different program and you got five days to get on mine."

At home, husbands fed children and boyfriends cleaned house—apprenticeships brought about by the demands of hula on their partners. Finally, in mid-February, the hālau invited family and friends to see the results of their devotion at an annual fund-raiser for the hālau held at a farm in Waimānalo.

Beneath the sheer green cliffs of the Koʻolau range, a thousand Mōhala ʻIlima supporters relaxed on a vast lawn. Musicians sang and jammed while the hālau served bento lunches. Children ran everywhere; in the adjacent plumeria orchard, their laughter rose into the perfumed air like unexpected birdsong. Then the hula began, and time disappeared into the clear blue sky.

"We're not just a hālau—we're a family," Māpuana tells her dancers every year. "If your family feels a part of what you're doing, they don't mind you doing it. You have to include them in everything you do, make them feel a part of it, and help them understand what you're doing, so they can support you and be happy that you're doing hula rather than feeling like it's taking you away."

The next week the women were back at rehearsals, and when Māpuana started the tape, they resumed practicing the art of moving as one. "Don't wiggle your fingers! Together! Stay together! Front row stay together!" Some of the older women struggled; one sat her aching body down.

Kīhei leaned against a wall, peering into a book. He made notes on index cards and catalogued them in a file box for the hālau's fact sheet, which the Merrie Monarch committee requires each group to submit to the judges. Many hālau turn in only a few pages. But Kīhei's index cards evolved into a thirty-five-page document followed by an additional ninety-four pages of appendixes, which discussed the hālau's chants and songs, its costuming, and the tradition of large group hula. Although Māpuana said she did not care what other people thought, the point of Kīhei's exhaustive fact sheet was to justify the choices of Mōhala 'Ilima for the judges.

The festival audience doesn't see the fact sheets, but every year they expect a certain feel-good style from Māpuana's hālau, just as they expect certain signature stylizations from the other "star" kumu and their hālau—Johnny Lum Ho's emotional and spiritual stories, Alicia Smith's controlled perfection, O'Brien Eselu and Thaddius Wilson's athletic prowess. Each one creates from different traditions and inspirations, making it impossible for judges or kumu to establish one standard, especially for hula kahiko, which has become the art form's most spectacular forum for interpretation and innovation. The argument that hula kahiko should be danced solely within documented traditional parameters irritates those kumu who believe hula is a living art form that can combine motions, costumes, and attitudes inspired by their own research and creativity.

In 1989, the year Māpuana's Mommies were scheduled to perform, the festival committee assigned "No'eno'e Maika'i Ke Aloha" (Beautiful in Appearance is Love) as the mandatory ancient chant to be danced by all women groups. The chant honors Kalākaua, the much beloved king who defied the missionaries and revived hula and other suppressed island arts during his reign (1874–1891).

The deSilvas care deeply about Kalākaua because of his efforts to perpetuate the Hawaiian culture, and before every recital, their hālau honors him by dancing "Kāwika," another chant in praise of Kalākaua. The deSilvas decided to pair "Kāwika," their "choice chant," with the required "No'eno'e" for a double tribute to the king.

"Kāwika" is the first hula to be learned by Mōhala 'Ilima students. Some aficionados consider its motions and verse suitable only for children, but Māpuana continues to teach the dance, even to her advanced students. She believes "Kāwika" always reveals more than what is evident in its simple moves and words.

"The value of 'Kāwika,'" Kīhei wrote in his fact sheet for the judges, "lies in the integrity of its music and choreography. 'Kāwika' is over one hundred years old. Our version extends through five generations of instruction; [this year] it suffers neither from neglect nor alteration."

Māpuana bases her choreography for unfamiliar chants, such as "Noʻe-noʻe," partly on Kīhei's discoveries about a chant's kaona—its second, sometimes sacred, meaning hidden within the active wordplay often found in Hawaiian verse. Kīhei's interpretations also reflect the ideology of Mōhala ʻIlima that hula is a gift.

"Māpu has a gift [from Aunty Maiki]," Kīhei said, "a tradition of dance that she believes is a treasure, an inheritance which she is obligated to uphold. . . . [For Noʻenoʻe] our fifty-two ladies weren't supposed to become the swooping ʻiwa [bird] or the flower that the ʻiwa swoops down on.

"Our interpretation of Noʻenoʻe was the boring hula pūʻili [bamboo rattle]: repetitive movements, very little drama, no significant changes in formation, no wheels or merges or unmerges. Just basically tap-tap-tap-tap, tap-tap-tap-tap [of the pūʻili]. That's [our] style—boring," Kīhei said, laughing. "There's nothing remarkable about that performance in a sense. It wasn't choreographed to be spectacular. It was choreographed to belong to the tradition."

It was also choreographed so the Mommies could do well at Merrie Monarch. Kīhei explained, "Once you get the choreography down, then the real challenge occurs. Can they dance it with the right amount of spirit and expression that can transform the stadium . . . and silence the audience and somehow put them someplace else?"

Before that was possible, the dancers needed to get to Hilo. On Wednesday afternoon, they gathered at Honolulu's airport for the forty-five-minute flight to the Big Island. Tourists in the terminal stared at the ladies. They were giggling and excited, dressed alike in blue jeans and hālau T-shirts. Heaps of good-luck lei, more beautiful than the usual Waikīkī garland, were draped around their necks. Māpuana had already passed out assignments for family and supporters once they reached Hilo—to make lei, watch children, drive eight vans, buy lunches and dinners, handle wake-up calls, and move equipment and costumes. She, Kīhei, the dancers, and musicians would concentrate on three nights of hula.

Jill Smyth was one of the Mommies. She had danced since she was six and had represented Mōhala ʻIlima at other competitions. Jill's friends knew she liked to have fun; they always heard her laughter long before they saw her. But when Jill first stepped into Kanakaʻole Stadium and onto the stage for the hālau's private rehearsal, she was petrified. "I did not want to dance anymore. . . . I wanted to get away. . . . Whatever made me think I had the guts to step on this stage with people at home watching their TV, and you know they are only looking for you, and people there in the audience, and you think, 'My God, what if I stumble? What if I make a mistake? What if everybody's turning left and I'm turning right?' A million things. I started hyperventilating. I broke out in a cold sweat."

Competing at Merrie Monarch is enough to make anyone nervous, but Jill was devastated and could not contain her fear. Kīhei talked to the women on the hotel lawn in the afternoon, after another practice. "I know a lot of you are nervous. A lot of you are questioning why you're here, but you're taking a very selfish attitude. You're thinking 'I' instead of 'we.' You're thinking, 'I am on that stage. I am dancing. I am going to be looked at.' But in actuality, there are fifty-two dancers. It's 'we' who are going to be on that stage. It's 'we'

Associate kumu assist two women into special pāʻū, skirts that Māpuana sews for each first-time Merrie Monarch performer. The skirt is an acknowledgment of the sacrifice the dancers make in preparing for the competition. Kekauʻilani Kalama, spiritual advisor to the hālau, watches from the back.

Mōhala ʻIlima performers and supporters gather in a prayer circle on the rim of Kīlauea Iki. Merrie Monarch dancers know their performance is possible because of support from family and friends—people who attend fund-raisers, handle competition logistics, and provide help at home during the long months of rehearsals.

who are going to be dancing. And it's 'we' who are going to be doing this."

The festival begins Thursday night with the Miss Aloha Hula solo competition of ancient and modern hula for unmarried women between the ages of eighteen and twenty-five. Mōhala 'Ilima would be represented by Valerie Māhealani Chang, who had danced with the hālau at six previous Merrie Monarchs.

As Val finished dressing in an assigned area beneath the stadium's concrete seats, sometimes laughing with Māpuana and Kahulu Ka'iama, her attendant, she could hear kumu onstage chanting for other competitors. The crowd cheered for especially dramatic and athletic moves—when soloists' bodies quaked in volcanic vibrations or when they sat on their haunches and swept the floor with their backs. Costume colors blazed in the bright television lights. Outer skirts of green ti or blond raffia billowed over multiple cloth skirts—red, gray, blue, yellow, purple, or lime green. The dancers' hair supported rainbows and geysers of flowers and greens; their bodies were drenched with the plants of the forest, even seaweed from the shore.

Val, a quiet, almost shy woman with a bubbling laugh and a master's degree in elementary education, would dance wearing another carefully reasoned Mōhala 'Ilima statement—a plain unbleached muslin skirt and blouse.

"This is to say that money can't do the important things; neither can fashion," Kīhei told the judges on the fact sheet. "Val won't compete against what she wears; her costume won't obscure her mele or hula. She wouldn't be our representative if we thought she needed that kind of prettying up."

If the judges wanted to know more, the fact sheet explained: "We [do not] go to extremes of time and expense to keep up with what is currently fashionable on the competition stage. . . . Our kahiko costumes cost less than $50 each . . . [and] with less than $50 each, we manage to achieve a distinctive and even expensive look; but that look is paid for with planning, busy hālau hands, and careful valuing."

Val's time to go onstage arrived. Māpuana and Kahulu accompanied her to center stage, chanting. Then they stepped back, not to the microphones that other kumu used, but a few yards away, where they sat down and began "Kalākaua He Inoa," a name chant honoring the king:

> *Kalākaua, he inoa*
> *Ka pua mae 'ole i ka lā;*
> *He pua mai la i ka mauna,*
> *I ke kuahiwi o Mauna-kea.*

Val became a flower blooming in the mountain forests of Mauna Kea, a flower too strong and beautiful for the sun to wilt, a flower reflecting the greatness of Kalākaua. For Kīhei and Māpuana, Val personified what the Mommies would be striving to achieve the next two nights. Kīhei said that when Val danced, her motions transformed the language into a tide gently ebbing and flowing. "That epitomizes our style at its best—the absence of sharp, rough, abbreviated, or broken gestures. . . . The dance encompasses more than herself. Rather than defining limits, it's more of a style that doesn't end at the end of the finger, that doesn't end at the end of the foot, but reaches out and encompasses and enfolds." When she finished, Val bowed her head politely to the festival's royal court and left the stage.

Next came the modern hula competition, and the stage became a ballroom of swirling satin and lace and velvet evening gowns as each soloist swept across the plywood floor, their hair bejeweled with floral headdresses and crowns. Val danced barefoot and happily in a simple white muʻumuʻu. Her hula felt as spontaneous and loving as a dance for a baby's first birthday lūʻau, and she was awarded fourth place among the solo performers.

For Friday night's group performance, the hula kahiko competition, the hālau prepared in the nearby Civic Auditorium. While supporters readied a buffet dinner, Māpuana sat her ladies on the wooden bleachers for a pep talk. "When you take off your own clothes, let a little bit of yourself go. Each time you put on a dress costume, get a little bit closer to each other. We all need each other."

Māpuana thanked the women for the wonderful feelings they had given her, told them how beautiful they were, and reminded them to enjoy everything. Some of the women started to weep.

"I said warm them up; not wring them out!" It was Kīhei's turn, and he told the ladies why this hālau differed from others, how at each Merrie Monarch, Mōhala ʻIlima tried to share something about hula, even if the audience couldn't see or didn't care.

Kīhei explained to the judges, "We come to offer enthusiastic praise of Hawaiʻi, to delight in the vitality of hula, and to find joy in being together. We certainly have no intention of bringing fifty-two [dancers] every year; the investment of time and money alone make that an impossibility. We do feel, however, that after a decade of competition there is more to say about ourselves than 'Here are the twenty dancers who give us the best chance of winning.'"

The Hilo evening rains smacked the auditorium roof as the women quietly dressed. They put on blue bloomers, blue tops, gold feather head lei, yellow and then red underskirts, blue overskirts, gold kerchiefs, white shell necklaces, gold wrist and ankle lei. Some of the women knew the customary old dressing ceremonies and chants, traditions Māpuana had learned from

Maiki, but this protocol was impractical for fifty-two dancers at Merrie Monarch, and Kīhei explained Māpuana's improvisation to the judges:

"Our attitude toward dressing and undressing is certainly one of order, care, and reverence. We use dressing as a time for quiet meditation, for leaving behind, with our street clothes, all that is not of the hula world. Each lady is carefully tied in, and the tying is checked, layer by layer, and step by step. . . . No one is allowed to become distracted from the spiritual preparation that must keep pace with its physical counterpart. . . . It is always our goal that each dancer—when she is fully dressed, our prayer-circle formed, and the pule [prayer] given—be transformed into her best self."

By 8:13 P.M. the dancers were dressed. Māpuana kissed each one and gave her the tip of a budding ti leaf to be secured within her costume, for good luck. Then she dressed in her kīkepa, a strapless sack dress that she made for her kumu hula graduation fourteen years earlier. The symbol of that accomplishment was a matching kīhei, or cloak, that she placed over the kīkepa and secured with a knot on her left shoulder. Her women stretched, chanted "we—we—we," and then went through the motions of their dance one more time before holding hands in prayer. When they stepped outside to the idling vans, the rain had stopped. Only stars filled the sky.

The vans took three minutes to reach the stadium. Intermission was almost over. Children ran along the sidewalks, and in the parking lot a bus pulled up to unload another hālau. People crowded the entrance, trying to get to seats. Thousands of ticket holders talked and laughed, sharing sodas, chili, and rice with friends unseen since the year before. Māpuana's women had arrived at Hilo's biggest party, and it was their turn to dance.

They got out of the vans silently and walked barefoot along a sharp gravel path still wet from rain. They lined up, arms folded and raised in front of their chests, waiting for Māpuana's signal to squeeze through the crowd loitering around the entrance. Eyes straight ahead, they walked past other costumed dancers, who were gabbing and posing for friends' cameras or staring as the hālau split in two and moved toward the ramps that would lead Mōhala 'Ilima onto the stage. Master of ceremonies Kimo Kaho'ano quieted the audience and announced, "And now, ladies and gentlemen, from Kailua, O'ahu, under the direction of their kumu hula Māpuana deSilva, welcome Hālau Mōhala 'Ilima." The dancers stepped into the heart of Merrie Monarch, formed their lines, and danced for Kalākaua as Māpuana chanted and beat out the rhythm on her ipu.

Afterward, the women filed offstage and quietly went back outside to their waiting vans. Finally, they could release their feelings, as the heat from their

Dressing before a hula competition may take two hours—for a performance that might last fewer than seven minutes.

Bottom: Valerie Chang sewed the lei and costume she wore for her kahiko solo. Māpuana (with ipu) and Kahulu Kaʻiama accompany Val in the style of their ancestors.

bodies mixed with Hilo's cool night air and steamed up the van windows. "It felt terrific." "It was so fun." "It was nice." "Wow." Even Jill Smyth survived. "I danced the whole kahiko set with very little scope to my vision. . . . I could see my hula sisters, left, right, forward, and back and that helped calm me down, and after it was done . . . it was like a tremendous weight got lifted from my shoulders and I thought, 'Wow, this wasn't as bad as I thought it was.'"

Back at the Civic, Māpuana and Kīhei beamed. "The best part of Merrie Monarch is you get to dance again," Māpuana told them, knowing they would experience the same joy the next night during the modern hula performance. "Now, you may have made a little mistake, your line may have been a little crooked, but you only get two minutes to think about that." She was proud of them, and told them their hula had exhilarated her. The ladies went to bed glowing.

The hālau did not place among the winners in the hula kahiko competition and took fifth place out of eighteen groups in the hula ʻauana competition. Kīhei and Māpuana did not care that the hālau had not won higher honors. "You were yourself," Māpuana told them in their closing prayer circle Saturday night. "I'm pleased. You did the best that you could, and that was very, very good."

On Monday, after Sunday's day of rest, the hālau traveled together to Kīlauea in Hawaiʻi Volcanoes National Park. As a special thank-you, the women would perform the ancient chants one more time for the contingent of family and friends who had accompanied them to Hilo.

Their stage was a pā hula, a special platform for hula that the Park Service dedicated in 1980. The pā was built of lava chunks and ʻiliʻili pebbles in a thicket of koa and ʻōhiʻa lehua trees. Many hands had helped gather the ʻiliʻili stones on the Puna coast and carry them through the Kaʻū desert up to the edge of Kīlauea crater. The pā overlooks the sulphur clouds rising out of Halemaʻumaʻu caldera and promotes a close communion with the ancestors of Hawaiʻi, especially Pele, the volcano goddess whose legends the hālau often dances.

Four of the ladies who would soon graduate as hula teachers danced for their Mōhala ʻIlima sisters and supporters. Val followed, sharing her kahiko solo. Then Māpuana called forward each first-time Merrie Monarch dancer to receive an unbleached muslin skirt that was hers alone, unlike the kahiko costumes worn during the festival, which belong to the hālau. The veteran ladies wept as they watched Māpuana tie the new skirts around the waists of the women who had just completed their first Merrie Monarch.

"By the time Merrie Monarch comes, most of my dancers have come to

Mōhala 'Ilima dancers share a final prayer together at the end of their Merrie Monarch trip to the Big Island. Māpuana thanks them for all they have given—to her and to each other. Two dancers wear dark blue overskirts. The color of the ocean depths, they symbolize the dancers' deep commitment to the hālau, and the deSilvas' gratitude to the dancers.

some kind of decision," Māpuana said later, "because it's so intense for so long that a lot of things get put off. For the majority of them, the decisions they've made show at the hula platform at Kīlauea. As that's being done, I see what's happening. . . . I'm getting a deeper look into them. I'm getting my own questions about them answered. I see and feel things about them that I wasn't able to see before."

The women tucked away soggy tissues, lined up in their Merrie Monarch rows, and stood facing Halemaʻumaʻu as Māpuana lifted her ipu to tap out the beats of the chant honoring Kalākaua.

The dancers' feet moved over the pebbles, and the clicking sound they made blended with the rustling of pūʻili, the split stalks of bamboo that flew in the women's hands. Birds in the koa and ʻōhiʻa lehua trees chirped like children, while a ranger's siren howled in the distance.

MELE NOI NA'AUAO

Poem Requesting Wisdom

Aia i Kumukahi ka lā e puka maila

> *There at Kumukahi in the east, the sun rises*

Ke ne'e a'ela nā helu i luna o ka 'āina

> *Sun rays touching everywhere, moving across the land*

Ke ho'opumehana nei

> *Bringing warmth*

Ke ho'omālamalama nei

> *Bringing light*

Ke ho'ōla nei i nā kini ē

> *Bringing life to us all*

Ua ao ka pō

> *Night has become day*

Ua eo ka pō i ke ao

> *Day has triumphed over night*

Ua ao wale maila ka hale kula nei lā

> *Daybreak brings light to our school*

E ola kākou a pau loa i ke ao ē

> *May we all receive life in the light of this new day.*

*Composed by
Kalena Silva*

4 THE WONG FAMILY

'Ōlelo Hawai'i ❧ Hawaiian Language

When Lilinoe and her husband, Kerry Laiana Wong, a construction worker, first enrolled their son at Pūnana Leo, a private Hawaiian-language preschool, they had no idea how their lives would change by the time he graduated. Today, Laiana teaches ʻōlelo Hawaiʻi at the University of Hawaiʻi, where he is pursuing a doctorate in linguistics. Lilinoe left her job at an animal hospital to become a certified preschool teacher for Pūnana Leo.

Preceding page: Respect for the flag is a daily lesson in first-grade immersion classes at Waiau Elementary School, where Lāiana Wong and his teacher, Lilinoe M. Kaʻahanui, lead the class in singing "Hawaiʻi Pono ʻī," the state anthem.

Kerry Wong was sitting in his mother's house one day, relaxing and flipping through a copy of *Honolulu* magazine, a slick city monthly. He stopped when he turned to a feature story with the title "Can Hawaiian Survive?" Although part-Hawaiian himself, Kerry was oblivious to his heritage, and the blunt headline needled him. His father had been Hawaiian Chinese, but Kerry wasn't even sure about the origin of his Hawaiian middle name, Laiana. He spoke English. Always had. At Iolani, an exclusive preparatory school in Honolulu, he had studied Shakespeare and Faulkner. He went to the University of Colorado, earned a business degree, and decided he did not want to wear a suit and play money games. He returned home and demolished buildings for a living. On weekends, Kerry played softball and drank beer with his friends. They spoke English. Everybody did.

The magazine article about the dire state of the Hawaiian language, and the struggle to keep it alive, stirred him. The article made it clear that Kerry's two-year-old son, a mixture of Hawaiian, Chinese, and Caucasian ancestries, was growing up in a Hawai'i where the native language was fifteen hundred people away from extinction. But the article described a newly opened preschool where everything was conducted solely in the Hawaiian language. The founders believed that when intellectually pliant keiki (children) were "immersed" in Hawaiian, they would learn to speak and think in the language, ensuring its survival. The new, bilingual generation would then become men and women who could see and feel as Hawaiians, and could pass on to others the language—and the culture inextricably bound to it.

In one quick read, Kerry Wong's life was changed. A sturdy man, intense by nature, thoughtful and articulate as a result of a good education and inspirational mother (a schoolteacher), the thirty-one-year-old laborer became a bulldozer determined to push his family into Hawaiian-language fluency. Kerry asked his wife, Jalyne, to look into the new preschool. Jalyne, twenty-five, had grown up in a family that spoke Hawaiian. She already knew about the immersion program—had known about it since before their son was born. And she also knew that she wanted their boy to attend it. But she hadn't mentioned any of this to Kerry because she knew her husband wouldn't be interested.

"I'll tell you something. That's true. I wasn't at all," remembered Kerry. He was sitting on his in-laws' lānai, talking while Jalyne served beef stew, rice, beer, and juice with a laugh that warmed the chill January night. "I didn't listen to Hawaiian music. I didn't go to watch hula. . . . Right after that article, my attitude changed slowly, [but] when we went, we went all the way overboard. . . . [I have asked myself] why didn't I do this ten years ago, fifteen years ago? Why wasn't I interested in [Hawaiian language] then? I don't know the reason. . . . Through Iolani and through Boulder, I never really was motivated. . . . Most of the time I was, 'I'll get by. I won't fail. The main thing I pass.' . . . I didn't think about the future. . . . I don't really understand why we did this [now]. We just did. It's just that I felt—the language is going to die.

"I've changed a lot. I've noticed my wife has, too. We've changed our attitudes towards a lot of things. . . . [Learning] is a whole different thing. I woke up and said, 'Hey, I want to learn.' It feels good to learn. It's something I've become addicted to now. Maybe I'll be able to instill that in my son so he won't have to wait ten years until after he graduates from college before he starts learning something."

In June 1987, Kerry and Jalyne enrolled their son, Lincoln Lāiana Wong, in Pūnana Leo o Honolulu (the language nest of Honolulu), the preschool that had been the focus of the revelatory magazine article. Within a year, Lāiana was fluent in Hawaiian. Within two years, Kerry and Jalyne had learned enough Hawaiian at night school to almost keep up with their son. Within five years, Jalyne became a teacher at Pūnana Leo, and Kerry returned to the university, earned a master's degree in linguistics, started work on his doctorate, and began teaching Hawaiian to undergraduates. In the process, the Wongs committed themselves to ka 'ōlelo Hawai'i, the Hawaiian language, and joined others in the community who were also rallying to save it.

The Wongs' new friends called Jalyne by her middle name, Lilinoe (the Hawaiian goddess of the mists), and Kerry by his, Laiana, the name his father had given him. Kerry had always thought Laiana meant Leonard, because that was his father's name. Later, a teacher explained that Laiana was the Hawaiian way of pronouncing Lyons. Before Kerry passed the name on to his son, Lilinoe's family asked her uncle what the name Laiana really meant. According to Hawaiian tradition, names must be carefully chosen, and the family wanted to make sure the boy's middle name would bring him good fortune, not ill. Lilinoe's uncle grew up speaking the language. He would know. "His Hawaiian seems to run deep, with ancient roots," Kerry said. "It's something I can't really understand. He broke the name down into syllables and gave us this meaning: 'The infinite vision of light reflecting the warmth of the sun.'

And I said, 'Well, that's fine with me and that's what we'll give to Lincoln as his middle name.'"

Both Jalyne and Kerry had been given their Hawaiian names in the 1950s, well before academics and others began adding kahakō (macrons) and 'okina (glottal stops) to Hawaiian words to clarify pronunciation and understanding. The use of kahakō and 'okina was popularized in the mid-1980s, on street signs and in printed material, after a decade of Hawaiian cultural activism known as the Hawaiian Renaissance. Then, in 1986, Hawaiian community leaders and scholars persuaded state legislators to revoke a ninety-year-old law prohibiting the use of Hawaiian as a primary teaching language.

The prohibition had been enacted in 1896, after the forced deposition of Queen Lili'uokalani and the seizure of her government by a band of pro-American businessmen. Although Hawaiians had spoken their language for at least fifteen hundred years, it took less than a century to almost completely destroy its vitality.

The process began in 1820 when Calvinist missionaries arrived from New England to spread the word of God throughout the Sandwich Islands and to transform the "pagan" kingdom into a Christian one. Six years after their arrival, the missionaries had created a written "Hawaiian language," an orthography that borrowed five vowels and seven consonants from the English language to convey phonetically what the missionaries thought they heard the Hawaiians saying. The Calvinists designed reading and writing rules to standardize the island dialects and eliminate some of the regionally distinctive consonant sounds that the people used interchangeably, such as T for K, D and R for L, and V for W.

Even before missionaries published the first Hawaiian Bible, in 1848, King Kamehameha II approved the teaching of the written language, wanting his people to acquire through reading and writing the same knowledge—and power—that the foreigners had. Literacy was a new concept for Hawaiians, who historically memorized their lore and passed it on in an oral tradition of chant and song. Many Hawaiians embraced the learning with the same enthusiasm they showed for the foreigners' god and hymns. Schools opened throughout the Islands, and by the 1830s most Hawaiians could recite the alphabet and read words. The more literate among them published chants, traditions, discourses, and histories in their own Hawaiian-language books and newspapers. Over the years, these documents accumulated in archives, libraries, and family trunks and became important resources for the cultural rediscovery a hundred and fifty years later.

As more and more foreigners journeyed to Hawai'i seeking access to island markets and goods, more haole took up positions administering the King-dom's business and political affairs. English became more than a status lan-guage for elite Hawaiians; soon, fluency was a prerequisite for dealing with the demands of outsiders and the new laws and treaties created to accommodate them. Missionaries learned Hawaiian and helped Hawaiians learn English, but most of them segregated their own children in English-only schools. Many of these haole students went on to become business leaders in the Islands' emerging agricultural economy and, as pro-American businessmen, worked to secure their Hawaiʻi ventures through the American annexation of Hawaiʻi. This eventually came about in 1898, five years after the overthrow of Queen Liliʻuokalani. English became the official language for the provisional, interim government, which passed a law prohibiting the use of Hawaiian in schools. Under the new government, most teachers ridiculed children who spoke Hawaiian; children were beaten or forced to recite one hundred times, "I will not speak Hawaiian," sometimes while holding a heavy stone in the air for emphasis. Teachers went out of their way to call on students' Hawaiian-speaking parents and warn them that they were depriving their children. Con-sequently, Hawaiian elders discouraged their children from learning Hawaiian or being Hawaiian. Most youngsters lapsed into the pidgin used by Japanese, Chinese, and Filipino immigrants. As native expression and native pride with-ered, real estate developers replaced old Hawaiian place names, rich in leg-endary meanings, with new ones designed to attract home buyers. Kaʻelepulu (the moist blackness) became Enchanted Lake; Puʻuloa (the long hill) became Pearlridge; Puʻu Keahiakahoe (the fire of Kahoe Hill) became Castle Hills.

By 1986, when the state Legislature legalized the use of Hawaiian in schools, 30 percent of the state's entire student body had some Hawaiian ancestry, but only 5 percent of the students in the University of Hawaiʻi system were Hawai-ian, and of the total number graduating, only 2 percent were Hawaiian. From that group, 1 percent pursued graduate studies. The Hawaiian language was spo-ken by about one thousand Hawaiian elders, plus a few hundred people on Niʻihau (a privately owned island off Kauaʻi that has resisted most government intrusions) and students who had learned the language at the university. Most hula masters and Hawaiian musicians who performed Hawaiian chants and songs either memorized them or used crib sheets during performances.

During the late 1980s, the future of the Hawaiian language seemed to depend almost solely on Pūnana Leo, the preschool that used the immersion technique introduced to Hawaiʻi from Aotearoa, the country better known as New

Zealand. Native Polynesians, or Maori, perpetuate their language through village-based preschools where no English is spoken. Within a few months of enrollment, Maori children are able to speak and understand Maori, despite the prevalence of spoken English in their country.

To make the concept work in Hawai'i, organizers of Pūnana Leo, mostly parents of the students, had to find Hawaiian speakers willing to teach for minimum wages—in a preschool they could not afford to build. They needed Hawaiian-language children's books that did not yet exist, and which they could not afford to publish. In Honolulu, the parents found two Hawaiian speakers from Ni'ihau and a third whose grandmother was from Ni'ihau. In 1985, the Kalihi and Moanalua Church donated space for the school, and friends helped tape Hawaiian words into English-language books. Twenty students were enrolled the first year, and the school's minuscule income required that parents perform eight hours of chores each month. Parents who could not speak Hawaiian had to attend once-a-week classes.

Pūnana Leo was just the beginning. Parents realized their children could lose Hawaiian fluency after they left the preschool and entered kindergarten in the public schools. They began a lobbying effort to persuade the state Department of Education to establish a Hawaiian-language elementary school program, thereby continuing the work begun by Pūnana Leo, and to give credibility to 'ōlelo Hawai'i as an official language of the state. Enough sympathetic officials supported the idea to overrule opposition from superintendents who had already tried (unsuccessfully) to stop a related program that placed Hawaiian elders in the schools to teach native concepts and values.

The Department of Education initially established two schools in 1987, each with a kindergarten through first-grade program and another class for second-graders. The department then sought funds for additional schools and grade levels, and its goal for 1999 was seven immersion centers across the state, offering Hawaiian through high school. English is introduced as a teaching language for some subjects by the fifth grade.

Support structures for speakers of Hawaiian are growing. Hundreds of students are now enrolled in Hawaiian-language classes. A few radio shows are broadcast in Hawaiian, and computer users can access Leokī, an electronic bulletin board. But the complexity of perpetuating 'ōlelo Hawai'i becomes apparent after visiting the Wongs. Laiana and Lilinoe, their son Lāiana, and his younger brother, Kumuhonuaikaueōkalani, live with Lilinoe's parents, the Kealohas, just off the freeway in central Honolulu, on a narrow side street in the district known as Kapālama. The place name refers to an enclosure made of lama wood that was a protected area for chiefs.

Immersion in Hawaiian culture is important for students learning the language in classrooms. These preschoolers from Pūnana Leo o Honolulu pull kalo in the remote village of Ke'anae, Maui.

The chiefs and their enclosure are long gone from Kapālama. The Kealoha home is squeezed between two others, all pinched into a neighborhood crammed into the urban sprawl that is Honolulu. Inside the family home, the walls are covered with mementos and photographs of children, family, and friends who over the years have passed through the house. In back, on the covered lānai, a barbecue, refrigerator, and cafeteria table stand ready for any guest who might stop by.

Here, during a visit in 1989, Lilinoe extended the aloha implicit within her family's surname. Smiling, she served more juice and beer while Lāiana ran around, sputtering and singing in a steady stream of Hawaiian and English, two languages he mixed freely to convey enthusiasm for that year's favorite video, *Ghostbusters.* His father relaxed on a bench, his hair still speckled with paint from the day's construction job.

When the Wongs applied for Lāiana's admission to Pūnana Leo, more than a hundred children were waiting for the twenty spaces at the school. Pūnana

Leo enrolled Lāiana because his mother had grown up listening to her uncles, grandmother, and great-grandmother speak Hawaiian. Two of Lilinoe's brothers had studied the language in college, and her mother played Hawaiian music. Pūnana Leo prefers family exposure for its children, to reinforce and encourage the use of Hawaiian.

After their son was accepted into the program, Lilinoe helped her husband to realize that they needed some immersion of their own to keep up with Lāiana. They both attended evening Hawaiian-language classes, where the first year was a headache of grammar and vocabulary study. They practiced by speaking with Lilinoe's uncle, their son, his teachers, and with a language support group.

"When we don't know how to explain things to him, we have to find out, and that pushes us to look for more knowledge," the boy's father said about their first year with the language.

"I'll be painting or something, and it doesn't take too much brain power, and . . . I just go into my head, you know, think of a situation and try to think of it in Hawaiian. That's what I tried to tell some guys too, and they say, 'Well, how you do it?' I say, 'Well, either you just go to talk to people over the course of years or try to talk to yourself or think about it yourself.' I look at things and instead of thinking about them in English, think in Hawaiian. Look at your pants. Instead of saying 'pants' to yourself, say 'lole wāwae, lole wāwae.' Leg clothes. Try do that with objects around you and eventually you'll get used to knowing those objects with a new name, not an English name but a Hawaiian name. . . . We had to get over being embarrassed speaking Hawaiian. 'Cause, you know, at first, you don't know that much. . . . That's a very big block. If you can get by that block, you can learn."

Lilinoe's uncle, who grew up speaking Hawaiian, did not help much. "He used to laugh at us when we first started because he said, 'Oh you folks sound like you're three years old!' which is normal when you start learning a new language."

"At first I was very limited," Laiana said. "Now I can carry on a conversation and say basically what I want and have it understood, and I can understand what people are saying to me. At that point I am happy, but I'm not going to stop there. I have a long way to go."

"I've decided to go back to school," said Lilinoe, who gave up her job at the Honolulu Pet Clinic to teach at Pūnana Leo. "I never thought I was capable of going to college. . . . [But that has changed] in being around these Hawaiian-language teachers, the Hawaiian language itself, and seeing the need [for more] teachers."

"She had no confidence," Laiana said. "She didn't think she was going to be able to do it. . . . Now she has confidence through the Hawaiian language. . . . Maybe other Hawaiians, through Hawaiian language, will gain confidence, a positive attitude toward things. If they now can say, 'In the English world I never would have made it. Now I got something through the Hawaiian world. Maybe I got a shot. Maybe I can make it.' Not everybody is an athlete. Not everybody is capable [of achieving what] we consider success. But as we open up new avenues, and you open up avenues that hit close to home, you'll be surprised what good things that can happen, and people's attitudes towards them and motivation factors will change drastically."

In 1989, about eighteen months after the family began the language immersion program, Laiana suffered a brain hemorrhage. Doctors told him he would never work construction-demolition again. During his recuperation, he visited the Pūnana Leo children inside the cinder-block walls of their school at the Kalihi and Moanalua Church and made a decision to return to the university, improve his Hawaiian, and become a teacher.

Except for the sounds of a fifteen-hundred-year-old Polynesian language issuing from the children's mouths, Pūnana Leo o Honolulu resembles many O'ahu preschools, with a carpeted area for songs and sharing; shelves for blankets, books, and toys; and small tables and chairs for learning and meals. The children's lunch pails and T-shirts advertise Barbie and Mickey and Donald, Hulk Hogan, and the New York Giants.

Two of the school's original teachers, Lolena Nicholas and Ipo Kanahele, grew up speaking Hawaiian on Ni'ihau. The third, Ululani Chock, had been raised on O'ahu by her grandmother, who was originally from Ni'ihau, and during the summers Ulu went to Ni'ihau to visit her relatives there. During a visit, when the teachers spoke to the children, words flew out in the accelerated Ni'ihau style, but the children didn't seem to have difficulty understanding. Instead, they challenged the teachers to keep up with their energy.

As the children napped, the Ni'ihau teachers sat outside and talked quietly. In English, with a stranger, they spoke in a humble, almost reserved, manner that transformed into smiles as soon as they returned to their first language. Ulu was happy to share in either language, mostly because her English is as fast as her Hawaiian and she loves to talk. She learned English because her father could not speak Hawaiian, which "came during the years when I was growing up [with my grandmom]."

People in Ulu's household never stopped speaking Hawaiian, and after graduating from high school in Wai'anae on O'ahu, Ulu went to work at Paradise Cove, a nightly commercial lū'au for tourists, where she greeted visitors and wove hats. When she heard about Pūnana Leo, she interviewed for the job even though the pay was low, and she became a teacher.

"I enjoy working with kids. I like to see more children speaking the language. Really, because when I was growing up you hardly heard anybody talking Hawaiian. . . . That was kind of boring because you only have you yourself and you have nobody to communicate with. . . . But now, there is so much people speaking it. Everywhere you turn. Sometimes you don't even know. . . . My grandma says, 'You see, you cannot gossip about anybody anymore [in Hawaiian] because you never know.'"

Ulu knew she could earn a better salary if she went to college and got a degree that would enable her to teach for the state Department of Education's immersion program, but instead she opted for preschool education classes at the community college. "I've been wanting to go back to school, but in another way I'm kind of afraid because if I leave it's only going to be two teachers here at Pūnana Leo, and it's kind of hard to find teachers for preschool. [When we first started] we had a lot of university students, but they didn't last very long. . . . We don't know why. . . . I don't know if the kids are too wild for them or what, but we're still here. I guess they are afraid, because we speak it fluently and some of them are just learning it, and they come here and then they hear us talk and they get shame, like: 'Oh my God . . . these people talk too fast for us.' Because we talk really fast among ourselves, and they just sit there and they watch us. 'Oh you guys are speaking too fast, can you slow down?' . . . We can't. That's our natural way of talking."

Teaching at Pūnana Leo has sometimes been difficult for Ulu. "Before, I never had blemishes on my face; now look at me. I go home all stressed out. We're teachers, mothers, nurses, fathers. We're everything. From seven to five. When they leave Pūnana Leo, they are with their parents two to three hours; then they go to sleep."

Ululani continues to teach because, as she said, "I like kids. Period. . . . I accomplish something when I see the kids speak. I feel real good about myself 'cause I say, 'Gee, I taught these kids Hawaiian.' Imagine that I taught these kids Hawaiian and they all speaking Hawaiian today. I can share my language with them, the younger generation.

"We have a lot of ears opening, but people have to be strong so that the language can continue for a lot more years. . . . I hope the language is not like a fad, to where [people] all get excited, . . . learn the Hawaiian language, and then, after that, it just disappears; they are not interested anymore."

Before Lāiana graduated from Pūnana Leo, in 1989, the Wongs planned to have their son continue improving his fluency through the state Department of Education's immersion program, the Kula Kaiapuni Hawai'i. The DOE initially set up the program in rural Keaukaha, a predominately Hawaiian community near Hilo on the Big Island, and at Waiau Elementary School, in the midst of the suburbanized central plain on O'ahu.

By 1994, 134 students were commuting to the Waiau campus from all over O'ahu to learn Hawaiian. Although more than seven years old, the state's program continues to be a novelty for visiting educators. One spring day, Waiau welcomed a group of teachers from American and Western Samoa, teachers who wanted to see the immersion program in action—they were considering the program for Samoa, to support the Samoan language. The group was ushered into teacher Alohalani Housman's portable classroom, where kindergartners had just finished pledging allegiance to the American flag in Hawaiian. The kids' valentines shared wall space with homemade educational posters and other posters from Disney and Sesame Street, modified for 'ōlelo Hawai'i with Hawaiian words taped over the English texts. On the chalkboard, smiley faces grinned next to the names of students who had performed well, and frowning faces scowled beside those who needed improvement.

As the children sat in their chairs, Alohalani asked them if she could speak English with the visitors. Then she explained to the Samoans that seven of her twenty students had arrived at Waiau from Pūnana Leo already speaking Hawaiian. The rest of the class, she said, could not. Alohalani explained how, as time and lessons passed, peer pressure encouraged the other thirteen children to use Hawaiian words; by spring, most of them were motivated to speak Hawaiian.

The Samoan group moved on to a reception in the library, where thousands of English books filled the shelves. The library in the Hawaiian classroom has slowly grown since 1989, when it consisted of thirty-five books, most of which were translated from English, with Hawaiian words taped in place.

At the reception, the visitors met Lilinoe Ka'ahanui, the other immersion teacher, who had learned Hawaiian at the university while becoming certified to teach high school. The Department of Education had waived its elementary education study requirements for Lilinoe because it needed a teacher at Waiau. In the beginning, the shortage of Hawaiian speakers was so acute that when Lilinoe or Alohalani got sick, no substitute teachers were available.

The principal at Waiau then was Diana Ka'apana-Oshiro. As at other schools, the students called Diana by her last name—Mrs. Ka'apana-Oshiro. Their respect was mixed with an equal amount of affection. Diana expressed a warm motherly concern for her brood and at the same time conveyed the expectation that loitering was not allowed. Diana has Hawaiian ancestors and she cared about the program's success, but she told the Samoan visitors that the shortage of Hawaiian-language teachers would continue to be a problem for at least five years. Eventually, there should be enough certified teachers, but even then, Diana suspected those new teachers might face another challenge: By the time the first-graders of 1989 become sixth-graders, they may be more fluent than new teachers fresh from the university. And the school needed more books to challenge the students' rapidly expanding Hawaiian vocabulary.

Diana also pointed out the problem of language teachers invariably interpreting and translating differently. She anticipated a standard for editing new Hawaiian textbooks, especially for science, which uses words that have no current translation in Hawaiian. She presented an example: Should the word galaxy be incorporated or translated into Hawaiian? Different combinations of Hawaiian words will yield the concept of galaxy, but someone has to decide what the standard will be.

Elders who still speak Hawaiian might be able to help, except that many

When Hawaiian-language immersion began at Waiau Elementary, in 1987, teachers and parents pasted Hawaiian words over the English in schoolbooks. Since then, federal grants have provided funds for new Hawaiian-language books with native themes.

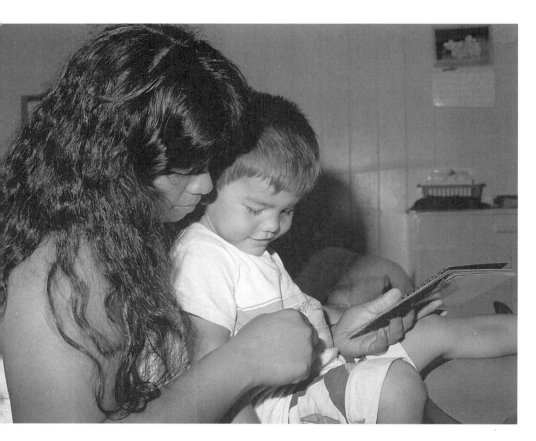

Lilinoe Kealoha Wong shares a story with Kalena Honda at a Pūnana Leo school in Honolulu. Parents of students at Pūnana Leo are required to know or study Hawaiian so they can reinforce their children's learning at home. Studies find that teachers in public-school immersion programs have difficulty maintaining Hawaiian as the teaching language with children who come from families where Hawaiian is not spoken at home.

immersion children speak the language differently than some kūpuna, most of whom learned their Hawaiian at home, as an oral language. The formal system for Hawaiian-language education had been dismantled, Diana pointed out, in 1896.

Before the Samoan ladies left Waiau, they went to the classroom where Lilinoe Ka'ahanui was in charge. The children said good-bye to their guests with a chant and a Hawaiian song as Lilinoe strummed an 'ukulele. The Samoan ladies shared some of their own songs with the children.

After class, Lilinoe described a recent field trip to see John Waihee, then the state's Hawaiian governor, at the Capitol. "My children are very confident. They think of themselves as very special. One student (a second-grader) pulled the governor aside and said to him in English, 'Just like you I'm part-Hawaiian, and I want you to know I'm not stupid. I am the future. The Hawaiian language will die if we don't speak it now.'"

Lilinoe regularly hugged her Waiau children, and she carried on a respectful relationship with them. She had them vote on whether they wanted to use lined or blank paper, and she remained positively attentive all through the long day. With no Hawaiian-language aides to take over for her during breaks and recess, Lilinoe put in a nonstop day, every day, and went home exhausted. She recalled a particularly awful school day when she felt sick and miserable, and her students knew it. "They were on their best behavior. They whispered to each other. I was just shocked. They were real sensitive."

With committed teachers like Lilinoe and Alohalani, with supportive parents and enthusiastic government officials and bureaucrats, the future of Hawaiian immersion should be secure, but it isn't. An influential daily newspaper editor voiced the fears of many people when he asked in a column whether Hawaiian immersion was the "first step towards a separated society like that of the French in Canada, the Catholics in Northern Ireland or the Indians in Fiji . . . with the same tinderbox potential?"

The fear resurfaces whenever the Department of Education has to beg for money from the state legislature. In 1989, the department needed an additional $521,000 to develop new immersion books, add classes, and hire Hawaiian-language teachers for Maui, Kaua'i, and for the third grade at Keaukaha and Waiau. Immersion parents followed the relevant appropriation bills through the House and Senate committees and discovered their representatives had eliminated funding for increased immersion and for teaching materials. Senators had attached an amendment to their appropriation bill requiring that government immersion funds be matched by other sources—possibly from the Office of Hawaiian Affairs (a state agency) or from the Bishop Estate, whose assets maintain the private Kamehameha Schools for Hawaiian students.

The budgetary politics angered the parents, and they organized a lobbying excursion to the Capitol. Chaperoned, the children visited Joseph Souki, then chairman of the House Finance Committee. He told them, "We must appreciate that we are Americans first."

Representative Souki's implication that the children should initially learn English infuriated the parents, who sought help from Hawaiian activists. Hawaiian students from the university painted protest signs, scheduled a demonstration, and notified the press. Parents, children, and supporters carried the signs through the state Capitol rotunda, held a press conference, visited politicians' offices, and spoke with the governor—in Hawaiian.

Governor Waihee later told a radio station that he understood the simple words, "But when they started to explain their mathematics lesson to me in Hawaiian, I got lost. . . . I didn't dare speak to them back in Hawaiian, because I was afraid these little children would start to correct my pronunciation. It's really quite embarrassing."

The demonstration and lobbying in 1989 eventually proved successful, but the process drained the parents—many of whom did not understand how politicians make decisions or why anyone would question the appropriateness of the funding request. How, they asked, could legislators not know anything about Hawaiian immersion or a $521,000 line item in a $4.8 billion budget that was being considered for the fiscal year?

Their frustration surfaced during a meeting in April that year at the Waiau school, where twenty parents showed up to discuss the legislative problems and the upcoming evaluation of the immersion program.

When Waiau parents get together, whether for meetings or barbecues, they usually speak English, except when talking with their children; then those who can, speak Hawaiian. Diana Ka'apana-Oshiro estimated about half of the immersion parents are dedicated to fostering the Hawaiian language. "Some parents don't have time to learn the language. . . . Those parents find it difficult to check the homework. They have no idea what their children are doing."

The parents who have time to care, however, care passionately. At a meeting with the immersion program's evaluator, one parent, a Hawaiian-language instructor at an O'ahu high school, said, "We are really very proud of our children, our teachers, and our curriculum. There are a lot of needs, but it's a success, and we'll do anything in our power to keep it going."

Another parent said that his daughter speaks Hawaiian in public. "School stays with her twenty-four hours a day. Teachers have done a tremendous job. She wants to come to school. She wants to learn. She finds it very, very enjoyable to be with kids who are so close-knit."

As they sat in their children's chairs at Waiau, discussing immersion issues, Robert Snakenberg asked if he could speak. Robert's ancestors were Caucasian, but when his family moved to Hawai'i from the mainland, when he was fifteen, a Hawaiian family adopted him. They named him Lokomaika'iokalani and helped him learn Hawaiian. "Loko" became a language teacher and was one of the first teachers in Hawai'i to offer Hawaiian to his high school students. After that 1976 debut, he moved on to administer the education department's Hawaiian studies program. At one time he had questioned whether the state should develop an immersion program, but later he became a vocal proponent for it. Loko knew that most immersion students thrive in school because their parents believe in education and encourage the children. "You go in the regular public schools and see how many Hawaiian kids are out there reading," he told the parents. "It's not a whole lot, because they are not getting reinforcement from home. . . . These kids in this immersion program are getting into the whole idea of reading and enjoying it."

Then Loko introduced an issue that concerned the parents more than the budgetary skirmish. Although peer and parental pressures encourage the bilingual children to focus on Hawaiian during the school year, English-speaking peers influence them to neglect the language after school and during summer vacations. They surf, play piano, and swat base-runs in English, which is also the language of their comics, Baby-Sitters' Club books, and Saturday morning cartoons. English dominates the fun in their life; Hawaiian is the hard-core curriculum. "What are we going to do," Loko asked, "if they begin to lose their enthusiasm? A lot of this has been parent-generated enthusiasm because we want to see the next generation of kids speak fluent Hawaiian, but as they grow up in this modern American situation, that may not be a high priority for them. How are we going to deal with that when the time comes?"

Laiana Wong had voiced a solution to the dilemma months before on the lānai of the Kealoha home. "I want a lot of people to be able to speak Hawaiian, so [my son Lāiana] doesn't feel like an oddball, that there's something's wrong, something's different about him. They get to that age they don't want to be different. You want to be like other people. You copy. . . . And if he's speaking Hawaiian and everyone else is speaking English, he might not feel good about himself. So we have to keep supporting him, showing him that we are into it too, we can do it too, and it's a good thing that he's doing."

The Hawaiian-language students and teachers on O'ahu—from Pūnana Leo through the university—gather together each year for a weekend of fellowship.

The retreat is similar to ones held on the neighbor islands, and in April the Wongs drove out with their son Lāiana to Camp Erdman on the north side of the island. A cold, wet wind kept everyone inside, bundled up in sweaters and jackets, where they focused on speaking Hawaiian as they made ti-leaf lei, shared hula and songs, and participated in the pā'ani 'imi'imi (scavenger hunt), Pā'ani Nīnau (College Bowl), and other games.

The Wongs discovered that some of the high school and university students could speak Hawaiian, but as with most beginning-language students, their phrases were basically memorized responses. Hawaiian did not flow from their hearts, as it did from young Lāiana, who ran away with his Pūnana Leo buddies, impatient with the older students' English-to-Hawaiian computations.

Most of the older students cared enough to try, though, despite the shortages of teachers and materials, despite counselors who advised students to study Japanese because there are "no opportunities" in Hawaiian, despite those students taking Hawaiian merely to satisfy a "foreign" language requirement. Laiana and Lilinoe Wong focused on those teenagers who really wanted to learn and speak Hawaiian better.

Students at the Mānoa and Hilo campuses of the University of Hawai'i can enroll in the largest Native American–language program in the United States. The university also has the nation's highest number of Native American–language majors, partly because the state is willing to pay Hawaiian-language translators, teachers, and textbook writers.

At the Hilo campus, students can learn to chant in Hawaiian and write poetry and literature. Hale Kuamo'o 'Ōlelo Hawai'i—the campus Hawaiian-language center—develops math, science, social studies, and language arts materials for the state's immersion program. Faculty members formulate ways of teaching Hawaiian syntax and orthography. They found, for instance, that if they use Hawaiian images (such as the tentacles-of-an-octopus pattern) they can convey Hawaiian grammar better than with the conventional sentence diagrams used in English. A Hilo faculty member also coordinates the production of pretaped Hawaiian-language radio programs that can be broadcast by stations throughout the Islands. Another professor tapes video lessons for children. And the Hilo language center also offers state immersion teachers Kāko'o Kaiapuni Hawai'i seminars to show them how to teach from a Hawaiian viewpoint so the children will learn Hawaiian concepts instead of translated Western ones.

One seminar, subtitled "You Are What You Eat," directed Hawaiian elders to take the teachers (many of them urban born and raised) around the Big Island to collect 'opihi (limpets), catch 'o'opu fish, build an imu (oven) to cook these and other island foods, and then eat everything in a traditional feast. Immersed, even briefly, in Hawaiian cultural practice, the instructors would become better able to help their students see the world as Hawaiians, so the culture and language would have a better chance of resonating as one.

Government efforts to perpetuate the language have the secondary effect of encouraging those individuals who teach ʻōlelo Hawaiʻi within hālau hula, who write Hawaiian poetry and song, and who organize important ceremonies such as the governor's inauguration and the reinterment of Hawaiian remains discovered during excavations for a hotel on Maui. No longer are these activities culturally isolated.

While all this is going on, Hawaiian enrollment in the university system is increasing. Hawaiian scholars are publishing English translations of older Hawaiian-language materials so a broader audience can learn what Hawaiian authors wrote a century ago. And poetry, stories, essays, and speeches written in English convey the challenge—and the meaning—of being a modern Hawaiian to those who cannot speak ʻōlelo Hawaiʻi.

More and more people are studying the language. About seven hundred are enrolled in the Hawaiian Language Department at Mānoa, where Hawaiian-language courses became so popular by 1989 that the university did not have enough professors to teach the students and still develop new books and learning programs. Earlier that year, when his brain hemorrhage had forced him to abandon his demolition job, Laiana Wong decided to enroll at the university to study Hawaiian language and linguistics. His wife left her job at the pet clinic to teach preschoolers at Pūnana Leo and take childhood development courses at Honolulu Community College. Their income came from her salary, Laiana's federal scholarship for Hawaiian students, and his work translating and later teaching Hawaiian to undergraduates. During his first semester, a language mentor got him a job researching turn-of-the-century Hawaiian-language newspapers. He reeled through the microfilms, looking for stories that could be used in immersion textbooks, because no one had time to write new stories. Whether the words were English or Hawaiian, Laiana read slowly, the stroke having impaired his vision. Laiana identified another kind of impairment. "I used to think, 'Man, reviving the language should be easy. If people were interested in the language, they should all feel the same way and we could just get together and start working.'" But his involvement with immersion had showed him that, while many people want to perpetuate the Hawaiian language, they follow different paths to the same goal. "As a result we have problems."

At the time, there were differences between the university's language scholars at the Hilo and Mānoa campuses. What materials should be translated?

Who should translate them? How should they be translated? How should they be taught after they had been developed into textbooks? Problems continued with some Department of Education officials who complained that inadequate staff funding, and curriculum would handicap the immersion students and their ability to learn English. The bureaucracy delayed funding for translations because of copyright concerns; hired Hawaiian-language translators, teachers, and substitute teachers whose level of fluency was considered inadequate by some immersion experts; and then—instead of adding more immersion classes—instituted a lottery selection system because more children wanted to learn Hawaiian than they could accommodate.

Sam No'eau Warner, Laiana's instructor at the Mānoa campus and one of the Pūnana Leo founders, said, "Every step of the way of the program has been a fight."

When a state Board of Education committee discussed expanding immersion for all subjects through high school, a Honolulu newspaper reported that an assistant superintendent for instructional services, a Filipino, had questioned whether the immersion program had enough "intensity and quality" to teach the students to become "contributing citizens, productive citizens in a competing world."

"What has ninety years of the Department of Education done for Hawaiian kids?" No'eau Warner asked him during the meeting. "Hawaiian kids are alienated, not doing well. . . . What we want for them is that they be competent, confident in themselves, motivated. That is what will make them competitive in this world."

No'eau teaches other people how to speak and read Hawaiian, but he maintains that he will always be a student of the language, as will his students. "The real life of the language is in these kids [learning Hawaiian], and their kids. We can never be native speakers."

No'eau regarded Laiana Wong as his best student in fourth-year Hawaiian, but for Laiana, the studies were frustrating. He wondered if his Hawaiian would ever become mature enough to match his sons'. At that time, he and Lilinoe felt they were still speaking to the boys as a child would speak. They recognized the need for young Lāiana and his brother, Kumuhonuaikauēokalani, to have more opportunities to hear adults speaking Hawaiian fluently and confidently so they could have adult role models for their language development.

Laiana and Lilinoe usually speak English to one another. "We try [Hawaiian], but it's difficult," for many reasons, Laiana said, though he was not sure why. Perhaps because English avoids confusion that can lead to misunderstandings and bad feelings or because it feels awkward with someone who knew you before Hawaiian became part of your life. "One of my friends hit the nail on the head. Your relations [with your wife] started in English, and you kind of go back to that. . . .

"Some people would consider me fluent [in Hawaiian], but there's just no way," Laiana said. "I could get by in a conversation, but there's so many times where you have to stumble and think in English first and translate it into Hawaiian, even to the point of using English words. . . . I couldn't hold this kind of conversation, like I am having with you, right off the top of my head, in Hawaiian.

"The [old] Hawaiians . . . recalled ʻōlelo noʻeau, wise sayings and . . . Hawaiian ideas [in their conversation], and they recalled stories from many, many years ago, and they used that in their conversations to emphasize a point, and it was all that metaphoric speaking. I think to myself, 'Well, I'd like to be like that one day.' But when? When is that one day? Many years from now, maybe. It's just such a slow process now."

E KŪ, E NĀNĀ I NĀ KAI ‘Ē

Arise and Look to the Faraway Seas

E kū, e nānā i nā kai ‘ē

Arise and look to the faraway seas

I ka lepa a ka lei me he manu lā

To the fluttering streamer as a bird

I Kahiki Kū, Kahiki Moe, Kahiki Nui

There at Kahiki-that-rises, Kahiki-that-rests, Kahiki-great

Kahiki Mamao

Kahiki of far away

Eia a‘e ka wa‘a holo

Here comes the worthy canoe

Composed by
K. Kalani Akana

He wa‘a ‘imi ola

A vessel that seeks knowledge

He ho‘ālahia ka wa‘a i ke kakahiaka

A canoe that awakens us at the breaking of the dawn

O kā i ka hoe e nā koa e paio ana

It is best that you paddle, warriors, who champion us

No Hawai‘i, no ke aupuni

For Hawai‘i, for the nation

Eia ka lawe wai, he ka‘apeha

Here is the sustaining water, an immense cloud

‘O ia ka hō‘ailona ē.

This is the sign that you look for.

5 ALBERT KAMILA CHOY CHING, JR

Hoe Waʻa & *Canoe Paddling*

Al Ching is one of a few Hawaiians in California still involved with outrigger canoe racing. He began paddling racing canoes thirty years ago, when the party after the regatta lasted longer than the competition. These days, his best paddlers train year-round so they will be strong enough to compete in the annual Molokaʻi to Oʻahu race.

Preceding page: After paddling forty-one miles across Kaiwi Channel from Molokaʻi, the women from Al Ching's canoe club reach the finish line at Waikīkī.

The cop driving along in central O'ahu couldn't believe his luck when the '47 Ford suddenly emerged from a canefield. Police had been trying to catch the canary yellow hot rod for months, but its four-barrel Mercury V-8 had been too fast . . . until now. Quickly, the officer blocked the Ford's escape and arrested the driver. The teenage speedster should have gone to jail, but the chief of police knew his parents and decided to give him a choice: Join the Marines and clear a string of drag-racing citations or spend some serious time in prison.

"The Marines? Why not?"

For Albert Kamila Choy Ching, Jr., the decision would mean leaving Hawai'i and starting a journey already taken by many other Hawaiians. It was 1959 and Al Ching was eighteen years old. His military basic training was in San Diego, and soon the Marines shipped Al to the Far East for three years as a radio operator. When he discovered that going to school could earn him an early discharge, he enrolled at Pasadena Junior College—and he never moved back to the Islands.

Of the 211,000 people with Hawaiian ancestry counted in the most recent U.S. Census, more than 72,000 live on the continental United States. And half of these expatriates make their homes in California. In places like Hayward, across the bay from San Francisco, and Gardena, near Los Angeles, Hawaiians and other former island residents have their own nightclubs, restaurants, grocery stores, radio shows, hula schools, and canoe clubs.

Many Hawaiians who have lived on the mainland for decades have not changed the patterns of their island upbringing. They can still speak in the Pidgin cadences of their youth. They wear rubber slippers. They stockpile rice in fifty-pound bags. In southern California, a group of Hawaiians holds an annual ho'olaulea, a celebration, attended by thousands of people. And some determined athletes meet regularly to paddle outrigger canoes, maintaining an aquatic link to their Hawaiian past. No matter that the traditional koa logs have been updated in fiberglass, resin, and nylon; paddling keeps them in touch with their island home.

Paddling outrigger canoes helped Al forge a deep connection with his

Hawaiian heritage, but it came about by accident. On a Friday night in 1964 at the Little Hawaii bar in Los Angeles, Al and his roommates were sucking up Coors when a friend introduced them to Sandy Kahanamoku, nephew of surfing, swimming, and paddling legend Duke Kahanamoku. He invited the group to join him in Santa Monica the following day to watch an outrigger canoe race. At the beach the next morning, they were having a good time watching the regatta when a coach singled them out and told them his team was shorthanded—would they pitch in and paddle in a race? Al Ching had never raced outriggers before, but his time in the Marines had kept his body strong and slender, and as a teenager he had crewed sculls for Kaimukī High and had paddled fishing canoes to diving grounds off Waikīkī.

Al and his friends took off their shirts and shoes, rolled up their pants, and climbed into a canoe. One minute they had been spectators, and the next, their paddles were pulling the canoe through the Pacific. They finished in second place. "It was fun," Al remembered. "[Afterward] we were held in high esteem by the Hawaiian community around here because not too many of us paddled then. It was a big thing, though we were just beginners."

Today, Al is in his fifties, but if not for his sun-crinkled eyes and the gray around his temples, anyone would guess he is thirty-five. His brown body is trim and fit, partly because he has paddled for three decades, but mostly because there is another side to Al's happy-go-lucky demeanor. He is intense and competitive, with the discipline to wake up at 3:00 A.M. Monday through Friday, clean office buildings before the workers arrive, go home, get his two sons ready for school as their mother leaves for her job, drop the boys off, then go to work on his canoes or house before picking up his sons after school and taking them to afternoon sports.

Beneath an umbrella at a Redondo Beach restaurant, Al relaxed, ate a breakfast omelet, and answered questions with stories about how his involvement with outrigger canoes had unfolded. "At first, I had no idea anything was going to happen beyond the next weekend. When you're single, you wait for the weekends and that's it."

After his impromptu first race, Al eased into the sport gradually. In the early days, most teams practiced just once a week. "We'd paddle out for about a mile, then paddle back in and drink the rest of the day," Al said with a laugh. "And that was our practice for the whole week." The competitions may have been intense, but the weekend regattas were basically an opportunity to socialize.

In 1970, after six years of enjoying the races and camaraderie, he and his older brother Ralph Hanalei, decided to start their own canoe club with three Redondo Beach paddlers who were tired of commuting fourteen miles to practice at Marina Del Rey. Al and Ralph asked their mother, Helen, a fluent speaker of Hawaiian, to come up with a name for their new canoe club. She chose the Hawaiian word for victory—Lanakila.

Ralph, an Air Force veteran and aerospace hardware designer, got the city to recognize the club and give them a place at King Harbor for their canoes. But financing was more difficult to come by. "We used our own money," said Al. "We built our own canoes. We just scraped money from here and there. . . . I liked everything about paddling. I liked the social life, the competition, the organizing, and of course I loved the water. I grew up near Kāhala Beach, and going to the beach was pretty regular with our family."

Al was a natural for paddling. He had keen eye-hand coordination and excelled as a steersman. He also loved to teach, and his high school coach John Kapua had taught him enough about paddling technique during his sculling year at Kaimukī for Al to want to improve himself and others. "I kept coming back [to paddling] because there was a desire to get better. There never was a desire to get to the very top—it just came. I wanted to get a little better, and then I figured maybe I can beat that guy and then the next guy. . . . Before you know it, there's a lot of guys behind you and you never intended to be that way. And people start looking up at you, and it's almost a shock, like 'Wow, how did I get here?'"

Al kept his days free for the canoes by working nights, loading and unloading trucks for United Parcel Service until he was crushed in an on-the-job accident and forced to leave. When he recovered, he began cleaning a woman's house and hair salon to earn money. That job led to connections with more and more companies until he and his crew of six were hauling mops, buckets, scrubbers, vacuums, burnishers, and polishers all over Los Angeles, scouring thirty-six company offices in the early morning.

Al spent his days training paddling crews, fixing older canoes, and building new canoes. The dry air and temperature extremes in California made the wooden-hull canoes crack, so Al concentrated on using fiberglass and eventually built twelve canoes, each with a Hawaiian name—Kūkini (the runner), ʻOnipaʻa (steadfast), Heʻe Nalu (wave rider). Ralph returned to Honolulu to live in 1975, and Al took over as head coach for Lanakila. He was determined that their club would win the California state championships that year—and it did. After the championship races, his paddlers were the first California crew ever to fly to Kona on the Big Island of Hawaiʻi for the annual Liliʻuo-kalani distance race. In a field of international competitors, Lanakila placed first in the fiberglass division, and in the years that followed they consistently took second and third place.

A Newport Beach paddling club called Blazing Paddles became the first non-Hawai'i team to win the annual Moloka'i-to-O'ahu men's outrigger canoe race, in 1978. The forty-one-mile sprint across treacherous Kaiwi Channel, where wind-blown swells on race day may reach fifteen feet, is considered the world's premier paddling event. In the years after Blazing Paddles' victory, more California teams won the prestigious event.

The Moloka'i victories by California teams raised the profile of the sport among southern California's legion of athletes, who are always on the lookout for a new ocean trend to keep them in shape. The sport quickly became more competitive. Most of Al's original crews had been Hawaiians, but Caucasians began moving into their slots. "I just don't see any Hawaiians living around the beach anymore," Al said. "I used to see a lot. Most live inland now. They are involved in a lot of other things, like hula and crafts."

Despite the change, Al did not worry about his sport becoming stranded in a haole world. "It never bothered me. I never thought twice about it. I just feel that nationality doesn't make any difference anymore. If you want to paddle, you're out there all the time."

Whenever a club had a new canoe to be blessed, though, they always called Al, the Hawaiian. "Now it's the standard, everybody wants me to do it. I can't believe it. I ask myself, 'Oh man, how did I get this job?'"

Like almost everything else in Al's life, canoe blessing began unexpectedly. One day Noah Kalama, the Hawaiian responsible for founding the Kalifornia Outrigger Association, telephoned Al to say he would not be able to drive up from Long Beach to bless one of Al's new canoes. Kalama urged Al to do it himself.

"'Me?' 'Yeah, you can do it.' 'Oh, I don't know how.' Then he told me, 'Just say things from your heart, say what you want to say, make things simple.' I've watched him bless the canoes, and he always read the Twenty-third Psalm from the Bible. Then he'd say the prayer in Hawaiian, the Lord's Prayer, then the whole group standing around does the same thing, but in English. Then there's a koa bowl filled with ocean water and he sprinkles it around, then names the name of the boat and blesses it. . . .

"Basically I do the same thing. I always mention to the people, 'There is no magic. . . . You are the people who make this boat blessed. . . . This boat will still be here if you take good care of it, after your years of paddling are done. And hopefully your children will get to use the boat. . . . And maybe their children will be using the same boat. So you kind of make a time machine. It just carries us from one generation to the next.'"

Al Ching instructs members of his Lanakila Outrigger Canoe Club, teaching them about paddling, canoe steering, and physical conditioning. Afterward, he will help the crews carry their canoes into the marina for practice.

Every year, Al coached the entire club—sometimes as many as seventy people in eleven novice teams of men, women, teenagers, and masters men and women. His life revolved around canoeing. He maintained that commitment until 1976 when he met Erin Shea, one of Lanakila's crop of new paddlers. He and Erin courted each other at races and at the parties that followed, and in 1978, Noah Kalama performed their marriage ceremony. It took place at sea off Los Angeles, aboard the *Buccaneer Queen,* an enormous square-rigged ship, with one hundred people in attendance. In the next few years Erin gave birth to two sons, and Al decided to train some new coaches in order to reduce his work load and have more time for his family. "When I was single I used to spend all of my time down at the harbor. I put all my energy into it," Al said. "Now I like to come home. . . . My family is number one."

Home base for the Lanakila Outrigger Canoe Club is about a mile from Al's house in Redondo, just north of Palos Verdes Point. There, at King Harbor, sixteen hundred pleasure craft are berthed in a maze of docks fronting an enormous power plant, its six emission stacks higher than the nearby hills. On a barren patch of dirt by the harbor, Lanakila's red outrigger canoes lie side by side in cradles resting on carpet remnants. The shiny hulls and spindly outriggers juxtapose centuries of Polynesian science and art with the severely urban landscape.

Each sleek canoe weighs no less than four hundred pounds and measures no more than forty-five feet long—standards set by the racing association. The outrigger, called an ama, is rigged off the hull's left side and is connected to it by two parallel booms, called 'iako. The whole assembly is secured to the boat by a series of complex lashings. The outrigger, Oceania's chief contribution to the world's marine architecture, keeps the slim vessel upright even in rough swells.

Three afternoons every week during paddling season, Lanakila paddlers lug their canoes to the harbor's concrete launch ramp and float them into the cold water. Hefting their paddles, the men and women climb into their seats and whisk quietly out to sea, past tugboats waiting to service the petroleum tankers anchored outside the harbor. As the canoes move beyond the break-water, the condo-smothered shoreline falls away into the darkening desert sky.

For a recent state championship, twenty-seven California canoe clubs descended on Leadbetter Beach in Santa Barbara, the fourteenth time for Lanakila since winning its first title. Oil derricks floated on the dim horizon, and kelp beds marked the water near shore, where the twelve-lane course was flagged parallel to the beach. The mostly haole crews pulled on Lycra shorts and tanktops over their swimsuits and did some stretches in preparation for the races. Loudspeakers pumped Hawaiian music into the morning air.

Al Ching moved quickly through the crowd of paddlers, preoccupied with a few team registration problems. His crews watched the half-mile sprints while waiting their turn. As the green flag dropped, the starting racers dug their blades into the water and pulled short, fast strokes, as many as seventy-five a minute. The practiced synchronization among the crews included a paddle switchover about every fifteen seconds, when the stroke—the paddler in the front seat who sets the pace and counts strokes—called out the signal for switching paddles over to the other side of the canoe: "Hut! Ho!"

The best crews moved as one, their muscles pulling precisely and quickly to move the hull and its outrigger as efficiently as possible around the markers and toward the finish line. At the finish, crew members collapsed, their lungs and muscles burning. Even the best teams were penalized now and then by slip-ups—a late start, a bad turn, poor timing. Al's senior women beat the favored club to the finish line, only to lose first place because of a time penalty for touching a flag.

Al was scheduled to steer a canoe in a master's division race. His carefree demeanor changed as his race time drew near. In the boat, he was all command and alertness. He yelled out the canoe's position and pressed the crew to paddle deeper and faster. At the turns, he maneuvered the canoe smoothly around the flag with a quick series of powerful side and back strokes from his long-bladed paddle. Al's canoe won the race by three feet. "I was like a maniac out there."

Although most paddlers in the championship races were haole, Hawaiians ran the meet. Kauhi Hoʻokano from the Newport club captained the committee boat. His brother Lucky, who left Kaua'i in 1970 to attend college on the mainland, announced the awards. The Marina Del Rey club, coached by Sandy Kahanamoku, won most of the trophies.

"I enjoy watching our people learn, how they came up from nothing," Al said. "And if any of them win a race in the state championship, that makes me happy, real happy. Just watching them. Because I remember when I won. . . . All the things that I learn through canoeing come from my Hawaiian side. How to look at the clouds. How to look at the ripples on the water and to see how the water is running. Even navigating backwards. . . . The canoes did a real lot for me, kept my health, kept my tradition, kept me in touch with Hawai'i."

Outrigger canoe racing is a legacy from an ancient voyaging tradition. The first Polynesians sailed to Hawai'i from the Marquesas Islands around A.D. 350. They crisscrossed the vast Pacific guided only by their knowledge of natural phenomena—the stars, clouds, birds, and ocean swells.

Early Hawaiians used canoes for fishing and interisland travel—and races, wagering their lives, belongings, and even wives on the outcome. Canoe racing declined after the death of King Kamehameha I, in 1819, as Western-style boats came into greater use. When King Kalākaua revived water sports in the late 1800s, the royals favored sculling barges for Regatta Day. Still, outrigger canoes could be seen dotting the rocky shores and beaches, and beachboys thrilled tourists with canoe rides on waves at Waikīkī Beach.

Canoe racing continued to be a haphazard activity until 1950, when leaders representing three hundred paddlers on O'ahu formed what later became the Hawai'i Canoe Racing Association. They set a minimum weight of four hundred pounds for koa-wood canoes and established rules against paddlers swamping or whacking each other. The sport attracted fifteen hundred people in the 1970s, during an historic resurgence of interest in all things Hawaiian known as the Hawaiian Renaissance. So many people wanted to paddle that a second, statewide association, called Hui Wa'a, was formed. By the 1990s, about seven thousand people were paddling in fifty-three different clubs. Since the Islands' koa forests have been denuded by ranching, logging, wild pigs, and grazing animals, wooden canoes are prohibitively expensive, and most clubs use fiberglass canoes for the racing seasons in Hawai'i and California.

The Moloka'i race and the Lili'uokalani distance race off the Big Island in September have become the annual goals for a handful of coaches in California and their paddlers. The local paddlers in Hawai'i no longer have an advantage in competition. Crews from Tahiti, California, and Illinois have finished first or second in almost every Moloka'i race since 1975.

Each spring, as the start of the California season approaches, Al Ching posts flyers in neighborhood stores and colleges and recruits novice paddlers from weight rooms and gyms. He typically begins a new season in April with three hundred eager people, but the number is quickly whittled down to about seventy or less. The sport demands a commitment few athletes can sustain.

Al and his crews began to compete in Hawai'i in 1975, usually in the Lili'uokalani distance race. They consistently placed first, second, or third. Moloka'i is another race altogether, and the few times his men paddled across Kaiwi Channel, eighteenth was the highest Lanakila placed. In 1989, Al's women decided to give it a try.

They set their sights on Moloka'i in March, allowing time for their bodies and pocketbooks to be ready by September 24, race day. For all paddlers, Hawai'i is the ultimate place to race. If Lanakila's women survived the Moloka'i race, the channel would transform them from mainland haole into nā wāhine o ke kai, women of the sea, carrying on a long-standing Hawaiian tradition.

The crew bought their tickets to O'ahu with money from a fund-raiser lū'au, their savings accounts, and the sale of eighteen hundred candy bars. To economize, they would forego hotels and sleep at Al's mother's house and with the parents of their steersman, Sheryl Au.

Two days before the crew was to leave for Hawai'i, Al got a call from Honolulu. Race officials had not received the papers to prove Lanakila's canoe hull conformed to race specifications. The canoe was unreachable—halfway to Moloka'i on a barge. With the race five days away, Al had to come up with another canoe. Maybe he was born under a lucky star; the canoe he arranged to borrow was a treasure, a deep reddish-brown koa canoe loaned by canoe-builder Paul Gay and paddling enthusiasts Mike Muller and Gaylord Wilcox.

Twelve years earlier, a precious, four-ton koa log had been shipped to O'ahu from the Big Island. A few men had tried to build a canoe from it, but they hadn't gotten beyond the rough outline stage. Paul Gay had been patching and restored canoes for thirty years, dreaming of the day he might build one. Muller and Wilcox asked him to carve a canoe from this magnificent log, and Gay's dream came true. Paul moved the log to Wai'anae, and for five-and-a-half months he and his friend Phillip Naone spent every weekend working to reshape the koa, using both handmade and power tools. The finished canoe was called *Ka'ala,* the name of the highest point on O'ahu—the mountain that rises behind Naone's house.

At Hale o Lono Harbor on Moloka'i the day before the race, the women of Lanakila rigged the outrigger to the hull, carried *Ka'ala* into the water, and tried it out. There was time to enjoy the moment, paddling easily along the arid, leeward coast, and they marveled at the sensation of the great hollowed log pushing through the water. Fiberglass hulls do the same thing, but *Ka'ala* allowed them to sit inside a piece of Hawai'i; their muscles and paddles gave new life to the koa tree as it moved over the sea.

In the evening, Lanakila joined the other 250 paddlers at the Kaluako'i Resort, race headquarters, to load up with carbohydrates and perform songs and skits touting each club's abilities. Race officials, supporters, and reporters joined them under the lū'au tent. The view across Kaiwi showed the lights of O'ahu sparkling on the northwestern horizon. The women were full of energy and excitement; the channel was calm and windless. A quiet sea might favor the mainland teams, some of whom were stronger on technique than the local Hawai'i teams but not as familiar with island waters. A notoriously short, steep chop often builds up unexpectedly in Kaiwi Channel.

Before the sun rose on Saturday, the race teams and escort personnel piled into buses and vans for the hour-long drive westward across the island's bumpy desert roads. They turned down a stony trail to Hale o Lono, where the canoes rested on a gravel beach. Paddlers and coaches checked and rechecked the canoes, tied spare paddles to outrigger supports, and positioned water bottles. They wished each other luck, then circled together to say a prayer of thanks and sing "Hawai'i Aloha" before the women stroked out to the line-up.

Everyone waited for the flag to drop—twenty-two canoes loaded with six paddlers each; twenty-two escort boats, each carrying a race official, coaches, and substitute paddlers; and a dozen committee and auxiliary boats with more officials, supporters, reporters, and cameras. At 7:14 A.M., the race was under way. California's Off Shore Canoe Club immediately took the lead. Within thirty minutes the canoes were scattered along the southern coast of Moloka'i. They moved westward toward Lā'au Point and cleared the protective Moloka'i shoreline. Kaiwi Channel opened up wide in front of them, stretching away to the stony southeast face of O'ahu.

Most canoes make their first crew changes at Lā'au Point. Typically, each escort boat motors about a hundred yards in front of its canoe, and when it's time for two or three relief paddlers to spell their teammates, drops the women into the ocean. The paddlers wave their hands at the oncoming canoe to help the steersman navigate alongside them, and as the canoe moves past, they grab the gunwales and pull themselves into the boat and the paddlers being relieved jump out. Like most tricky athletic maneuvers, when it is executed precisely it looks easy and is beautiful to watch. When the changeover goes badly, the canoe stalls and loses valuable time.

The Lanakila women's team was strong; this was the year they had placed

third in the thirty-two-mile Newport to Catalina Island race. But Kaiwi was unfamiliar territory, and even though paddlers who had crossed it before said the ocean was flat this year, it felt rougher than any water the Lanakila paddlers had ever known. The club's escort boat bobbed and churned on the sea, and three of the relief paddlers threw up breakfast. When two others jumped into the ocean and waved their hands for the steersman, the swells blocked their view of the canoe until it almost plowed into them.

Canoes sprint for the finish line at a Kalifornia Outrigger Association State Championship at Leadbetter Beach in Santa Barbara. Contests in California are like those in Hawai'i, except for the kelp beds, frigid water, off-shore petroleum derricks, and predominantly Caucasian crews.

After Lā'au, the flotilla spread out across the channel, and Lanakila lost track of the other boats. Al's directions for his two steersmen were simple: Aim for the back of Koko Head until Diamond Head comes into view, then steer for the back of it; Waikīkī and the finish line would be thirty minutes beyond.

The Off Shore Club from California had paddled this race ten previous times, winning three of them and placing second or third in the others. Some people said Off Shore succeeded because it used only "professional" paddlers;

others sniffed at its high-powered phalanx of coaches, managers, and corporate donors. Al Ching admires the club. "They set the standard in California."

Al also recognizes the benefits of training with the best, and before heading to Hawai'i he had asked Off Shore coach Billy Whitford if the Lanakila women could practice with Off Shore. Whitford agreed. They towed a couple of canoes to Catalina Island, and Off Shore and Lanakila raced the thirty miles back to the mainland. "They smoked us," Al said. "We came home exhausted. But it got us ready. We were in tip-top shape for Moloka'i."

In the official race boat, the *Maggie Joe,* reporters listened as race officials talked to the escort boats over the citizen band radio. Number sixteen's outrigger was loosening; could the crew repair it? Yes. And could it be true?—an oil tanker was heading straight for the canoes? *Maggie Joe's* skipper radioed the tanker's captain, who understood a little English but not enough to comprehend that on his present course he would probably swamp a fleet of outrigger canoes. The Coast Guard intervened, and the tanker altered course.

The *Maggie Joe* drew near O'ahu, and the Ko'olau valleys—Kuli'ou'ou, Niu, Wailupe, Wai'alae Nui—yawned in green-to-brown succession along the suburban coast, mileposts for measuring the racers' progress as they pulled for the famous Diamond Head cliffs.

As the canoes rounded Diamond Head, they entered a three-ring circus of well-wishers. Hundreds of spectators had gathered in boats to greet the paddlers and escort them to the finish line. Helicopters hovered overhead, windsurfers raced in and out, their neon sails flashing and snapping in the breeze, and kayakers skimmed over the water. Whitford realized that his Off Shore crew had a chance not only to break the women's Moloka'i record but also to finish in under six hours—a phenomenal accomplishment. By now his voice was hoarse and the women were tired, but still he shouted encouragement to them, directing them to pick up their pace as they skirted the Waikīkī reef, pulled past the thicket of hotels, and entered the shallow green waters near the Hilton Hawaiian Village hotel and the finish line.

Five hours, fifty-nine minutes, and thirty-six seconds—a new record by twelve minutes. The Off Shore women whooped and hollered in triumph, and hugged one another and the crowd of husbands, boyfriends, family, and friends who waded out from the packed beach to congratulate them.

When Lanakila's canoe crossed the finish line, forty-one minutes later, they placed sixth overall, second in the koa division and ahead of sixteen other canoes. The women threw their paddles into the air and cheered with as much joy as if they had won the race. They crowded their relief paddlers into the canoe and maneuvered it across the finish line a second time, all twelve

Lanakila women finishing together—the whole team in the elegant, gleaming canoe, *Kaʻala*.

In the years since the Lanakila women celebrated their personal victory in Hawaiʻi, Al's team has returned for the Molokaʻi race and continues to place first or second in the koa division. After each race, Al contemplates moving Erin and the children back to the Islands. The temptation is strong. A koa racing canoe that he and two friends purchased is in storage on the Big Island. His sons, Danny and Kawika, would be eligible to attend Kamehameha Schools, the private academy for Hawaiian students. "I don't want them to grow up not knowing anything about Hawaiʻi . . . but time keeps slipping away. Before you know it, three years gone by, then five years."

Al is not the first Hawaiian to move to California and find himself teaching his children about their Polynesian lineage. He explains to the boys who they are named for, that they should be proud of those names and the ancestors they represent. "I read 'em a lot of stories . . . about Kamapuaʻa the big Hawaiian pig god. Mele and the Mongoose. Of course I'm always telling stories about my childhood days and what I used to do. . . . I'm teaching them something about the ocean. . . . I want them to become steersmen; it's the most difficult job of all, but a career as a steersman can last you a long time."

KA NALU

The Wave

Eia ke kū mai nei ka nalu nui

Here now a big wave rises

He ʻonaulu loa

An ʻonaulu loa, a wave of great length and endurance

Hoʻohua Kūhela i ke awakea

It swells, sweeping unbroken in the noonday sun

A pae kuʻu papa i ka ʻakoʻako

My board mounts the crest

Lele lā ka pola i ke ehu o ke kai

My loincloth flies in the spray of the sea

ʻO ka ʻiwa kani leʻa koʻu like

I am like the ʻiwa bird crying wildly

Kikaha ana lā i luna loa

As it soars so high above

Hoʻokahi nō naʻe māhiehie

But the finest delight

Aia i ka poʻina ʻale

Is there in the wave's cresting

Me he mahiole aliʻi lā

Like a feathered helmet

E kau ana i ka lae

Upon my brow

Composed by
Larry Lindsey Kimura

6   BRIAN LOPAKA KEAULANA

He'e Nalu   *Surfing*

Brian Keaulana at Mākaha Beach with his father, surfing champion Buffalo Keaulana, who helped him become one of the best watermen in the world. Today, Buffalo shares those same lessons with Brian's nephew, Stanley.

Preceding page: Brian (left) waits with Darrick Doerner for a lull in the sets at Waimea Bay before paddling out through the shorebreak to surf mountainous waves.

Mākaha Beach is on the leeward coast of Oʻahu, just beyond the northernmost reach of urban sprawl. Over time, storms have blown away most of the shoreline trees, leaving the broad arc of sand shadeless and open to the cobalt sea.

The water is cool and clean at Mākaha, irresistible for leeward youngsters on summer vacation. Children splash and swim in the shorebreak all day long, and their parents picnic and relax on the beach, grateful for an ocean that never tires of playing with their keiki.

In winter the scene changes. Great Pacific storms send ocean swells pulsing to Oʻahu. Waves wrap around the North Shore and build into mountainous surf as they trip up on reefs and rocky points. The truly big winter waves rarely reach Mākaha. When they do, the inside shore break explodes on the sand, and the beach becomes an arena for spectacular surfing at Mākaha Point, about a half-mile off the coast. Unlike the celebrated North Shore surf breaks at Pipeline, Sunset, and Waimea, Mākaha is rarely jammed with sightseers. When Oʻahu residents go to beaches on the leeward side, they go as a guest or with a friend, with humility. If they don't, the phrase "Locals Only" may take on physical ramifications.

"We got a bad rep this side," said Brian Keaulana, a thirty-five-year-old lifeguard captain in charge of overseeing all the lifeguards along the leeward coastline. "You go down to Mākaha, you get raped, you get murdered, you get ripped off. But that's just the reputation. That's not really how it is. But in one way the reputation is kind of good. [Mākaha] gains a lot of respect from a lot of people real fast. They don't seem to take advantage. When they go North Shore, they take advantage. . . .

"Over here, if you really get to know the people, the people are nice. They help one another. Like the lifeguards that work on the west side; they kind of feel at ease because if something happens in the water, the whole majority of the community, everybody, kicks in and helps if somebody's life is in danger. People over here think differently. Life is precious to these guys."

Brian Lopaka Keaulana is more than a lifeguard to the people on the leeward coast. He is the friend who watches their children. He is the waterman who risks his life to save others. He is the surfer who trains constantly for the ultimate ride. He is the son of "Buffalo" Keaulana, the pure Hawaiian surfing champion who showed the world he could ride the best Mākaha could offer. He taught Brian how to live with the sea and share it with others. "Mākaha is my first home," Brian said. "I was born and raised right there. I know every single [underwater] rock and crack, how the currents move and the waves change."

For Brian, Mākaha is family. He grew up on the beach. The ocean kept him fit as he matured. It gave him the knowledge and skills to support himself and, after his wedding on Mākaha Beach, his growing family. When Quiksilver, U.S.A., a surf-wear company, announced it wanted to revive Mākaha's big-wave glory days with a prestigious surfing event called the Point Challenge, Brian understood why some Mākaha regulars grumbled about the news. The one-day meet would showcase Mākaha's legendary surf and offer an exclusive opportunity for the world's best big-wave riders. But the local boys felt the break was their spot, their surf, their turf; they resented having their waves—the best waves of the season—off-limits because of a surfing contest, even for a single day.

Brian and his family supported the Point Challenge. They wanted to see the break recognized once again as a great surfing spot, the way it had been when it was the site chosen for the original International Surfing Championships. But there were limits to how much Brian was willing to share his home and way of life. When surf magazines asked him to write about the beach where he was raised, Brian recalled that he "thought about it. After that, nah. We get so much stories already. I figure, just keep the feeling the way it is. I don't need to explain it, tell them how it is down here. When they come down, they find out what it is. . . . We don't need to get hyped-out like North Shore."

Brian told a story about a convoy of tour boats motoring up the coast with paying customers intent on snorkeling and diving in the waters off Mākaha. The skippers tossed anchors onto the reef, damaging the coral heads. Surfers filed a complaint out of concern for the living reef and for their waves, which are shaped by the coral. Boat operators agreed to put in a single permanent mooring with a buoy, but when the waves were big, it bobbed right in the middle of the surfers' impact zone. Someone went out and cut the buoy rope.

"We kind of live day by day and take it as it comes," Brian said. "The thing is, we gotta kinda keep control of whatever situation happens. The guys down here, they're real tight. If the water gets too crowded, then the guys down here are going to do something about it. If the guys earn their waves, then that's all right. But down here can get pretty ugly. Guys can really get nasty if they wanted to."

Brian knows both worlds, the good and the bad. Mākaha Beach is just a few blocks from his house, and people constantly stop by the lifeguard towers to check the surf, drop off family or friends, swap stories. Some arrive clear-eyed, with athletic bodies toned and tanned from years of surfing Mākaha. Others shamble in a fog, bellies drooping over their shorts as they gulp another Budweiser. Businessman, derelict, or high school student—Brian regards everyone equally. "You treat people nice," he said, sitting in the lifeguard tower while his eyes remained focused on the beach, "people treat you nice. We get treated accordingly."

Brian joined the Honolulu County Department of Parks and Recreation as a lifeguard in 1978. After serving at various Oʻahu beaches for eleven years, in 1989 he was promoted to lieutenant for Leeward Oʻahu, and then captain in 1993. His lieutenants supervise all the lifeguards on the coast, making sure the beaches are staffed and equipped, while Brian testifies before politicians about the need for improving water safety. Then he goes back to the west side and continues his study and charting of currents, shorelines, and hazards. Brian is compiling the data so the traditionally reactive lifeguards can be taught to foresee problems and reduce future risks.

Before, when Brian was on duty at Mākaha, he kept watch over children at the water's edge and occasionally rescued tourists from the rip. On work breaks and weekends, he paddled his surfboard out for a few sets. If the surf was meager, Brian bodysurfed. If there was no surf, he sailed his canoe or a board. If the wind wasn't blowing, he paddled, dove, or fished. After buying a WaveRunner III (Yamaha's version of a Jet Ski), which dramatically reduced the time for performing sea rescues, he and three friends circled Oʻahu on their jet-propelled craft. Many people focus on one ocean sport and denigrate others, but "we on the west shore are bred as watermen," Brian said. "We enjoy the ocean regardless of what we are doing. Our ancestors weren't just surfers. Their whole lifestyle was based on survival—'We have to feed one another. We have to get water. We have to fish.' When there was time to relax and surf, they went out in the water and played. For us guys, it's the same way of living, in a modern sort of way. My friends who work on the beach, they living from paycheck to paycheck. The career lifeguard is not really doing it for the money. They like to help people.

"And [while helping people], we try and perfect each thing that we do. That's where I think we got our competitive attitude. I kind of like to compete and see where I stand, what caliber. If I'm not good in that [sport], I kind of concentrate on that more. . . . I like to enter events, any kind events, just to keep the competitor in me up. You can always learn more strategy. You

Brian has developed a rigorous conditioning program for the lifeguards he supervises. They sprint along the ocean floor, carrying boulders. When their lungs cry out for air, the lifeguards surface, then dive again to pick up eighty-pound rocks and sprint another forty yards. Up, down, lift, and sprint, until they are a quarter mile from the beach in water thirty feet deep.

always can fine-tune your ability in contests. For me, I enter everything and anything. . . . It's kind of like sharpening the knife so it doesn't dull."

Brian is six-feet tall, slender, and deeply tanned, with reflexes and muscles honed by the ocean. And when he smiles, he shows the relaxed confidence of the great Hawaiian watermen—the same smile and confidence you see in photographs of Nainoa Thompson or Duke Kahanamoku.

Brian's familiarity with the ocean, his training to become a waterman, began in 1961, when his father, Richard "Buffalo" Kaloloʻokalani Keaulana, first took him surfing; Brian was three months old. From 1960 to 1968, Buffalo (nicknamed because of his affinity for water) was the county caretaker for Mākaha Beach Park, a job that provided his wife, Momi, and their five children with a house on the sand.

Buffalo, a barrel-chested man with reddish brown hair bleached even lighter by years in the sun, grew up in Haleʻiwa and Nānākuli, rural Oʻahu towns where children had lots of time and not much to do. Life was hard for the young Buffalo. His father had died saving three men from a plunging wrecking ball at Honolulu Harbor. The ocean became Buffalo's preferred environment. He often slept at the beach. The water cured him when he felt sick, refreshed him when he felt tired, exhilarated him when nothing else could. He became one of the best bodysurfers in Hawaiʻi, but he wanted to ride a board and regularly traveled eight miles north from Nānākuli to Mākaha to learn how.

In the mid-1950s, California surfers began taking their fancy boards to Mākaha, where Buffalo and other Hawaiians surfed on older versions made of plywood, Styrofoam, and fiberglass. Californians had revolutionized the sport by adding skegs to the boards, bottom-mounted fins that increased maneuverability and tracking. In 1958, boards got lighter and faster when light polyurethane foam replaced wood as the core material. As interest in surfing grew, prompted by the Hollywood infatuation with surfing and beach movies, experimentation increased. With each modification, previously unsurfable waves were challenged, and mastered. Boards got shorter and shorter, and the once stately art of surfing evolved into a gymnastic display of athleticism and courage.

Mākaha locals continued to favor longboards, and Buffalo became a world champion on the waves at Mākaha, along with George Downing, Rabbit Kekai, Conrad Cunha, Peter Cole, and Wally Froiseth, among others. The International Surfing Championships were held at Mākaha every winter from

Brian Keaulana drops down a twenty-foot wave at Waimea. When a surfer wipes out in a swell this size, Brian says it feels like "being one ant flushed down a toilet." Brian survives by having the right surfboard, being in top physical condition, and, mainly, knowing the ocean. Bernie Baker photo.

1953 to 1973, drawing the world's best surfers to the leeward side long before any hundred-thousand-dollar contests were taking place on the North Shore. This was Buffalo's world, and he became a legend in it—a masterful long-board surfer riding the sleigh-ride waves that shouldered up off Mākaha Point. But Buffalo was more than a legend. With his wife, Momi, they took in and fed boys who were in trouble, just as their home also welcomed famous visitors from around the world. On the beach, Buffalo kept the peace and taught people how to live with and off the ocean, while Momi made the house a refuge.

Their son Brian grew up on the sand watching his dad ride the waves, which would rise to thirty feet every few winters. "When I was small, surfing to me was huge surf," Brian remembered. "I used to look out the window of our house on the beach and see George Downing or Buzzy Trent or my dad streaking across twenty, thirty-feet Mākaha. Even now, when you see some-body doing that, it's one awesome sight. . . . I always used to say, 'I can't wait to enter those contests.'"

Even though the family moved off the beach in 1968, Brian's father continued working as a lifeguard at Mākaha. He insisted that his children go to the beach after school and get out in the water—it was a good way to avoid the temptations of drugs and trouble onshore.

Brian needed no prompting, but ocean sports were not recognized as legitimate physical education by his school, which focused on land-based studies and athletics. For Brian, organized school sports looked like a dead end. "My best friends and cousins were football stars in high school, but they couldn't afford college. After that it's like, what happens? What's next?"

At Wai'anae High, Brian's coach told him he had to choose between football and surfing. There was no choice. "I lived right next to the ocean. I learned more [there]. I learned how to feed myself, to feed off the ocean. I learned how to stay in shape. I learned how to survive. I learned how to save people."

Brian was lucky. The watermen who hung out at Mākaha looked out for him and gave him their support. Dennis Gouveia, a Mākaha lifeguard who grew up on the coast, remembers how they encouraged the boy. "'Good wave Brian.' 'Nice ride Brian.' Not all the kids get that opportunity, get that kind of praise. To be recognized now, you gotta do the drugs. By the time they figure that one out, the competitive edge is gone. They cannot get that back. All that time is gone. Local kids can surf, fish, dive unreal. But they aren't recognized, so they think it's nothing."

Dennis remembered seeing a boy called Danny Kim surfing a bodyboard at the Tumbleland break in Mā'ili. The boy rode well and Dennis took him to a competition at Sandy Beach, which was ninety minutes away in east Honolulu—unreachable for most leeward coast youngsters. Danny made the finals and was persuaded to try harder. "Now he's touring all over the U.S.," Dennis said. "Of all the kids from Tumbleland, he's the only one that is recognized. Eight other kids could be world class Boogie Boarders, but they just stay at their spot and do their thing."

As Brian learned about the ocean, he also dreamed the teen surfer's dream of being on the cover of a surf magazine. Because his father was famous, he had a better chance than most. During high school, in the late 1970s, a photographer approached him about doing a feature story about him—the hot young surfer, son of a legend. Before the writer could proceed, Brian needed his father's permission. Being Buffalo's son was not easy. As with the children of other celebrities, the public did not expect Brian to be as good as his father, but demanded that he be better. Everybody expected more, including his father.

Brian recalled the offer from the magazine. "I was all excited. I thought I'd tell my dad and my dad would tell me 'Yeah.' So I told my dad, 'I get these guys from this magazine. They going take pictures of me and put me in a magazine, but I gotta ask your permission. They like call me Baby Buffalo.' My dad, he wasn't saying anything. 'So what? I'm going tell 'em, Yeah? Can?'

"He tell me, 'No.'

"'Why?'

"He go, 'No. I'm just telling you no.'

"I was all mad, just stomping out because he give me no explanation, nothing. And then, after, he tell me, 'You know what. I no like you living off my name. Later on, you make your own name for yourself.'

"But I was ticked off and mad, just pissed to the max. I didn't even bother going back to the magazine guys. . . . I went to school. I got into fights. I got beat up from classmates and then came home. 'What happen to you?' And I never say nothing. Just kept to myself. Went back the next day to school, fought the same guy, got licking again, came home. Dad kept asking me, 'What's the matter?' and I would tell him nothing.

"Later on, fighting the same guy that was licking me, I got to beating up him. In that way, I learned how to really fight my own battles. . . . I never did use my dad's name. I always did things on my own, tried to be more independent; but he helped me out in a lot of stuff. He taught me a lot of things in surfing, sailing, and fishing—all the basic knowledge that I know. I just progress as I go on."

Brian's math teacher encouraged his students to make a list of goals they wanted to accomplish. Brian's was to win a surfing championship from every O'ahu beach, and soon Brian's trophies stood alongside his father's. After high school Brian traveled around the world, surfing the professional circuit, but his father urged him to get a steady job and become a lifeguard. "In his time, surfing wasn't a thing you could survive on," Brian said. "I told myself I can still do the lifeguarding stuff, taking time off when there is a surf meet on weekends. . . . Until you go out in the world and look at what other people are living in, you can't really appreciate where you come from. I never saw a Third World country before [surfing the circuit]—people living in cardboard houses and no sanitation and hepatitis just running around like a cold. It's good to travel, but I cannot see myself anywhere else. Mākaha is such a special place for me. I like to come home. Home is where my sanity is."

Dennis Gouveia remembered when Brian decided to stay in Mākaha. "When he got out of high school, he'd say, 'I can do this. I can do that.' I'd tell him, 'Brian, show me, no tell me.' Last five, six years, he would just progress so fast. All this confidence he was talking about, he had 'em.

"He took the sport of sailing and surfing canoes, and it was just like he went another step. Handful of guys surf canoes and go straight. Brian rides across the wave. He's trying to challenge bigger waves. Ride, cut back with canoe, back and forth. Surf 'em like one surfer would ride 'em. Canoe surfing was one old sport. He took it one more step.

"His attitude is more of a traditional type. It's not like today's surfer—not out there for competitiveness of it all. He is challenged by bigger waves, to be on top of a bigger wave. . . . Brian always looking for the biggest wave. He gives away waves. He's taking it a step more. 'I want to ride the big wave and make 'em; not just ride one of the waves.' That part of his surfing is special. In the [big surf], there are only a handful of guys that really go after the waves with confidence, and Brian is one of those guys. Even in really heavy surf, he's relaxed."

Brian's ambition to improve himself, to train constantly, and to always treat others with courtesy and a smile gives him opportunities that make living more comfortable for his wife, Nobleen, and their two children. It also compensates Brian for not trying to be ranked among the world's top three hundred competitive surfers. Photographers, whose image-making is critical to a surf professional's career, call Brian when they need help, and he readily gives it. In return they focus on him for Mākaha stories or photograph him surfing in a lounge chair, on top of a ladder, with his pet pig, Chop Chop—images that have been published around the world.

Brian's supervisors needed a lieutenant to oversee all the lifeguards along the leeward coast, and Brian said he would take the promotion if he got time off for winter surf meets and any large waves that rolled in. They agreed. When organizers of the North Shore contests needed a new water patrol association to rescue surfers and clear noncompetitors from the waves, they groomed Brian and lifeguard Terry Ahue for the part-time job because promoters and surfers respected them as people, and more important, as watermen. They got a loan for a $5,000 jet-propelled WaveRunner so the business, Hawaiian Water Patrol, Inc., could do its job faster; a surfboard rescue that once would have taken forty minutes might require only forty seconds with the WaveRunner. After he and Terry performed two hundred rescues with their own machines, the ensuing newspaper stories helped the county Parks Department decide to get six WaveRunners for other lifeguards on duty at dangerous beaches. When the director for Kevin Costner's film "Waterworld" needed stuntmen on the Big Island, Brian was hired, and that lucrative work led to additional television and film roles that required more time off from his lifesaving responsibilities.

Brian Keaulana gets plenty of publicity without surfing competitively, which is why Duke Kahanamoku Surfwear provides Brian with sponsorship and clothing, and why Russ•K Mākaha surf company gives him equipment and boards and sometimes pays for travel expenses abroad. Brian's success on a Russ•K board and wearing Duke Kahanamoku trunks mean buyers for the companies' products.

Unlike his brother Rusty, whose natural surfing talent earned him the Oxbow World Longboard Championships in 1993, 1994, and 1995, and the opportunity to open Russ•K, his own surf shop, Brian is a great waterman and surfer because he constantly works at improving his strength and abilities. "If I had [Rusty's] talent, I'd be world champ. He can pretty much do anything. I got to really train and fight hard to achieve what I want to get."

Gaining a top ranking from the Association of Surfing Professionals (ASP) requires a few additional skills that Brian does not want to have: the ability and patience to travel the world and compete year-round on short boards in small waves. "Shortboarding—it's more like work," Brian said. "You go from surf meet to surf meet and everybody's competing. It's an intense kind of competition. Longboarding is more fun."

During the past fifteen years only two or three men from Hawai'i have been rated among the world's annual top twenty shortboard surfers, and it was not until 1993 that a Hawaiian, Derek Ho, won the ASP world championship.

About 450 men and women from all over the world surf the ASP circuit, at about thirty sanctioned surf meets in Europe, Japan, Hawai'i, Australia, South Africa, and the west coast of North America. Surf culture is an international phenomenon; brand names like Quiksilver, Billabong, and Local Motion can be found on T-shirts in Fiji or France as easily as in Malibu. Nationally, the sport and its related industries generate up to $2 billion in annual sales.

Worldwide in its fashion influence, the surf industry often focuses on Hawai'i, traditional home of the sport and scene of the world's most photo-genic and accessible big waves. For ambitious athletes, Hawai'i—specifically, O'ahu—is where careers, legends, and money are made. Surfers want the big waves, the attention, the publicity. Or they just want to be able to say they have surfed Hale'iwa, Pipeline, Waimea, Rocky Point, and all the other North Shore spots they have read about for years. The number of surfers at the famous breaks on O'ahu has grown relentlessly, and surfers have become ever more aggressive to stay ahead of the pack. During the winter season, riders cram the lineup, steal waves, and bump away others' boards as they slalom through an ocean filled with photographers treading water.

Each December, the ASP's ten-month, around-the-world pro-tour comes to a climax in Hawai'i with a three-contest series called the Triple Crown. At least one of the meets is traditionally held at Sunset Beach, where steep waves break in shifty, unpredictable patterns that elude newcomers looking for the lineup. Neophytes can get trapped in the vicious rip current, which sends lost boards eighty-five miles away to Kaua'i. The contest organizers hire Brian Keaulana and Terry Ahue's Water Patrol to make sure the surfers remain close to O'ahu.

Sometimes Brian competes in the preliminary heats to see if he can reach the finals. When he is not competing, he or one of his colleagues scoots about on a WaveRunner, clearing noncompetitors from the area and ferrying surf photographers to the lineup or back to the beach. When the waves peak, he moves out of the competitors' way and watches to make sure no surfer is in need of rescue before the next set. Although the WaveRunner improves the Patrol's ability to save lives, once in a while Brian and his machine get caught inside the impact zone, where waves smash man and machine.

Above Sunset Beach, the competition officials set up a portable viewing complex on top of an air-conditioned trailer housing the computers that record the judges' scores and heat-by-heat results. Announcers sit on the trailer, offering play-by-play and color commentary for the five thousand people watching the meet. On the beach, competitors watch their opponents and wait. When each heat ends, packs of Japanese women tourists run down to snap photographs as contestants emerge from the water. Kids eager for autographs push contest programs and posters into the faces of surfers, who stop for a quick scribble.

In the water for the next heat, competitors once again transform shivs of fiberglass and foam into antigravity machines. They dance down the face of the waves before twisting into heavy g-force bottom turns that zip them back up to the lip for a cutback and a floater over the topside.

Surfing is no longer just a water sport—it has become airborne, too. Professionals normally try to catch the judges' attention with a variety of acts that use the waves and air as surfaces on which they display original choreography or the season's latest gymnastic trick. This approach works in smaller waves, but when the swells reach overhead, the more outrageous moves become unsafe, and some surfers, fearing a reef thrashing, strap on helmets for protection.

The risks, especially at the nearby Banzai Pipeline break, make Hawai'i one of the most spectacular places to witness a surfing event. At Pipeline the swells leap up to pound the reef with an intensity that matches the competitors' single-minded desire to score the most points. Sometimes the wave wins with a swallow and a shredding against the reef, while everyone on the beach groans in sympathy. When a surfer escapes unscathed from a collapsing tube, the crowd's cheer rises over the roar of the ocean. They love the show. Sponsors love the publicity. And the winning surfers love the prize money and an end to the grueling season. "It's great," Brian said. "It's like sharing. Everybody gets something out of it."

For fun and camaraderie, Brian prefers longboard competitions like his father's Big Board surfing classic in February, the week-long Biarritz Surf Festival in France, or the annual big-wave contest at Waimea Bay, the Quiksilver: In Memory of Eddie Aikau. It is held only when the surf exceeds twenty feet.

The Waimea contest honors Eddie Aikau, a Hawaiian who lit up the surfing world in the 1970s when he rode the biggest of waves with a heart-stopping gusto equaled by few. As a lifeguard, he saved hundreds of lives along the North Shore but shrugged off his heroism the same way he ignored compliments from fellow surfers, who considered him a legend.

In 1978, Eddie joined the crew of *Hōkūle'a,* a replica of the double-hulled sailing canoes that once sailed from Tahiti to Hawai'i and New Zealand. Its voyages of rediscovery confirmed ancient Polynesian navigational techniques and mastery of the sea. Five hours after leaving Honolulu bound for Tahiti, a huge swell swamped the canoe in Kaiwi Channel. Then a bad squall hit, throwing up twenty-foot wind-whipped swells that began pushing *Hōkūle'a* away from any hope of rescue. Eddie's surfboard was lashed to the canoe, and he believed that he could paddle through the storm and reach the island of Lāna'i, perhaps twelve miles away. The captain decided Eddie should go. A search plane found the crew clinging to *Hōkūle'a* the next day, but Eddie had disappeared into the storm and was never seen again.

The annual Eddie Aikau memorial competition is held in December, January, or February, whenever a North Pacific storm generates a day of rideable gargantuan waves. Nature does not always cooperate, and between 1985 and 1995, surfable Waimea waves exceeded twenty feet only three times. Each December, the three-month waiting period begins with a late afternoon ceremony at the beach in Waimea. Most surf contests in Hawai'i begin with a prayer, but for the Aikau, all thirty-three invited surfers partake of ritual. First, each one receives a lei. Then a kahu (pastor) blesses the men and their boards. Each surfer is given a handful of salt and instructed to cleanse his board. Then the surfers, friends, and Aikau family members launch themselves into the shore break. The group paddles out 250 yards, just off the bay's northern point, which serves as the lineup on those rare days when the swells shoal into thirty-foot cliffs breaking across the bay, crushing anything beneath.

Big-wave surfers, the "men who ride mountains," prepare for a blessing at Waimea Bay, where an annual surfing contest is held in waves exceeding twenty feet. After the ceremony, the surfers paddle out, form a circle, and remind one another that this competition means more than the $50,000 first prize. It honors the memory of Eddie Aikau, a legendary big-wave surfer and waterman.

As the sun drops to the horizon, a glow warms the coast from Ka'ena to Kahuku, and the participants sit on their boards and hold hands, forming a large circle. Incoming swells roll beneath Brian Keaulana and the other surfers, who work as board shapers, lifeguards, businessmen, or professional competitors. They are an exclusive group, linked by their understanding of the speed, height, danger, and force of big waves. During the Aikau ceremony they listen as their colleagues speak about the Aikau contest and offer prayers of thanks and hope. One year, before calling out to Eddie three times and tossing their lei into the circle, the surfers heard the words of the competition director, George Downing. George, who won the world surfing championship at Mākaha before most of these men were born, reminded the group that this annual event represents a fellowship for surfers, a gathering in honor of the memory of Eddie Aikau. It was not about the $50,000 first prize or fame, but about love—for a man who had loved to surf big waves.

"I wouldn't really care if the purse was $50,000 or $5," Brian said after the blessing one year. "The money is great, but I'm more stoked about what this contest is all about. This contest represents the person, the man—Eddie Aikau. It's a special thing."

Anyone who has surfed big waves has a story about an awesome ride, a horrendous wipeout. Brian has had his share. On a morning when the Mākaha seas were calm and vacant, Brian sat in the shade of the lifeguard tower and talked story. Sunglasses protected his eyes from the glare reflecting off the sand, almost as bright as the fine gold chains around his neck. Brian enjoys telling stories, and they spill out in a mix of his childhood Pidgin English and the King's English required for adult responsibilities.

He recalled the previous weekend when he took his WaveRunner and towed some friends from Mākaha to a secret surf break down the coast—a wild and arid strip of land that cannot be reached by car. They found ten-to-fifteen-foot waves breaking clean and empty. As they surfed without buildings or crowds to distract them, Brian suddenly realized he was sharing the same water enjoyed by his ancestors; his body and their spirits in harmony with the waves rolling beneath the sky. Brian knows of no sport that affects his senses the way surfing does, and on that day, his ancestors touched him. "It was heavy."

He talked about his vision for a canoe surfing contest (which eventually became a reality down the coast from Mākaha at Mā'ili). There would be Hawaiian arts and crafts, food and music, and instead of trophies, winners would receive a kukui or monkeypod sapling, or a sprouting coconut. Brian would tell them to plant the trophies and care for them until they became shade trees for their grandchildren and dropped seeds that would grow and become new trophies for the next generation of watermen and women.

When Mākaha's waves scrape the sky, Brian's dreams stop, he wakes up, and he goes out into the water. He recalled one night at home when he awoke to the sound—the feel—of the ocean reverberating through the darkness, pounding the nearby shore. In the dark, he got out of bed, picked up his board, drove to the beach, and waited for enough light to paddle out to the lineup. Whenever Brian sees the big waves, his feelings contradict one another. "[The surf] looks nice. It looks intense. It looks powerful, mean. It gives me a heavy rush that I'm gonna get out there. [But] for me surfing big waves really takes out a lot of stress. Surfing big waves gives me a peace of mind, because I understand so much. I'm comfortable enough to play around, to practice different sorts of things out there."

The giant waves at Waimea require a surfer to plunge down the face and execute a quick bottom-turn to escape to the safety of the wave's broad, safe shoulder. But Brian says surfing Mākaha is like racing down a long hallway as fast as you can before the door at the end slams shut in your face. To survive, a surfer has to stay as high as possible on the wave, picking up maximum speed as the wave builds into the long, peeling cliff wall that delivers surfers into Mākaha's notorious bowl. That's where the water over the reef shallows abruptly, where the waves peak suddenly and break prematurely before rolling into the channel. If a surfer does not have enough speed and height to get across the bowl, he wipes out in it, and the wave rolls and punches his body over the reef, all the way to shore. In the *Surfer's Guide to Hawai'i,* surf journalist Greg Ambrose describes it: "A wipeout [at Mākaha Bowl] is the most serious moment you will ever experience surfing."

On the thundering morning when the surf roused Brian from sleep, he paddled out and waited for his wave. When it came, he took off and hung in close to the lip until the wave bulged and pitched his board into the air. Brian's feet stayed on the board as it free-fell into the trough. Back on solid water, Brian maneuvered the board back up the face and gathered speed. He had to beat the bowl. "I went back up and the thing pitched me out again. I fell back down and went up for the third time."

When the lurching wave finally reached the bowl, Brian encountered the surfer's ultimate nightmare. "Suddenly it changed shape again and pitched me way out to the point. I was just flying. When I landed, I tried to turn. My skeg slipped and then I fell, just tumbling, tumbling, and then the wave hit me. Boom! I went under. The only thing you think is just to relax, save your oxygen. Don't fight it because the ocean is way stronger than any Olympic swimmer. I was just tumbling down, tumbling, tumbling. All of a sudden I hit the bottom. Boom! Boom! I started rolling on the bottom of the reef. I got my grip, stood up, and tried to get back up. But the thing just kept shoving me down, and I was thinking, 'Wow. I'm under kinda too long.' Then, all of a sudden, my eyes, everything, just started blacking out; started getting weak; this tingling, like needle pokes all over my body, and this numbing feeling. I got kind of mad with myself like, 'Oh no, I ain't going like this.' So I got this extra kick and just started powering out, powering out, and broke the surface.

"And as soon as I came up and got a breath, the next wave was right there, a twenty-footer. Boom! It took me down again, and I was tumbling, tumbling, tumbling, but this time I went blackout a little bit faster. So I reached for my leash and started pulling myself up. Finally I got ahold of my board, which was underwater with me, and we was tumbling around until my board came shooting up. When it shot up, I took a breath of air real fast—and the next wave came and pounded me. I got whacked five times. The same thing, over and over until I reached the channel. I was like low power, dead, like one piece of dead meat just floating. I rested there for like half an hour.

"Most guys, if they freak out on that kind of wipeout, they paddle in. That's it. They'll never surf again. So I went out and stayed in the bowl and caught one of the biggest bowl rides, free-fell down, made the turn, and got this humongous barrel and came out. All my fears were like gone.

"If anybody is going to die outside in the ocean, it ain't going to be me. I'm probably the most conditioned guy out there. It's not bragging. It's like psyching yourself in your own mind.

"When you get out there—hah, your mind goes blank. You forget your name. You forget where you live, who you live with, your wife's name. You forget everything. Your basic instinct is just survive. That's all you thinking about. Point A to point B—how I'm gonna survive. And once you wipe out, the next instinct is just air. That's how I release my tension and pressures.

"People, they sometimes come down to the beach and tell us we're crazy. I'm not crazy. Crazy is the guy on the streets, smoking crystals and destroying his mind. [It's not crazy] exercising and training and trying to eat the right foods and not taking any kind of drugs and no drinking, and then going out and catching thirty-foot waves."

This is the message Brian takes into the schools, where he shares his surfing experiences and urges students to avoid drugs and take advantage of opportunities for learning. Preparing for big surf, he tells them, is no different than getting ready for any other challenge in life. "My training is like just nonstop training. You just keep training your body, training your mind, keeping everything focused into one point. Big surf, really big surf, only comes maybe four times a year, so you have to be ready."

Before Brian paddles out, he already knows the beach, its surf, his abilities, what his board can do, and the risks that may come with an unexpected gust stalling a takeoff, the freak set of gigantic waves that prevents escape, the shark no longer willing to share his home. This awareness, added to a lifetime of experience, enables Brian to surf the waves before getting wet and provides an emotional safety net that landlubbers cannot appreciate.

Yokohama Beach is six miles beyond Mākaha, where the asphalt road disintegrates into an isolated beach park. Fishermen go there to cast for ulua from the rocky ledge. On days when the surf runs higher than ten feet, tourists like to stand on the ledge, watching the surf and spray, feeling the waves smash against the rocks. Fishermen never turn their backs on the ocean because an unexpected set can climb over the twenty-foot ledge and swiftly drag you into the sea. Anywhere else, a local waterman would try to freestyle through the waves and stroke over to a nearby beach, but the Yokohama ledge is riddled with sea caves, and if you do not swim away fast enough, big surf can pulverize you against the rocks or—if it chooses a slower death—push you inside a sea cave and block your escape until you die of hypothermia and exhaustion.

When disaster struck in 1967, WaveRunners and cellular phones had not yet come along to transform lifesaving. Buffalo Keaulana and rescue officials were called to Yokohama after three people became trapped in one of the sea caves. Through the roar of rapidly rising surf, they could hear a man inside the cave shouting for help. Buffalo waited while his superiors debated what to do. They agreed Buffalo should try to paddle his surfboard into the cave. He managed to get in and bring out two boys, but before he could go back for the man, the surf increased to fifteen feet and blocked the cave entrance. All anyone could do was wait until the man's shouted pleas stopped. The surf subsided the next morning, and Buffalo paddled in and retrieved the man's body.

Twenty-six years later, on the afternoon of January 25, 1993, a big wave washed a man named Hugh Alexander off the Yokohama ledge, and the relentlessly pounding waves pushed him into a cave. Each time he tried to swim out, the surf battered him against the rocks and forced him back inside the cave.

Brian Keaulana knew the area well. He and the other lifeguards had been there six months earlier, practicing rescue techniques in heavy surf. At that time, football pads and a helmet had seemed like a good idea until they discovered what happens to the equipment when it gets caught between an immovable object (coastline) and an unstoppable force (surf). The lifeguards practiced with a line tied to a rescue tube and tried floating it into the cave, where a person in trouble could grab the tube and be pulled out, but the surges and backwash kept pushing the tube away from the entrance. They tried using the jet-propelled WaveRunner; it can carry two people, tow a rescue sled, and elude vicious surf. One man drives and the other rides in the sled, ready to haul the victim aboard.

When the lifeguards arrived at Yokohama to rescue Hugh Alexander, they decided to use the WaveRunner. On Brian's first approach to the sea cave, the WaveRunner hit a submerged rock and was swamped by an incoming set. Brian and his partner, Craig Davidson, escaped harm, but the Air One helicopter from the Honolulu Fire Department had to tow the WaveRunner away. As they waited for another craft to arrive from the North Shore, Brian swam into the cave with fins and a rescue tube, but it was impossible to locate the man amid the high surf in the dark cave. Brian could hear him, though, and before diving underneath the incoming surges and fleeing the cave, Brian told the man to try and swim out so they could grab him at the entrance.

Firefighters used megaphones to let the rescuers know when they spotted a lull between the sets, and Brian and lifeguard Earl Bungo were ready with the new WaveRunner when the badly bruised man appeared at the mouth of the cave. They raced in and Earl pulled Hugh onto the sled. Brian accelerated the WaveRunner through an incoming wave, but the impact knocked Earl and Hugh off the sled. Brian circled around and pulled them to safety. After treating Hugh for multiple head and body cuts and bruises, the hospital released him the same day. The U.S. Lifesaving Association awarded Brian its Medal of Valor.

"I hardly ever think about things [during a rescue]," Brian said later. "I know exactly what my body can do. I know exactly what the machine can do. I know everything there is to know about the area and what might happen. I know I can utilize all that. I'm not even thinking about it. It's in me already. If you think about things, it's too late. . . . The ocean is never predictable. You have to be flexible. You have to be just like the water. Smooth and calm. Also strong and ferocious."

KĀNAʻE O KA PUA

The Flower of Kānaʻe

Aia i ka moku o Keawe

There on the island of Keawe

Ka ʻāina aʻo ka lehua

The land of the ʻōhiʻa lehua

Me ka maile aʻo Panaʻewa

With the maile of Panaʻewa

E noho i ka pua mamo

Resides the lehua mamo

Nohona i ka pua ka lehua mamo

It resides here, this lehua mamo

E ʻike aku i ka nani

One can see the beauty

Nō ka pua ka ʻilima

One need only look for the ʻilima flower

Ka pili a e Kāʻana

To be joined together to share a common love

Composed by
Tony Conjugacion

Hoʻopili kāua hāliʻaliʻa

Together we shall recall

Pāheahea i ka leo

Of that welcoming voice

O ka ua Kanilehua

Of the Kanilehua rain

Hoʻokipa a ka malihini

Welcoming all visitors

Mālie i ke kai aʻo Kūhiō

When the sea is calm at Kūhiō Bay

ʻAuhea wale ana ʻoe

If you listen carefully

I uka i ke kuahiwi

There in the uplands

He leo kuʻikuʻi lima

A voice of the pounding hand

A he leo wale nō ʻo Kānaʻe

It is only the voice of Kānaʻe

Ka lehua mamo i ka nani

That rare lehua mamo blossom

Puana kou inoa

Whose name will be remembered

Nō Hilo Hanakahi

Throughout the land of Hilo, Hanakahi.

DENNIS KANAʻE KEAWE

Kapa & Tapa

A drum's voice must be as fine as its appearance. Kanaʻe Keawe evaluates the sounds resonating through a drum made from sharkskin and kamani wood. He adjusts the sennit lashing (braided coconut fibers) until he is satisfied with the tone. Hawaiians no longer make large quantities of sennit, so craftsmen sometimes import it from South Pacific islands, where traditional crafts are more alive than in Hawaiʻi.

Preceding page: Wood is pounded against wood, and in between is the bark that will become kapa. Similar pieces will be used to make a ceremonial costume for a Cook Islands chief.

Kana'e Keawe has spent much of his adult life retrieving the neglected skills of his ancestors and sharing that knowledge. Nonetheless, he was intrigued by an unexpected request: A German woman in the remote Cook Islands in the South Pacific wanted him to fly three thousand miles to teach the making of kapa (barkcloth) to the native women there—the "mamas." The mamas did not care much about beating kapa, the woman wrote; they preferred appliqué and sewing. Perhaps Kana'e, a fellow Polynesian, might persuade them to revive this art from their past. She, a papa'a (foreigner), could not.

Kana'e was unsure whether he could help. He knew that creating kapa was not easy. Hawai'i had lost the art long before 1944, when he was born. He learned the skill only after much research and practice led him to finally and literally hit upon the technique that transformed his beating of bark into an art. And he was apprehensive about sharing his knowledge. First, his personal Prime Directive prohibited Kana'e from interfering with the normal development of any culture. And second, he had not picked up a kapa mallet in more than a year. His job with Hawaii Electric Light Company kept him busy five days a week, and there were other distractions on weekends—finishing his house, learning a new craft, visiting family, delivering lectures, participating in cultural festivals, and entertaining friends of friends of friends passing through Hilo during their travels around the Big Island.

But Kana'e was already planning an October vacation in Tahiti, and the once-a-week flight included a stopover on Rarotonga in the Cook Islands. He wrote to the German woman and told her he could stay for six days. If she could somehow get him to her nearby island of Atiu, Kana'e would try to help the mamas.

Hawai'i and the Cook Islands have more in common than British explorer James Cook, who visited both island groups in the late 1700s and for whom the Cook Islands are named. Polynesians settled both island groups. Two hundred years later, Cook Islanders, called Maori, and Hawaiians still look alike, and their languages echo each other. But major differences distinguish the two cultures. Although the Cook Islands have had an ongoing relationship with Great Britain as a protectorate of New Zealand, a member of the

British Commonwealth, Cook Islanders still speak their native language, practice their traditional culture, and retain ancestral lands.

The tie with New Zealand assures the Cook Islanders comfort and security, but in return, planeloads of Kiwis fly up to the capital island of Rarotonga each week to vacation in the motels, hotels, and hostels scattered along the coast. The sixteen-thousand-acre island is a third smaller than the Hawaiian island of Ni'ihau, and Rarotonga's main road is barely two lanes wide and only twenty miles long. Tourists on scooters need less than an hour to circle the island, and the road allows visitors to peer into homes and yards along the way. This unavoidable daily parade is an intrusion for some Rarotongans, who look through visitors with a malevolence engendered by Rarotonga's physical transformation by tourism and by the Rarotongans' growing subservience to tourist dollars.

This was not where Andrea Eimke and her husband, Juergen Manske, wanted to remain when they first visited the Cooks in 1983. They had left their home in Germany to escape the pressure and hustle, and lived for almost a decade as expatriates in Africa. They wanted to find a new home, where people and the land had not yet succumbed to greed. While on Rarotonga, they heard about a smaller island called Atiu (ah-too), 72 miles northeast of Rarotonga. They decided to pay it a visit.

From the sky, Atiu resembles a six-thousand-acre pancake, green except for the bright white crushed coral airstrip that scars the jungle. Swamplands and a raised coral reef surround the island's highest point, a basalt plateau 236 feet above sea level—all that remains of a submerged volcano.

A thousand people live on the island of Atiu, and they welcomed Andrea and Juergen as friends rather than foreigners. Atiu's mayor encouraged Juergen to lease the abandoned coffee plantation and revive the export crop. Juergen was not a farmer, but the possibility intrigued him, and he sent some beans off for analysis. The coffee was rated excellent. Juergen and Andrea returned to Germany, packed all their belongings, and moved to Atiu.

On Atiu, they joined fewer than a dozen Caucasians who live among the Maori, deriving most of their income from government wages, grants, and pensions. Money and gifts from their families abroad supplement their income, along with profits generated by exporting coffee, fruits, and vegetables to New Zealand in exchange for tins of fish and meat, and other products. The imports augment their diet of taro, arrowroot, bananas, coconuts, kamara, yams, and garden vegetables. When there is not enough food for local consumption, the island council initiates compulsory planting.

The people of Atiu once lived along the lowlands near the taro swamps, but the first Christian missionary, John Williams, saw the advantage of pros-elytizing from a central location. In 1823, he encouraged the people to move their five villages onto the island plateau. Atiu's isolation allowed the villages to evolve slowly through the century and two World Wars. Today, most peo-ple live in hollow-tile houses with tin roofs that are capable of withstanding the hurricane season better than the thatched huts used for storage or rest houses in the gardens. Catchment provides water; a freighter takes in most of their supplies; and telephone service, which arrived in the 1990s, connects them to Rarotonga and the rest of the world.

While Juergen resurrected the coffee plantation, Andrea, a dressmaker's daughter, taught two sewing projects at the Atiu school. She is a slight woman with short, cropped hair and endless energy. Encouraged by her teaching suc-cess, she envisioned a plan for the Atiu Fibre Arts Studio, a private company in which members would own shares and receive dividends. She also saw the studio as a place where the island women would gather to create traditional works to sell to tourists on Rarotonga or the occasional visitors to Atiu. Four island matrons, including the mayor's wife, became founding members and shareholders in the company. Andrea's interest in papermaking then led her to examine Atiuan kapa made from banyan and breadfruit trees, and soon she began interviewing the few people on the island who still practiced the art. She wanted to ensure that their knowledge would not be lost.

"The white man came and took it all away from them, and now the white man comes and tries to give it all back to them. I don't know what's right or wrong," Andrea told a visitor. "Some people blame people like Juergen and me for doing the same job as the missionary by not leaving the people in peace. On the other hand, we've seen many things [lost] in our country, and we've seen things go down the drain. Luckily, we had books so later on we could learn them again. But there are not so many books available here. Our contribution [here] is to make any recording of it—whether it's book, video—so at least they have something to relate to and look at it and go back to their own past."

Before Andrea moved to Atiu, the island people had already lost much of their cultural knowledge, and they were either too busy or disinclined to pass on what remained. Even today, as soon as school is out and chores are done, many daughters and sons go to the mayor's house and pay to watch videos. The children long for the world beyond the reef. As soon as teenagers have enough money, most of them move to the nearby main island of Rarotonga. Later, if they can, they go on to the United States or Australia, but more often to New Zealand, where more Cook Islanders live than the eighteen thousand remaining in the Islands.

A similar migration takes place worldwide, with young people abandoning rural areas and crowding into the capital cities, searching for the life they see on videos or imagine from relatives' stories. "I don't know what to say [to the people about saving their culture]," Andrea said.

In early 1988 an Australian papermaker told Andrea about a kapa conference she had attended that year on the Big Island in Hawai'i. Andrea wrote to the conference organizers and asked for their assistance. They passed the message on to Kana'e, who was already planning his vacation in Tahiti. He derives great satisfaction from his trips throughout the Pacific and has made many friends across the region. He wrote to Andrea and told her he would be in the Cooks and would help however he could.

Whereas Kana'e acquired his kapa-making skills through research and practice, the Atiu women's knowledge came from their mamas, who had gotten it from their mamas. American scholars classify craftsmen such as Kana'e as native revivalists—the term for those who want to prove the ancients were capable of artistic genius. The Hawai'i revivalists often study original works in museums and private collections and then try to duplicate the arts at home—a much different context than on Atiu.

Kana'e developed an interest in Hawaiian crafts during his childhood in the urban Honolulu community of Kalihi. As a young boy he showed skill with his hands—he put together model planes with such precision the glue never dripped. On weekends and holidays, he went over the mountains to rural Lā'ie, where his grandparents lived an older Hawaiian way. They spoke Hawaiian with him, and he ran around the village with his cousins, stopping by the beach to help the church people haul in nets for the monthly hukilau. On Mondays, Kana'e was back in Kalihi, eating breakfast, already dressed in the starched khaki uniform then required for boys at Kamehameha, the private school for Hawaiian students.

"When I was going to school, I wasn't very involved in normal student affairs," he recalled at his present-day home in Hilo. "I was always pursuing art courses, and I was doing things [other students] weren't interested in. I enjoyed slack-key guitar. It wasn't popular then. I was a surfer. A lot of [my friends] just started surfing in their junior and senior year, and I was pretty accustomed to a board at that time, and I had some great-looking boards.

"After Kamehameha, I went to a year of college in Los Angeles. It was called Woodbury College. It was geared basically to business and art courses; right on Wilshire Boulevard in the heart of Los Angeles. When I got home in the afternoon my clothes and hair just reeked of smog. So after one year of it, I said, 'This is it. I think I am going home.' I didn't like California all that

An ancient-style Hawaiian cape begins with thousands of tufts of feathers. Using twine, Kanaʻe secures each tuft into a net framework. Once braided from olonā, a native shrub, the original netting material has been replaced here with cotton netting from a fishing supply store.

well. The water was freezing cold; the people were different. I didn't feel like I belonged. It's kind of a shock to your values and your ethnic background when you get mistaken for another race. They thought I was Mexican. They thought I was Greek. They thought I was Jewish, Lebanese. At home in Hawaiʻi we know who we are and it doesn't have to be explained."

After four decades of crafting objects, Kanaʻe has refined a balance of quiet strength, patience, and dexterity that seems remarkable in today's clumsy, hurried world. You can see the balance in his hands, which slowly chisel a stump of kamani into a drum or carefully tie microscopic knots around bunches of feathers for a cape.

Before Kanaʻe learned such skills, he attended Honolulu Community College, where he earned an architectural drafting degree; then he took a job at Hawaiian Telephone designing telephone and cable circuits. At night he partied in Honolulu clubs, until the excursions exhausted him, financially and mentally. Kanaʻe decided to enroll in a Hawaiian-language course. "My grandparents had given me inspiration for understanding things Hawaiian, and the language class reinforced it. I decided, why not learn how a lau hala mat is woven; how a feather lei is put together; how a hula instrument gets completed?"

The Queen Emma Hawaiian Civic Club offered craft classes, and Kanaʻe excelled. The following year, in 1973, civic club members asked Kanaʻe to teach some classes of his own. His new day job with Hawaiian Electric had him hiking the Koʻolau ridge for the surveying department. On lunch breaks he picked leaf buds, ferns, and maile vine to weave into lei. When the company advertised a job opening at its Big Island affiliate, the Hawaii Electric Light Company (HELCO), Kanaʻe decided to leave Oʻahu.

"The Big Island was wide open and had such a diverse geography, so I welcomed the change. It was a rather maturing experience being out on my own, buying a lot and designing a house, making a go of it, keeping up the mortgage, trying to get things done. . . . Nothing is dull here. You make your own fun, and for craftsmen like myself, the Big Island still has a lot of resources available. We still have the trees and woods in relative abundance. But there is a sense of conservation that we feel we have to practice.

"If it's possible, don't pull plants up by the roots. If you cut something, put some pulapula [seedlings] back in the ground for next year's crop. Some of the palapalai [fern] patches in the mountains are getting trampled by the hula hālau who need it for competition, a hōʻike [show], or something. A lot of people are now growing it in their own yards for their immediate use or to help out some hālau and conserve the forests. Hawaiians are going to have to start looking at this more carefully. We can't keep plundering. We've always got to repay and give back."

Kanaʻe was fortunate that on the Big Island he had opportunities to deepen his Hawaiian spirit while he was still a young man. His mind and hands became wise in the ways of making kapa, drums, hōlua (sleds), and model canoes. He learned how to weave makaloa and lau hala, and he learned how to get close to—and protect—the natural source materials necessary to pursue these projects. But it is his life as an American that makes these pursuits possible.

Monday through Friday, Kanaʻe serves HELCO as its commercial service representative. The job requires that he learn about customer power needs and help them understand his company's problems generating and transporting electricity. In a sense, he is HELCO's ambassador. He is always punctual, prepared, easy to talk to, and neatly dressed. Kanaʻe lets clients call him by his English name, Dennis. But when work is over, Kanaʻe leaves HELCO behind. On free weekends, he puts on boots, jeans, and a T-shirt, climbs into his pickup, and drives up the mountains looking for materials.

Lynn Martin, the Folk Arts Coordinator with the Hawaiʻi State Foundation on Culture and the Arts, acknowledges that Kanaʻe is "very highly respected" because of his commitment to his culture, his versatility and ability in making a range of crafts and the tools necessary to create them, and his desire to share. "He's so good," she said, "just a gifted individual. He can discipline himself to really concentrate on something. That's not a common ability in any of the arts."

"I have a rule," Kanaʻe said. "There is no way to do a job but to do it well. If you are going to do kāpulu [careless] work, it's going to be your signature. If you want your name to be respected, you must do good work. [The crafts world] is competitive. You would like to be better than the next craftsperson. . . . Of course, we always give each other that respect and distance and admiration because these are fields that are sometimes not popular."

In recent years, Hawaiʻi delegations have invited Kanaʻe to join them as they participated in festivals of Pacific Island arts in New Zealand, Tahiti, and Australia; an international paper conference in Japan; and the Smithsonian Institution's Folklife Hawaiʻi celebration.

As skilled as Kanaʻe and a few other Hawaiians are, only two, Malia Solomon of Honolulu and Pua Van Dorpe of Lahaina, have produced kapa matching the nine-by-seven-foot sheets beaten by the ancients. In 1982, Pua began to create one of those giant sheets, but after five hundred hours of labor she asked Kanaʻe to help her with the overprinting. She did not attempt that type of kapa again.

Non-Hawaiian academics point out that although revivalists' kapa may be technically proficient and thoroughly researched, it usually lacks a cultural imperative. Malia Solomon created a huge kapa sheet for display at the Mauna Kea Beach Hotel. Most contemporary pieces are too valuable and rare for use in ceremonies or by hālau hula, which often substitute fabrics such as pellon. But an imperative—a real, culturally authentic use—arose in 1989, when Hawaiians needed to rebury the remains of a thousand ancestors disinterred from the West Maui dunes of Honokahua by a resort developer. According to tradition, a proper reburial requires that the bones be wrapped in kapa shrouds. But in 1989, that much kapa was not available, and the Hawaiian community did not know who would make it.

Besides work by Pua Van Dorpe, Kanaʻe Keawe, Kawaikaulāʻau Aona-Ueoka, Malia Solomon, and her granddaughter, Lisa Kalahauoli Jack, only two Hawaiʻi groups in 1995 were dedicated to kapa—Kapa Aloha Perpetuation Association (KAPA) and Nā Hoa Hoʻāla Kapa (The Friends of the Reawakening of Kapa). The last had difficulty sustaining interest in the craft. Moana Eisele, one of the original Nā Hoa members, first learned about the art from Kanaʻe in 1978, when three Hawaiian Civic Clubs jointly sponsored a series of classes. "Out of thirty people I remember," Moana said, "I would say about six people went from day one to the end and completed all their tools. I'm the only one who stayed actively with it."

Moana helped form Nā Hoa with thirteen people in 1982, and of that number five remained somewhat interested in kapa. "It has a real good possibility of losing what little flicker of life the recent interest has caused," Moana said. "I don't see people sticking with it long enough to carry it or keep that light on. I see it completely dying out and eventually nobody knowing anything at all, because the books that have been written are so inaccurate—something that you don't find out until you try it yourself."

Kapa making is a difficult craft to master because tradition requires that the craftspeople make their own tools from wood. They typically make the kapa from wauke, the paper mulberry tree, which they cultivate in straight stalks so the bark will peel off easily. They roll the bark inside out and into coils, and soak it. Then they can scrape away the outer bark and soak the inner bast again in salt water or fresh water (depending on the type of kapa desired). After several days of beating and soaking, the bast ferments; its pungent odor discourages some newcomers from kapa beating, but the smell is a signal to the kapa maker that the bast may be ready for final beating. Then, the craftsperson (traditionally a woman) beats the bast with a wooden mallet against a long, rectangular wooden anvil. The kapa maker must moisten the bast as she beats it into ever thinner and wider sheets, though not so thin that they become holey. A different kind of mallet is used to mesh sheets together and to imprint watermarks, visible when the dried kapa is held up to the light. Kapa makers create dyes from many plant sources, including kukui root, mountain fern, ʻōlena (a ginger), or red earth, which they use to color kapa and to decorate it using hala-nut brushes or stamp designs carved onto bamboo strips.

Given the labor-intensive kapa-making process, and the few people who know how to do it, the Office of Hawaiian Affairs, which was responsible for reburying the people of Honokahua, wondered how 1,011 sheets of black kapa, each three feet by three feet, could be made within a few weeks.

Fortunately, Pua Van Dorpe had eight hundred basts of Maui wauke, which she had stored for eight years. She got additional bundles of bast from friends in Tonga and Fiji, where the Melanesian people still make kapa for ceremonial purposes and for tourists, as they do in Samoa, where the craft was revived in the 1930s. The niece of a daughter of an aunty of Pua's called around and located fourteen Hawaiian women willing to help. They somehow managed to learn in fourteen hours the basics of what Pua had learned in fourteen years. They agreed to beat kapa without pay, without men, without gossiping, for up to ten hours a day until they had finished the work and dyed it black in the dark mud of nearby loʻi kalo—all in an effort to bury ancestral bones properly. Their patient and dedicated work received much publicity in Hawai'i, and it inspired people to ask Pua and other kapa makers such as Kawaikaulā'au Aona-Ueoka to help them learn the art. At last, the Hawaiians had reconnected the craft with a culturally important application. Thousands of bones removed from other sites still await reburial.

The women of Atiu do not feel compelled to beat kapa. They make bark-cloth costumes only for the coronation of a new ariki (chief) and for the annual pageant celebrating New Zealand's 1965 decision to allow the Cooks self-government. The women beat kapa for these occasions with encourage-ment from Andrea, who is willing to drive around and get whatever they need. She hoped the arrival of Kana'e might make the mamas as enthusiastic about kapa as they are about making tīvaivai, the quiltlike fabric bedspreads and pillowcases that are the primary craft activity at the Atiu Fibre Arts Studio.

Tīvaivai are the jewels of Atiu's five villages, so precious that visitors only see them during Christian holidays or when each home has to open its doors for Tutaka, the government's quarterly health inspection. Then families empty their linen chests to drape beds and couches with the floral-patterned coverlets that glow with the women's handiwork.

A similar but heavier quilt version of the tīvaivai evolved in Hawai'i after missionary women introduced fabric and sewing to the chiefly wives in 1820. As more Westerners arrived in Hawai'i, island artists and craftspeople applied other traditional skills to making Western articles (the Hawaiian word for quilt is kapa) and began to fashion objects with tools and materials their ancestors had never known.

Hawaiians used their featherwork, cordage, and kapa as tax payments until the mid-nineteenth century, when the Kingdom's economy shifted from subsistence farming and fishing to plantations and markets. Men then had to pay taxes in land or cash—usually earned by working for haole busi-nessmen and landowners. Knowledge that had evolved over the course of a thousand years disappeared in a single generation. Skills that persist today do so because people need certain things—foods, hula drums and implements, canoes, feather and flower lei—or because the craft has been adapted to meet a new necessity, such as lau hala hats instead of mats. Eventually—with mandatory public education and the growth of the Kamehameha Schools and the University of Hawai'i—a contemporary group of Hawaiian artists developed. These self-taught or university-trained potters, painters, sculp-tors, designers, and craftspeople create new aesthetic forms that reflect Hawaiian cultural imperatives as often as Western and personal ones. Sean Browne, Momi Cazimero, Rocky Jensen, Deborah Kakalia, Herb Kane, Mary Lou Kekuewa, Marie McDonald, and Levan Keola Sequeira are among the better-known Hawaiians whose contemporary or traditional work equals or surpasses that of the state's best non-Hawaiians.

Some Hawaiian crafts, the labor-intensive quilts and Ni'ihau shell necklaces, for example, have been refined to the point where replacement costs prohibit regular use. Other, more traditional pieces have roles in modern Hawai'i that are not too far removed from their past. Sculpture, for instance, was an integral part of ancient Hawaiian culture, but Hawaiians did not carve temple images for more than a century and a half after 1819, when the Kingdom's religion was outlawed. During the Hawaiian Renaissance of the 1970s, woodworkers began carving images of gods for use in rituals or to preside over restored heiau. Kana'e Keawe made a pahu (drum) for instructors at the University of Hawai'i at Hilo, who use it in teaching students how to chant.

Kana'e knew enough about Pacific customs and languages to prepare for the Cook Islands visit. He filled his suitcase with books, pareu, aloha shirts, and macadamia nuts—thank-yous for hospitality, both planned and impromptu. For the Atiu women he made shark-tooth knives to carve bark from trees, and hand-grooved kapa beaters. For their husbands, a friend gave Kana'e fish-hook pendants made from bone and fine cordage. Then Kana'e went to the Bishop Museum in Honolulu to examine samples of Cook Islands kapa, which the museum stores along with two thousand specimens from Hawai'i and a thousand more from other Pacific islands.

The kapa collection ranges from family heirlooms of bedding and sleeping kapa to skirts, loincloths, and capes collected by royalty and gifted to the museum. Wearing white cotton gloves, Kana'e slid out the trays of bark cloth and examined the Cook Islands pieces. He took notes and photographs to supplement the twenty color slides he had ordered from the museum, slides he would show on Atiu. He wanted to demonstrate that some Cook Islands kapa is as good as any produced by the Hawaiians, who were considered the finest artists in the ancient Pacific.

The Atiuans were busy preparing a welcoming feast at the Fibre Arts Studio in honor of Kana'e when his airplane landed at the Atiu airstrip. One of Juergen's coffee workers met him and greeted him with a lei, and drove him in a pickup truck up the coral road onto the village plateau to the house where he would be staying. For a reasonable cost, Kana'e got a screened bedroom, an outer house with a toilet and shower, and a cook who fried flying fish over a fire for the visitor's breakfast.

The feast began, as most formal Cook Islands gatherings do, with a series of welcoming speeches from several Maori. "Welcome to our shores," said Ngatamariki Manu, an Atiu schoolteacher. "On our shores, we are not as bad as you are, to be honest, in our tradition and custom. But in one or two aspects within our culture and custom, it's more or less running down the drain. . . . For example kapa-making is one good and fast example. It's almost running off because our elderly women have just gone down and all the knowledge has gone down with them. . . . That's one of the biggest disadvantages down here. [Our crafts have] all been done practically. It's never been written down in black and white whereby we can refer to it at a later date. . . . This is a real failure. . . . Our people are not keen to sit down for even a bit of their time and write about it. I myself have this interest in developing our culture in school, in order to maintain it in the young generation. The upcoming generation of tomorrow are the very important people who will keep our culture and customs alive. . . . Andrea deserves a pat on the back. In the short time she has been here, she has done a lot in reviving our customs, our arts. Congratulations for the efforts you are doing as far as traditions and customs."

After the host speeches, Kanaʻe rose and spoke, thanking the Atiuans for their welcome. Then he told them that, sadly, his mother and grandmother had not known how to make kapa—his knowledge of kapa was not handed down from them. He had learned from books, which were not much help. Only after much trial-and-error practice did he master the art and become a teacher. He said he taught so that the knowledge would not be lost.

Speeches and eating and prayers of thanks continued until twilight, when the men of the Matavai Tumu Nu invited Kanaʻe to join them in their thatched shack, a hundred yards from the Fibre Arts Studio. Atiu did not have a restaurant or bar at the time Kanaʻe visited, but a club of young men gathered at the Tumu Nu on Monday, Wednesday, and Friday nights to sing songs and drink. Steinlager was expensive, so they preferred "swipe"—a homemade brew prepared from hops, malts, sugar, and yeast bought at the store and fermented inside a hollowed-out coconut trunk called a Tumu Nu. Papa Toki, an elder, presided over the young men, and a designated barman sat beside the Tumu Nu and used a coconut cup to dole out the swipe. If anyone got too drunk, he didn't get any more brew, as villagers often hired the Tumu Nu boys for day jobs around the island. But in the dim light of the oil lamp smoking away the mosquitoes, inebriation was difficult to gauge as the men played ʻukulele and sang through the night. Before the evening ended, the group closed with a quiet prayer and a common request to visitors: "Tell us who you are."

When confronted with this question, Kanaʻe paused. He knew what he said and how he said it would be important to the men, who would pass his words around the island. He gathered his thoughts out of the haze in his head and told the men, "I am Kanaʻe Keawe of Hawaiʻi. I am one of ten master craftsmen sent to Australia for the Festival of South Pacific Arts. I go to Papeʻete Friday. I am one of five people in Hawaiʻi who can still do kapa. I had to learn it. It wasn't taught to me by my grandmother. They lost it back in their generation."

"Even today here," Papa Toki interjected sadly.

"Andrea asked me if I could come over and show your women our Hawaiian type. I want to learn their style, too. It is going to be a sharing, educational experience. I am happy to be here."

"Are you married?" one of the men asked when Kanaʻe finished.

"No."

"Do you have a sister?"

And so it went through the night, with long, rambling speeches in Maori and Papa Toki's kind insistence that Kanaʻe return on Wednesday when the Tumu Nu resumed.

That night Teumere, the mayor's wife, dreamt about finding a grove of trees off a trail still ragged with the coral that had risen from the sea thousands of years before her people had sailed to Atiu. In her dream, the jungle had trapped the heat rising from the island, and the air buzzed with bugs that nipped the skin of her companions, including the stranger, a Hawaiian named Kanaʻe. All Teumere knew about the man was that he had been found by Andrea, the papaʻa woman who had moved to Atiu from Germany with Juergen. Kanaʻe, Teumere had been told, knew some things about making kapa. When she awoke, Teumere decided she would show this Kanaʻe how to make cloth from her island's trees.

The next day Andrea picked up Kanaʻe for an island tour with Teumere, who was joined by the senior agricultural officer on Atiu, and his barefoot assistant, whose soles were as tough as the shoes Kanaʻe wore. They rode in a truck, first going down to the landing where islanders launch hand-hewn outrigger canoes into the night, using hoop nets on poles to catch flying fish, which they attract with lanterns.

Along the coral roadside, Kanaʻe spotted plants and trees in abundance that were rarely seen in Hawaiʻi. He knew their uses back home but hesitated to share that knowledge, fearing it might influence and alter Atiu's culture. Kanaʻe had seen how the mixing of cultures at Pacific arts festivals had changed traditional dances and crafts—hula took on Tahitian movements,

The Tumu Nu, which began as a clandestine clubhouse for men during decades of temperance on Atiu, now attracts tourists seeking a native experience.

Andrea Eimke explains to Kana'e Keawe how this dead coral once provided the lime used by Atiu islanders to plaster their homes. These days, the islanders use paint.

and Polynesians appropriated Hawaiian lei-making techniques. The blurring of cultural distinctions disturbs the purist in Kanaʻe. Atiu's agricultural assistant was less concerned. With pantomime and a few English words, he explained how leaves from this tree can induce a mother's milk, roots from that one alleviate stomach disorders, those over there cure ulcers.

The sun soon burned away the clouds, and heat withered the group. Teumere wove a wreath of leaves to shade her head. The truck stopped beside a coconut tree so everyone could have a drink. The assistant climbed the tree and cut some coconuts, which he husked on a stake chopped from the brush. He cracked the nuts open with a rock, and the group drank.

The road gave out after the coconuts, and the entourage continued on foot up the Vai Momoiri path, through the makatea—the coral that had risen from the sea to surround the island. The Atiuans showed Kanaʻe a large stone formation—the testicles of the god Māui—and the cave where the sons of Chief Ruapunga once lived.

Teumere headed down the trail, swinging the machete and laughing as her green dress fluttered around her stout body. Suddenly, she stopped. There on her right were the trees in her dream—the long, straight stalks of mati, a species of fig suitable for bark cloth. She struggled to cut through the bark until Kanaʻe gave her one of his shark-toothed knives; then she quickly pulled the edge down the length of the tree and with the assistant's help pulled off the split bark. They found more stalks, stripped off the bark, and rolled them into bundles, which they secured with vines and stacked on the path.

Atiu enchanted Kanaʻe. He was far from the demands of his American life—mortgage, bankers, building codes, and power grids that represent walls for so many people. On Atiu, life is still deeply rooted in the land and the old ways. Earlier, the group had passed a crew of men who laughed as they worked on the island's coral runway with shovels. The men waved, and Kanaʻe recognized several of them from the previous night at the Tumu Nu. Through the sun's glare, he could see they were sweating, but the men seemed unconcerned. Like Teumere, several had stepped into the jungle to weave wreaths to cool their heads. The night before, Kanaʻe had heard them sing with a joy that comes only from the heart, and now, as they labored, the joy was still evident.

After the group left the jungle, the truck took them down to Oravaru Beach on the other side of the island, where Captain James Cook had landed in 1777. Teumere cut a fresh palm frond and wove a basket, stripped the bark off a hau tree to secure her slippers to her ankles, and walked into the tide pools. She helped the others gather a lunch of opihi, wana, limu, and paua, which they supplemented with a tin of meat from the store.

That evening Teumere and Papa Tu, her husband the mayor, went to Andrea's house along with Mama Tepu, Mama Ate, and Manu, the schoolteacher, for the slide show Kana'e had planned. They presented him with a lei of bell pepper slices, basil leaves, and gardenia blossoms, and the aromas perfumed the room. When the bulb in Juergen's carousel projector burned out, the German couple fumed and apologized for not having a spare. The Atiuans waited patiently while Manu drove to the school to borrow an old projector. Then they watched the screen uncomplainingly as one by one Kana'e pushed the slides into the machine and removed them. Two nights later, when the island generator conked out and interrupted another slide show, they again sat peacefully, still independent of the technology that was slowly transforming their island.

Since Kana'e could not take the Bishop Museum kapa collection to Atiu, he showed slides of Cook Islands kapa from the museum collections, including a sample of one beaten in 1930. As Juergen tried to silence his dog, which was barking at passing neighbors, Kana'e showed images of a man's wedding-day waistcloth, and a yellow kapa poncho. The slides revealed other ponchos perforated with patterns, including one with a serrated edge around the neck opening. Most of the ponchos appeared to be lightweight and apparently designed for ceremonial use rather than labor. One was imprinted with the image of a biplane. Kana'e explained the size, origin, and apparent use of each sample as noted by the Bishop Museum curators.

Kana'e ended his presentation by showing the islanders the kapa-making tools he had made from kauila, a Hawaiian hardwood. And he told them of the old days in Hawai'i, when sorcerers used a staff of kauila wood to imprison a dead person's spirit: After the sorcerer contrived to obtain a piece of the enemy's clothing, hair, or discarded food, he could command the spirit to leave the wood in the form of a fireball, which would attack the victim. "We still have some of them flying around our island. Not everybody can see it. It's one of those things that is still hanging on. As long as you have a good heart and believe in God, nothing will hurt you. My grandfather was one of those kāhunas who could dissipate the bad luck that was prayed onto you. He was always getting calls at two o'clock in the morning, three o'clock. He had to go to somebody's house to chase away the spooks. . . . If your bone was broken—your arm or your leg—he could put his hand on you and pray, and the bone would heal right then and there. It's too bad my grandfather never left that gift to any of us. . . . I admonish you people to save whatever you have left. You still have all of the influences from your old world still around. If you lose your language, you lose your whole culture. Keep talking your language to your children. They can always pick up English in Rarotonga."

Andrea questioned Kana'e about sharing knowledge. She said there are people on Atiu who do not want to share. "We have lots of people in Hawai'i who don't want to share," Kana'e said. Some craft masters only pass the knowledge within their families. Others feel no one deserves it unless they practice the knowledge with respect. "I teach [my students] everything that I know. If my students become better than me, I feel I have done my job. The best teachers I've known are the ones who say they don't know everything."

Ngatamariki Manu asked Kana'e to deliver a lecture the following morning at Atiu College, the island high school. Manu believed strongly that the college should pass Atiuan culture on to the youngsters and help them become self-sufficient in Maori ways. But throughout the Cook Islands, the standard government curriculum is imported, designed by New Zealand educators for Caucasian children heading toward college. Manu feared that without a meaningful and relevant education that incorporated their local culture, many of the Atiu children would end up like their older cousins and siblings living in Rarotonga, Auckland, or Brisbane—performing manual labor at minimum wages.

In big cities everywhere in the Pacific, the values and prejudices of Western culture surround and influence native people. These influences make it "enormously difficult" for them to maintain a healthy cultural identity, according to Dr. Kirini Moko Mead, professor of Maori at Victoria University in Wellington, New Zealand. Dr. Mead delivered that message in Honolulu when he gave the keynote address at the Fourth International Symposium of the Arts of the Pacific.

"The more the world around us changes, the more important it is to maintain those parts of our culture which we value highly. . . . The spreading tentacles of commercialism . . . are creating a sort of uniform international culture of people who wear the same brand names, watch the same videos, eat the same sorts of food, drink Coca Cola, fly in the same jumbo jets, and drive the same models of automobiles. The people of the Pacific are caught in the fishnets of international trade. . . . What chance does heritage have against the strong invading cultural influences which come from Japan, the United States, Britain, and Europe? These high-status international giants are experts at political manipulation and commercial exploitation. . . . Citizens who grow up in a multicultural society often place a false value upon the right to choose a culture. There is no real choice. . . . There is one heritage above all others, which has great significance for the individual in an emotional and spiritual sense. This heritage is found when one is true to one's self. There is no deception, no dodging or avoidance of the issue, no pretense, and no posturing for political or social purposes."

In one of the Atiuan classrooms, students had hung fabric across the windows to block out the morning light. The boys were on the right, the girls on the left. Kanaʻe sat down among the green-and-white uniforms, turned on a cassette of Hawaiian music, and began showing slides of Cook Islands kapa, which he used to illustrate his lecture on the tradition and continued value of the arts in the Cook Islands. He could have shown other slides—perhaps one of a fabulous Hawaiian cloak made with 450,000 yellow bird feathers. But Kanaʻe purposefully avoided this and other images that displayed the vitality of pre-Western Hawaiian life. He did not want to sidetrack the students with stories from a different culture; again, he did not want to influence the uniqueness of Atiu.

After the lecture, Kanaʻe told the students, "What I want to leave you with is the message, Don't ever give up your language. If you lose your language, you lose everything. Support crafts[people], go and learn from them if you can. It's good to learn the papaʻa ways—you can get good jobs—but never lose your cultural identity. If you get to be very good at making tapa or whatever it might be, eventually at some point in the world they are going to want to take people from here . . . to show how you do your skill. Learn what you can from the grandparents, because they are the ones with the most knowledge. No matter what the skill, learn it . . . [and] do well in school. You'll be able to do well for yourself, your parents, your country, and your island as well."

Students at the Atiu high school watch a slide show about kapa made by their ancestors.
The kapa pieces are in the collections at Bishop Museum in Honolulu, where they may
be viewed only with special permission and handled only with gloved hands.

Kana'e had no idea whether he had reached the students. Except for a recitation of thanks from one student and profuse praises from the papa'a teacher, not one Maori teenager had said a word. Andrea drove Kana'e back to the Fibre Arts Studio, where the mayor introduced him to Papa Rongo, a man whose strong, tattooed arms continued the old tradition of weaving vines into baskets for trapping eels and braiding hau bark into reef sandals. The mayor explained that he had once known how, but had forgotten. After beginning the session with a prayer, he narrated as Papa Rongo pulled bark off the hau with his hands and silently braided it into three-eighths-inch rope. Within fifteen minutes, he had woven it into sandals. Kana'e watched in amazement. No one in Hawai'i still had this skill. "I wish for our Aloha Festivals [court] they would wear these instead of slippers and shoes," he said. The same kind of rope had once been used to tie up animals, but, the mayor said, "Now our lazy boys go to the shop and buy the rope."

Sometimes, Andrea asked Papa Rongo to make sandals and eel traps so the studio could sell them to visitors, but she said most tourists will not spend thirty dollars for such an item, or even more for the tīvaivai. With few customers

On Atiu, rubber slippers have taken the place of sandals that the islanders used to braid from hau bark. Papa Rongo can fashion a pair of sandals in fifteen minutes, but few young Atiuans are interested in learning the skill.

for their work, Papa Rongo and the others lose interest. "Most of the tourists are not after crafts," Andrea told Kanaʻe. "They are after souvenirs. Many of them say it's wonderful to have a place like this [Fibre Arts Studio] where you can actually see the people make things, but when it comes to paying for them, they say, 'Oh they're beautiful, but you see my budget won't allow for it.'

"This is the point where crafts get lost, because people don't want to make it anymore. There is no real need to make it for the family, and they can't earn a living with it as well as they can with other professions, so they drop it and it's gone."

Kanaʻe acknowledged that the same problems exist in Hawaiʻi. Niʻihau shell necklaces can cost up to $5,000, and most visitors pass up even the $100 versions. "Crafts" sold in Waikīkī stores are often cheap, mass-produced trinkets shipped in from other places, like the Philippines and China. Most island craftspeople in Hawaiʻi are weekend hobbyists until they can retire and pursue their love full-time. Some receive help from the federal government, which funds apprenticeship programs and efforts by the Native Hawaiian Culture and Arts Program to research and recover forgotten knowledge. One of their projects included building *Hawaiʻi Loa,* a replica of an ancient, double-hulled voyaging canoe.

It was mid-afternoon after Papa Rongo's demonstration, time for the three mamas of the Fibre Arts Studio to beat kapa from the bark that had been cut in the jungle the day before. Mama Tepu sliced palm fronds and wove them into mats for sitting on the ground. They carried two wooden beating anvils out of the studio. The women unwrapped the bundles of inner bark, which had been kept moist inside ti leaves, and began pounding, tentatively at first, then with confidence. They remembered remnants of a kapa-beating song sung by their mothers and grandmothers, and they sang it again for the tape recorder Kanaʻe had with him. The beating mallets were supposed to keep time with the song, and for a few moments the voices and mallets became one. Kanaʻe listened to the rhythm and imagined the poetry that had accompanied the beating mallets of his own ancestors a century and a half before. This is why Kanaʻe has enjoyed his journeys below the equator. Andrea may have thought Kanaʻe had come to help the mamas, but the mamas were giving him glimpses of a Polynesian past rarely visible in Hawaiʻi.

Before Kanaʻe arrived on Atiu, the women had difficulty beating out pieces of kapa wider than a pants leg. Kanaʻe leaned over the anvils and showed them a technique to join several pieces together, creating a sheet more than three feet wide. The mamas caught on quickly, and their sheets began to grow.

Smoke drifted over the glade where the women worked. They interrupted

Three Atiuan "mamas" pound banyan bark into cloth on an ironwood anvil. In days gone by, songs used to accompany rhythmic beating, which resonated through the earth.

Opposite page, top: Mamas Teumere and Ate work their kapa, and Kana'e removes bark from a breadfruit branch that has been roasted over a fire to help separate the bark from the xylem. The breadfruit branch ideally should be no more than an inch and a half thick, or the bark will be too old and hard to pound into cloth. In Hawai'i, the inner bark of mulberry is often used to make kapa.

Opposite page, bottom: Mama Tepu (center) laid down a carpet of coconut fronds so she, Teumere, and Ate could manipulate a large, wet sheet of kapa without tearing it. Rather than making kapa, most Cook Islands women today prefer to sew piecework and make appliquéd tīvaivai, quiltlike coverlets.

their pounding when they learned that a nearby rubbish fire had blown into the dry brush, threatening the island's pineapple crop. The women felt safe, but Andrea—protective of her mamas—insisted they move to the studio's screened-in porch. They placed the anvils on the floor and continued working, but the concrete prevented the beating from resonating through the wood to the earth. Eight ladies showed up to watch and then picked up mallets to join in the pounding. This was rare, observed Andrea—to see so many women working the old way and laughing as they did it.

Kanaʻe got lost in the moment and forgot his Prime Directive. "When nobody's watching," he told the women, "I use a spray bottle and I get a nice even coat of water. But for cultural purposes, I use a bowl. But that's the Hawaiian style—I don't want to change your culture."

That night the Tumu Nu greeted Kanaʻe with a five-minute song. They sang it from their hearts, these men who knew they were "Toke-enua no Enuamanu" (worms-of-the-land-called-Enuamanu), the ancient name for Atiu. Conviction reverberated in their voices. They wanted Kanaʻe to feel the island where they had been born and would be buried.

After singing the Lord's Prayer in Maori, Papa Toki said to Kanaʻe, "We are very pleased to have you with us tonight. Although there are many differences, we are here, and I don't think these differences would have kept you from sitting with us. We are almost the same. These customs we are very proud of, and at the same time you ought to be proud of too. The similarities in our customs and languages prove, I am sure, as was said before, that we all came from Avaiki. Maybe in Avaiki that we came through and through and through, we stood together."

Kanaʻe responded in Hawaiian, the drinking resumed, and for the first time the swipe relaxed the control Kanaʻe usually maintains over himself. He borrowed an ʻukulele to sing for the men, who responded with more Maori songs until it was time to close and slosh through a number that everyone knew—"My Bonnie Lies Over the Ocean."

The following day and night would be the last for Kanaʻe on Atiu. The mayor, Papa Tu, wanted to offer him a formal good-bye dinner, even if Kanaʻe would only be able to stay briefly before moving on to the next house and another farewell. Teumere heaped her husband's tables with eel, bread, coconut, pig's intestines and feet, and three different types of banana. A young girl stood alongside to fan away the bugs. When Kanaʻe arrived, Papa Tu talked proudly of the coming year, when his island would have twenty-four hours of electricity and a satellite dish for phone calls. His people would no longer have to wait three hours for an operator to transmit or receive calls by radio.

A coconut shell forms the body of a Cook Islands 'ukulele, made by inmates at the Rarotonga prison and sold to tourists. Kana'e borrowed one to share a song with the men at the Tumu Nu. Members of the Tumu Nu drink and sing together during the evening, when they also share hymns, prayers, and Scriptures.

The evening continued at Andrea's home, which was filled with Maori, new friends for Kana'e. The women already had hidden away their gifts—the kapa beaters and shark-toothed knives. The men came with shirts open so everyone could see their fishhook pendants. After Kana'e showed them his slides of Hawaiian artifacts, he thanked the group for all they had shared with him and for the many gifts (a pair of reef sandals, an eel basket, among others). "I would like to thank you from the bottom of my heart for all these sharings and friendship. . . . Now I don't want you folks to go take your cultural skills and [start using] the Hawaiian tapa beaters. Leave those alone. May your tapa making go on and improve. Get the younger ones interested so [your culture] can be preserved. . . . You are the only ones who know how to do it. You are the remaining master crafts[people]. You are cultural repositories."

It was getting late; the Maori had to be at church by 5:30 A.M., so Papa Tu summed up for Kana'e what the women would feel the next day after the service, when they would place lei upon lei around his neck, until he would barely be able to see the twin-propped Excalibur that would take him back to Rarotonga. "Although you are leaving tomorrow," Papa Tu said, "you are remaining over here through all these craftswork that you have given. The ways of tapa making are now improving. Before, they couldn't make anything wider than these pants. They could only make a foot and not more than a foot. We thank you very much on this because certain ways of tapa making, improvement, and widening-up got lost. They got it through the way you were dealing with them. So this is very much appreciated. We hope we can pass it on to the young ones, if the young ones are interested to come. Again we thank you very much. You are leaving tomorrow; our hearts will be with you and our prayers. God will take care of you until the end."

HAʻAHEO O LAPAKAHI
With Pride for Lapakahi

Haʻaheo o Lapakahi
It's with pride for Lapakahi

Ua ʻike maka ʻia
Where many eyes have seen

Ka laulima hana
The working hands met

Pioʻole ka ʻiʻini a iloko
With endless flame within

No nā Kūpuna Lāʻau Lapaʻau o Hawaiʻi
For the Kūpuna and the Healing Herbs of Hawaiʻi

Composed by
Kupuna Katherine
Kamalukukui Maunakea

Ulu wehiwehi ka nani
With its splendor and beauty

No ka pā ana mai
And the cool trade winds

Ka makani o Kohala
Swirling over Kohala

ʻOluʻolu ka pūliki ana mai
We did huddle together

No ka lehulehu no ka ʻāina
Like they did for many generations on this land

E ho'opa'a 'ia nei
Let it be recorded now and ever

No ka lōkahi ka mana'o
The unity and its morrow

Hui pū me kealoha
Mix with much Aloha

Mai ka Makua o ka Lani
For our Heavenly Father

Ka mākou Makua Ka Haku
He is our Lord and Savior

Pua ana mai Lapakahi
Bloom out for Lapakahi

Ua 'ike maka 'ia
Where many eyes have seen

Ka laulima hana
The working hands met

Pio'ole ka 'i'ini a iloko
With endless flame within

No nā Kūpuna Lā'au Lapa'au o Hawai'i
For the Kūpuna and the Healing Herbs of Hawai'i

8 WILLIAM KALUNAKEAKI KAHU'ENA

Lapa'au & *Healing*

When William Kahuʻena was a boy, his grandparents taught him how to find and gather plants from the mountains, shore, and sea to use in medicinal preparations. Because these plants are hard to come by in urbanized areas, healers today grow some plants in their own gardens.

Preceding page: Hands prepare the medicine, but many healers believe faith in the remedy and in God are the most important ingredients for a patient's recovery.

Twenty million tourists have visited the island of Maui in the past decade. The island has been so transformed by condominiums, resorts, and newcomers that its sunny, leeward coast barely resembles Hawai'i any more. A drive from the Nāpili condos to the Wailea resorts, with Kā'anapali hotels, Lahaina honky-tonks, and Kīhei apartments in between, leaves people wondering where the Hawaiians live.

Many Hawaiians make their homes in faraway Hāna, isolated by sixty miles of narrow road that squeezes through lush forests perfumed by guavas, mountain apples, ginger, and liliko'i. The road to Hāna twists through six hundred curves and across fifty-six one-way bridges; the journey may take three queasy hours or more, especially when the asphalt is crowded with rental cars and vans filled with tourists. Intrepid visitors do not despair. Tour guides may share a song by Aima Aluli McManus, which promises sightseers mythic beauty and unspoiled Hawaiian hospitality in a land steeped in a traditional history and folklore.

> *I lost my heart to Hāna by the sea*
> *Where nature sang to me in sweet soft harmony*
> *Her gentle waterfalls caress her mountains strong*
> *It's there I lost my heart, it's there where I belong*
> *Oh how she smiles so peacefully*
> *Her voice reflects tranquillity*
> *And her fragrances fill the air*
> *Reflecting times that we have shared*

Once visitors arrive in Hāna, mesmerized by the fragrant air and gentle waterfalls, they do not realize that the lives of many Hawaiians there are far from ideal. Since 1848, Hāna has suffered the consequences of laws that disenfranchised most Hawaiians from the land, while allowing foreigners to buy vast land parcels, create plantations, and profit from the demands of a growing and hungry western America.

The Danish owner of Hāna's first sugar plantation severed villagers' ties with their land when he offered them housing and jobs in return for low wages and long hours of monotonous, exhausting labor. A company store fed the families, but high prices indebted the Hawaiians until they finally understood what had taken place and became unwilling to continue working for the Dane. This situation forced the plantation—and other plantations in the Islands—to import immigrant laborers, who introduced diseases that killed many of the islanders they had been hired to replace. Some of the Hawaiians who still owned land in Hāna leased their plots to the plantation and departed for what they hoped would be an easier life in the cities. A few remained.

In 1944 a wealthy San Francisco businessman named Paul I. Fagan converted the withering Hāna sugarcane plantation into a cattle ranch. Fagan also built the exclusive Hotel Hāna-Maui, an expensive hideaway for tourists attracted by the quiet isolation and cordial ways of the small, one-company town.

In some respects Fagan was a generous boss. The hotel and ranch provided the most jobs for Hāna's people. He donated $100,000 for a community center. His wife's estate supported a trust fund benefiting the Hāna Community Association. He and the subsequent owner of the plantation-ranch-hotel complex permitted the town's two thousand residents access across company lands to reach the ocean and mountains; it was important for the Hawaiians to continue their traditional fishing and hunting, to supplement food they purchased or grew. But this changed in 1984 when the Rosewood Corporation from Texas acquired the 4,700-acre ranch and hotel and closed many accesses because of liability fears. Five years later, Rosewood sold the property for $63 million to a consortium of Japanese, British, and Hawaiʻi-based businessmen. The new owners promised to resolve the access dilemma, but other problems continued to frustrate the local residents. Ambitious expansion plans for the ninety-seven-room hotel initially included a golf course and condominiums. A group of one hundred workers objected, telling the consortium they desperately needed housing for their own families. In 1995, the consortium sold the Hotel Hāna-Maui to another corporation. As the rural area has become an exclusive retreat for wealthy outsiders, land values have escalated beyond the reach of the low-paid hotel workers, many of whom were born and raised in Hāna. Some workers acknowledged the benefits of a golf course—it would attract more visitors to the hotel, help keep them and their children on the payroll, and perhaps help pay for employee housing. But not everyone in Hāna wants a golf course or more visitors. New people moving in prefer to see Hāna maintained with the qualities that enticed them to go there in the first place. Five hundred thousand visitors a year is enough, even if most of them drive in and out in a day.

Enchanted by the beauty of Hāna, tourists rarely see the extent to which the hotel and ranch and influx of outsiders have affected the lives of many local Hawaiians. They might catch a brief glimpse—say on a Friday afternoon at the company store in Hāna town when workers line up to buy cigarettes, beer, and frozen food, along with videotape movies for another low-cost weekend in front of television.

This scene is repeated in many Hawaiʻi and American communities, but for those who care, the situation in Hāna is especially troubling. Hāna is still a beautiful, rural place, populated predominately by Hawaiians in a rich landscape capable of supplying much of their food. Some have started a health center that is improving residents' nutrition, while others have obtained $2.8 million in grants to start a village marketplace that will sell locally produced goods and crafts and provide services to the community. These Hawaiians are vital, committed, and enjoying good health, but many of Hāna's other Hawaiians are not.

Hāna was a natural choice when a group of Hawaiian healers, doctors, and kūpuna thought about where they would hold a gathering to discuss Hawaiian health and healing. They didn't meet at the luxury hotel, but at the Hāna Hawaiian Village, an oceanside complex of fishponds and gardens subsidized by the vanloads of tourists who stopped there for lunch. The proprietors, the Noa family, appreciated the opportunity to host the healers—people who still practiced the wisdom of their ancestors. Participants in the group included Harry Kunihi Mitchell, Sr., from nearby Keʻanae; Agnes Kalanihoʻokaha Cope of Waiʻanae, Oʻahu; Kalua Kaiahua of Lahaina, Maui; and an elder whose story deserves close reading—William Kalunakeaki Kahuʻena, a plant-medicine man who had recently returned to Oʻahu after an eighteen-month effort to settle in Florida. In all, about forty people traveled to Hāna for the talks.

On the opening day of their 1989 gathering, the healers stood in a line, ranked by age and expertise, outside the entrance to Hāna Hawaiian Village. Kamaki A. Kanahele III, trained in healing and hula, chanted an ancient oli as he led them across a fishpond bridge onto the Noa property. He conveyed the guests' respect to their Hāna hosts and called upon their ancestors to join them, so that their knowledge, essence, and mana would enhance the group's sharing and healing. Hāna schoolteacher Parley Kanakaʻole, also speaking Hawaiian, greeted Kamaki and the others and welcomed them to Hāna. Then Parley and Kamaki stood beside the fishpond and mixed together waters that had been carried to Hāna from each island. Non-Hawaiian observers stood off to the side while the rest of the group walked single-file past Parley, who sprinkled the water over their heads; after this blessing they were free to move onto the land. They climbed a slope toward an arrangement of picnic tables under a canopy of green and blue tarps stretched over bamboo and metal frames. After more prayers, they sat down for a ho'oponopono ceremony to clear the air of any bad feelings and then allowed the non-Hawaiian observers to join them.

This was not the first such gathering of modern Hawaiian healers, nor the last for the concerned men and women seeking ways to apply the wisdom of years gone by to the health crisis faced by kānaka maoli (native Hawaiians) living in today's westernized Hawai'i. They know that in Hawai'i, America's healthiest state, the Hawaiian population is the most unhealthy ethnic group, living an average of seven years less than other residents. This has been documented and publicized so often by haole researchers that some Hawaiians no longer permit examinations and study by outsiders. Instead, they want to undertake healing for themselves, and rather than talking about how sick they are, they prefer to emphasize the progress being made to improve their lives. But according to a 1991 report prepared by Hawaiian internist Dr. Richard Kekuni Blaisdell, more—much more—needs to be accomplished. Dr. Blaisdell reported that kānaka maoli have the highest overall death rate in Hawai'i, especially from the major causes—heart disease, cancer, stroke, accidents, diabetes, and infections. Kānaka maoli also rank highest for mental retardation, suicide, child abuse, and infant mortality.

Other studies have found that among the eight thousand remaining pure Hawaiians, the death rate is 146 percent higher than for other races in the United States, and the death rate for the estimated 211,000 part-Hawaiians is 17 percent higher, with even higher percentages for specific diseases and populations. Pure and part-Hawaiians represent about 19 percent of the state's total population, yet in 1989, twice as many Hawaiians had incomes beneath the poverty level when compared to all other families. Most of the homeless in the Islands also are Hawaiian. Many of them live in rural communities where health care is underfunded and scarce.

The U.S. Congress examined these serious problems and passed a bill in 1988 that eventually provided $2.3 million to fund five Hawaiian health centers. The bill mandated that the centers focus on the prevention and control of diabetes and high blood pressure among Hawaiians, improve overall nutrition, provide prenatal and infant care, including immunization, and reach out to the community wherever possible. The bill also encouraged the centers to provide access to traditional Hawaiian healers and healing—an option that was included in the bill partly because a few knowledgeable healers were still alive in 1988.

The congressional staff report blamed Hawaiian health problems on Hawaiians, claiming they did not control their own obesity, smoking, and drinking. It also faulted Hawaiians for avoiding doctors until it was too late— a behavior typical, the report said, of Americans with low incomes. But some Hawaiian health professionals believe the reasons for poor health in their community are more complex than simple negligence and low income levels. They see harmful behaviors as the result of 150 years of oppression by a dominant Western society and government, a dominance that denies Hawaiians access to resources and opportunities that would enable them to pursue a more traditional lifestyle, such as medical centers where they could seek Hawaiian healing methods. Kekuni Blaisdell and others propose to reduce problems with culturally sensitive healing, but success will be limited, they say, as long as the dominant society prevents Hawaiians from being kānaka maoli.

Ever since the arrival of traders, whalers, and missionaries in Hawai'i, most foreigners have expected—often demanded—that Hawaiians conform to new values. Early European explorers described the islanders as exceptionally healthy, as could be expected after fifteen hundred years of subsistence living and isolation from outsiders and foreign diseases. Among all Pacific people the Hawaiians were considered the most humane, sociable, friendly, and hospitable to newcomers. The reason for pre-contact Hawaiian health and civility, according to Dr. Blaisdell, stemmed from a simple belief: "To intentionally harm others or anything in nature was to harm oneself. . . . Pono, or proper order or harmony . . . required conscious effort of each individual kanaka. . . . Imbalance of mana or loss of pono accounted for misfortune, such as illness, sparse catch of i'a [fish], or crop failure. . . . While there was collective lōkahi [unity] and interdependence with self, others, and all of nature, nevertheless, individual self-reliance was expected."

During the nineteenth century, 80 percent of the Hawaiian population (at least 160,000 people and many more by other estimates) died from newly introduced bacterial and viral infections. Hawaiians needed time to develop immunities to the various plagues, from influenza to smallpox, that had ravaged other parts of the world in previous centuries. In the course of the Hawaiian depopulation, the local lifestyle disintegrated. Chiefs sought Western mana when their traditional political and religious systems collapsed, and the Hawaiian ways were replaced by a European-style monarchy, by the idea of private property, by capitalism, and by the Christian god. The 'āina, the land, became a commodity exploited by Hawaiian and haole owners or lessees for exportable goods—produce, sugar, then pineapple.

Unfortunately, Western medicine could not help the thousands of Hawaiians dying from the physical and psychological upheavals that were the nineteenth century in Hawaiʻi. In 1859, Queen Emma and King Kamehameha IV established a clinic in Honolulu to help their people, but the Hawaiians distrusted Queen's Hospital and the Kapiʻolani Home (founded later by Princes Kalanianaʻole and Kawānanakoa). Western-trained doctors focused on diseases, rather than trying to help Hawaiians cope with the rapid changes in their daily lives, changes that resulted in abnormally high rates of diabetes, hypertension, cancer, and heart disease. These problems continued during the Territorial years as urbanization increased and American rulers enacted laws that further alienated Hawaiians from their language, culture, and lands. Many kānaka maoli simply gave up trying to survive, and died.

Today, as Dr. Blaisdell and some others see it, the effort to restore good health to Hawaiians is doomed unless Hawaiʻi chooses and encourages the development of native gardens rather than golf courses, fishponds rather than yacht harbors, villages rather than casinos—Hawaiian models of living rather than Western.

Passage of the 1988 Hawaiian health bill was lengthy and arduous (eventually it funded a native health center in Hāna)—some participants at the Hāna conference wondered why the elders, the healers, would ever want (or be allowed) to integrate their skills and wisdom into a Western medical system which can be so politicized and impersonal.

Several kinds of healers attended the Hāna gathering, and to the outsider, each one seemed to have a slightly different healing method. There were those who use hoʻoponopono, which involves family discussion, reflection, and prayer to cleanse the mind and spirit of trouble that often leads to disease; the kūpuna lāʻau lapaʻau, who heal with medicines made from plants; the practitioners of lomi, a form of massage; and the practitioners of lāʻau kāhea, who use their voices to channel God's strength into healing—all techniques with parallels in other cultures.

Some parents in the group had raised their children without ever taking them to a doctor, keeping them healthy with medicines made from native and introduced plants. Leaves from one plant had been used to cure a son's ruptured spleen. Sap from another plant had relieved a granddaughter's constipation. A certain combination of plants had helped repair someone's bleeding heart after doctors said nothing could be done. But the most important ingredient for all healing, the Hawaiians said, was faith—faith in the healer, in the spirit, and especially in God. Said one kupuna, "Prayer is the key."

Sabina Mahelona shares her knowledge of traditional healing plants and techniques at the 1990 *Folklife Hawai'i festival on O'ahu. For many years, Mrs. Mahelona assisted Henry Auwae, a respected healer, with his practice and lectures. Some traditional Hawaiian healers offer simple remedies, but a few masters, like Papa Auwae, have also devised medicines that interest Western medical researchers.*

The Hāna conference was something of a summit meeting for the emerging group of healers gathered from around the Islands, and William Kahuʻena was a special case. His modest story—how he became a kupuna lāʻau lapaʻau—describes the widespread dissipation of traditional Hawaiian wisdom and the challenges to keep it alive.

Before plantations covered the island slopes with green sugarcane fields and neat rows of pineapple, indigenous forests flourished. Hawaiian families used the plants and trees for medicine, as well as for food and shelter. According to Hawaiian historians, good health for the Hawaiians depended on the well-being of the forest, so they took care of the kukui groves, where they planted kalo; the hala trees, whose leaves were plaited into mats for their houses; the coconuts, bananas, and breadfruit, which helped sustain them; and the ʻōlena, ʻawa, pōpolo, noni, kī, kō, mamake, hinahina, hau, koʻokoʻolau, limu, and other plants and shrubs, which healed them.

Foreigners planning to expand the sugarcane business regarded these people as poor. They did not understand how the wealth of the land enriched the Hawaiians' spirits and bodies in ways that Western "improvements" could not. Perhaps that is why the mother of William Kahuʻena decided in 1919 to send her pure Hawaiian infant away from downtown Honolulu. He went to live with his grandparents in Wailea, an isolated hamlet in the Hāmākua district on the island of Hawaiʻi.

The Hawaiian-speaking elders welcomed the child into a house thatched with pili and paved with stones. Wherever Grandfather went, the boy followed, usually on the old man's back as he walked up the mountain to cultivate kalo or down to the beach, where Bill played and fished from the stream. Everywhere they ventured, Bill absorbed strength and knowledge from the rugged land, and he grew into a robust and independent boy. On Bill's first day of school, he encountered a teacher who beat him because he spoke Hawaiian. The boy threw a desk at the man and never went back.

"And from then on," Bill remembered decades later, "my grandfolks taught me how to live off the land, which consists of going up the mountain and getting all the things that we had up in the mountain or down at the beach, in the river. We traveled out in the deep ocean, out in canoe."

Along the paths of land and sea, Bill learned how to use plants to catch lunch from a stream, how to build a fire to cook, and how to turn bamboo into a spear to catch dinner from the reef. His grandparents also showed him which plants can heal and how to prepare the leaves, roots, bark, and fruit as medicines.

Bill grew into "oni kalalea ke kū a ka lāʻau loa" (a tall tree that stands above others). Even in his seventies, gray-haired, he mirrored the forests of his youth: tall, robust, brown, silently offering visitors shade, fruit, comfort, or medicine. From a Western perspective, his humility did not make sense. This man grew up Hawaiian, as fluent in the language as he was in the indigenous crafts and medicines. He had adapted to the changes brought about by annexation, World War II, and statehood, yet Uncle Bill endured with the steadfastness of a giant koa tree, observing the world in a quiet, friendly manner, shy in the presence of strangers eager to learn his knowledge. His voice, barely audible but always polite, shared without embellishment, even with family or his friends at the Church of Jesus Christ of Latter-Day Saints. When others might have bragged before the reporter's tape recorder, he simply said, "What I know about medicine, it took me quite a while. I had to grow up with it. I used to go to up-mountain and pick the medicine up . . . and bring back and prepare it for my grandfolks and my granduncle, and they showed me how to apply it."

Back then, in the 1920s, Bill knew the tension between his world and the encroaching haole world. "Some doctors," he said, "when I was growing up, they only use pills and they found that the pills didn't heal the people, so they went to the Hawaiian people that knew about the [plant] medicines and they would be taught. The doctors that came and learned about that medicine, they use that medicine for their patients, but somehow or other the medical association found out they was using herbs, some other medicines besides what they was supposed to have, and they were reprimanded for it. I don't know why. They killed a lot of people with their pills. I can remember those days. They used to call the doctors 'Dr. Pill.' For any kind of sickness you had, they would give you a pill."

Bill's grandparents transformed plants into medicines that kept the boy healthy. Pōpola got rid of colds. 'Ōlena juice took care of earaches. They healed burns and cuts with the ashes from a dry coconut husk, strained and then mixed with water. "There's lots more," Bill said. "But all in all our medicine is not used only for one type of sickness. It's used for all types. It's a dual purpose 'cause our medicine, when it goes into the blood system into the body, it goes through your blood system and cleans you all the way from the top of your head, all the way down to your toe."

Bill was a young boy when his grandfather died, and his grandmother moved him up the coast to Waipi'o, an enormous valley where Hawaiians still grew kalo and fished from the sea. His grandmother died there in 1931 when Bill was twelve. By then, Bill said, "I knew how to live off the land and not depend on anybody for food. I knew all the things that I was taught by my grandfolks—how to make a living for myself and take care of any sickness I have. . . . When they passed away, some other family had . . . sickness and I did the healing for them."

For a brief time Bill lived in nearby Kamuela with his father. He worked for the Parker Ranch and at various jobs in Hilo until someone discovered that this tall young man was a minor. He moved on to the harbor village at Kawaihae, staying with an uncle who taught him what he knew about canoes, fishing equipment, how to trap wild cattle, and how to catch feral pigs with a hook and a lariat made from the morning glory vine. "Sometimes I tell people that and they laugh at me until they went up and tried themselves, and then they found it was better than having a rifle. It's quiet and you won't disturb anybody up there with that loud noise, although sometimes it's dangerous. It depends on the size of the wild hog you have."

During World War II, the Army sent Bill to the Solomon Islands, to Guadalcanal, where thousands of Americans and Japanese spent months slaughtering each other for control of the island. During one battle, enemy shrapnel shredded the body of a friend. Because the daily bloodshed had drained the medics' supplies, all Bill could do was watch his companion suffer. Then he looked down and discovered lettucelike leaves growing on the ground and recognized them as laukahi, which Bill had used as a boy to cure boils. He prepared them for his friend, and the wounds soon healed.

After the war Bill returned to Hawaiʻi, and in Honolulu he became a driver-mechanic for the Pacific and Hawaiian dredging companies. He continued operating heavy equipment until his retirement in 1985 from the state Department of Transportation, Harbors Division. During those years, the man who as a boy in Hāmākua had learned the traditional methods of plant medicine healed only two people—a cousin with tuberculosis and a sister whose neck had become infected and swollen after an operation. "I made the medicine for it; got all that thing out of there. That took three days. It healed without the operation. Didn't have to cut her up."

Bill's first wife suffered from diabetes, a disease that affects many Hawaiians. "I tried to make the medicine for her, but she wouldn't take it. She was strong-headed." She died in 1972. The following year Bill remarried and moved to Windward Oʻahu, where he and his second wife, Alapaʻi, lived for sixteen years. After Bill retired, his pension and social security paid the rent until the house was sold and the Kahuʻenas found they could no longer afford to stay in Hawaiʻi. Encouraged by a relative who lived in Florida, they decided to retire there, with the hope that the Sunshine State would be affordable and tolerable for them. When they left Hawaiʻi, Bill did not know that his vast knowledge of Hawaiian ways had become something rare among Hawaiians; nor did he realize there were people who wanted to preserve and perpetuate the things he knew.

Bill and Alapaʻi Kahuʻena stayed in Florida for eighteen months, until they could no longer endure the racial intolerance they suffered there. A cousin offered them a studio behind his Kāneʻohe home on Oʻahu, and the state Department of Education's Kūpuna Program gave them jobs teaching Hawaiian culture to children. They joined a group of Hawaiian elders, who told a leading kupuna, Harry Kunihi Mitchell, about their new friend's mastery of Hawaiian healing.

Harry and Bill became friends. They were the same age and shared similar backgrounds. Harry had been raised in remote Keʻanae on Maui, where he had learned the traditional ways of fishing, planting, and healing. But whereas Bill was quiet and had kept his learning to himself, Harry was busy and involved. He initiated the first modern gathering of Hawaiian healers. He helped form the statewide healer's organization Papa Lāʻau Lapaʻau (which became Kūpuna Lāʻau Lapaʻau o Hawaiʻi), and two other key groups, Papa

Ola Lōkahi (Board of Health and Harmony) and E Ola Mau (Live On), the sponsors of the gathering in Hāna.

In the Hāna discussions, the question was simple: Could Hawaiian healing methods be recognized by and institutionalized within the Western political and medical systems that dominated Hawaiʻi? The answers were difficult. For instance, besides having different levels and different kinds of expertise, the healers had been trained differently. Some, like Bill Kahuʻena, had learned as children. Others had received the knowledge or healing gift through their mentor's last breath. Several believed their abilities came from God.

How, one participant asked, would the Lāʻau Lapaʻau association certify someone like Kalua Kaiahua of Lahaina? Kalua explained to the group that his father had taught him the use of herbal remedies, while his mother, a registered nurse, had shown him how to care for the young and elderly using both Hawaiian and Western medicines. His aunt, a blind woman who was a healer, had touched Kalua's hands and examined his palms and fingers. She had sensed a gift within him and told him that if he wanted to know how to use the gift—what he could do with it, its cautions and blessings—then he had to pray to God in order to receive the knowledge.

The group pondered which part of Kalua's training was certifiable and which was not. Who would judge? A committee of his peers? A panel of Western doctors?

Obtaining certification for today's kūpuna is important to the Kūpuna Lāʻau Lapaʻau because their association wants to ensure that others will learn correct healing techniques and medicines and because they want to protect patients from fake healers. Some kūpuna are cautious about the idea of certification to satisfy the organization or the Western medical community. Others will have none of it.

Agnes Cope, for one, explained that her knowledge is not for examination or dissection but only for sacred learning by her son, Kamaki, and her grandson. When interviewed by the Kalihi-Pālama Culture and Arts Society about his knowledge of the healing arts, Kamaki described the nonacademic nature of his training. "We learned by watching and repeating. Sometimes doing it daily or only in the mornings. As children we practiced our healing lessons on our dogs. They were very good patients, and because we loved them the healing lessons were very wonderful. . . . In sickness we healed ourselves. For some things you can heal and cleanse, for others we must first return to the teacher or suffer from kāpulu [careless] work. We never realized what we had learned or been given until we were adults. Like all children we just wanted to play. Our lessons were our games."

At the Hāna gathering, Kamaki reiterated his point. "The keepers of the healing are you and I. Our healing knowledge is not on exhibit for the whole world. It's between healer and patient. Practicing kāhuna doctors never went out in public and made a spectacle of themselves. . . . Some ideas must not be shared."

Despite resistance to the idea of measuring up to a Western system of acceptability, the Hāna conference pursued the idea of certification as necessary to allay doctors' concerns about integrating traditional Hawaiian healing methods with Western medicine.

Four Hawaiian doctors attended the gathering in Hāna, offering their sympathies and expertise; they warned the kūpuna about the resistance they might encounter from the medical establishment. As lawsuits and economic pressures increase, Western medical practice becomes more specialized and standardized. Many physicians restrict themselves to narrow fields of practice and are often ignorant about healing approaches that are outside their standards of care. The national and Hawaiʻi medical associations reinforce this isolationism through political lobbying that tries to limit authority and reimbursement for other Western practitioners—including advance practice nurses, certified nurse midwives, chiropractors, and naturopathic doctors.

The kūpuna will face other challenges, too. Different patients do not always respond to medicine the same way, whether plant medicine or modern drugs. Penicillin saves millions of lives, but kills the allergic few. "The problem of medicine [Western or traditional] is that it is not entirely predictable," said Dr. Blase B. Lee Loy, a Hawaiian general practitioner from Kona. "Even though you try your best, sometimes you are not successful and the patient dies. If it happens to [kūpuna] lāʻau lapaʻau, it could throw the whole thing back into the fire. You have to look at it objectively, without getting emotional. It will be a tough job introducing traditional healers to Western medicine. That doesn't mean it won't be successful, but it will be a long, uphill battle. It will take a lot of ingenuity. It will take a lot of patience."

Cedric "Rick" Akau, a Honolulu-based doctor whose specialty is sports medicine, raised the thorny issue of liability. "I am supportive, but the Western medical-legal system makes it difficult. Physicians may open themselves up to liability problems if they bring in lāʻau lapaʻau."

Some healers flatly rejected any discussion of liability, dismissing it as a Western concept alien to their traditional ways. True healers never pondered liability, they said, because they had achieved harmony and balance within themselves, with others, with nature, and with the universe. Holistic by nature, Hawaiian healers used herbs only after the source of disharmony had been singled out and removed from a patient's life. Anger among relatives could provoke illness, as could the simple action of taking a neighbor's tool. By bringing a family together through hoʻoponopono to discuss someone's anger or hurt, a kupuna could eliminate the psychological cause of an illness without the need for treating the physiological symptoms. Medicinal herbs only became necessary when the symptoms progressed too far.

The healing process of hoʻoponopono can take days or months, and the healers pondered how they could pass on the old ways of life and healing to a younger generation leading busy lives. The children of some kūpuna are not interested in learning the old ways, even though they know the knowledge will die with their parents. The Kūpuna Lāʻau Lapaʻau organization tried assigning apprentices to some of its members, but the students are busy surviving modern Hawaiʻi, and have difficulty finding the time to devote to learning from the masters. The older Hawaiians wonder whether they—like elders around the world—can ever turn their grandchildren's attention from television and video games long enough for them to learn anything about their traditional culture, much less the intricacies of native healing.

Discussing these issues in Hāna, the healers and doctors became so focused that few of them acknowledged the passing rain showers, even when the water beat loudly upon the overhead tarps and cascaded down the sides. During breaks, participants relaxed and took time to wander along the shore, where they saw medicinal plants cultivated by the Noa family. Near a small ocean cove, Bill Kahuʻena came upon some ʻuhaloa. Most people regard it as a weed, but Bill knew how to use its roots to make a cure for sore throat. Bill also explained how to steam the leaves in water, using the vapor to clear away congestion and headache. A woman attending the conference acted on his suggestion and felt better after deep draughts of the vapor.

In Honolulu and similar urbanized areas, Bill and other healers have had a difficult time finding the plants they needed. And Bill advised kūpuna to be careful that plants for medicinal use have not been poisoned by automobile exhaust or contaminated by herbicides that county road crews spray to destroy weeds. Obtaining clean plants usually requires access to remote areas, a task hampered by landowners who block trails to reduce liability.

Claire K. Hughes, a Hawaiian nutritionist, told the Hāna group that proper nourishment is the easiest step toward better health. She also pointed out that in Hawaiʻi, as in most American communities, low wages, the Western lifestyle, peer pressure, and mass merchandising of junk and fast foods encourage harmful consumption.

Bill Kahuʻena uses a stone pestle and mango-wood mortar to grind plants he will incorporate into healing mixtures. Traditional Hawaiian healers share their skills at five native health clinics established with federal funding in 1992. In 1996, budget cuts jeopardized the future of the clinics.

As an experiment, the Wai'anae Coast Comprehensive Health Center on O'ahu in 1989 devised a traditional Hawaiian diet. Twenty Hawaiian participants promised to abide by it for twenty-one days. They consumed as much poi, kalo, squid, sweet potato, breadfruit, fish, fruits, and lū'au leaf as they wanted. After three weeks, they had reduced their weight by an average of seventeen pounds. Their health, complexions, and energy levels improved. Their cholesterol counts dropped by 14 percent, and one pure Hawaiian man eliminated his need for insulin injections for diabetes.

"The first day, [we] were very gung ho," said Kamaki Kanahele, a participant in the Wai'anae study. "Lunch, same thing. By dinner, people were screaming for salt, shoyu, and milk. Halfway through the study, everyone was swearing a lot."

By the end of the twenty-one days, most of them craved Western foods. Kamaki went to McDonald's and ordered a soda. For the first time in fifteen years, he could not drink it. A week later, he tried to eat spaghetti. His body threw it up. "If we went back to the traditional diet, I'm positive our health would improve," he said.

The Wai'anae Diet Program organizers have moved beyond experimentation and now encourage the entire Hawaiian community to use more kalo, sweet potato, lū'au leaf, fresh fish, and other traditional foods in their diets. If those foodstuffs are unavailable or too expensive, people in Hāna and other towns are urged to substitute brown rice, potatoes, vegetables, beans, tofu, chicken, shrimp, and turkey. A few communities have built communal gardens and fishponds to reduce dependence on grocery stores and processed foods. At Pūnana Leo, a private school in Honolulu where preschoolers learn the Hawaiian language through immersion, administrators decided to prepare lunch for the students instead of asking the parents to do it. They use fresh vegetables, fruits, and Hawaiian staples from a Windward O'ahu farm and soon discovered the children were napping better, learning more, and fighting less.

Another issue challenged the group of healers attending the Hāna conference: Could the kūpuna knowledge help Hawaiian families affected by abuse, alcoholism, or crime? Or in other families where social and economic pressure take their toll? A survey of Hawaiians living in west Kaua'i found that about half the households earn less than $15,000 a year. Rents on Kaua'i are high— a two-bedroom house can cost a thousand dollars a month. As in Hāna and other communities, many Hawaiians in west Kaua'i are barely subsisting— even more so after Hurricane 'Iniki damaged or destroyed six thousand homes on the island in 1992.

To help them, west Kaua'i health care providers and community leaders created an organization called Ho'ōla Lāhui Hawai'i to improve health services for Hawaiians. The group supports efforts to improve access to lā'au lapa'au expertise, because it knows that Hawaiians facing medical problems are as likely to seek the help of traditional healers and family members as they are to go to a doctor. The organization believes Western and traditional health care providers need to develop a relationship of mutual trust and respect. It will take time and patience—and recognition by Western practitioners that traditional healing techniques, such as ho'oponopono and lomi, help Hawaiians. And Ho'ōla encourages traditional healers to acknowledge the value of Western diagnoses and therapies. The organization hopes that by working together, Western and traditional practitioners can alter harmful life-styles and improve the overall health of Hawaiians.

Alu Like is a nonprofit corporation that seeks to help Hawaiians become self-sufficient. Largely through the efforts of its Big Island director, Everett "Sonny" Kinney, Alu Like embarked on an islandwide ho'oponopono project. The courts and the state Department of Human Services and its agencies refer clients to the project, where a group of elders use ho'oponopono to try and resolve problems among them. Sonny Kinney observed that Western-style group therapies tend to alienate Hawaiians, who prefer to have a kupuna help them acknowledge the true reasons for their pain or addiction and make amends to those they have hurt. It is the Hawaiian way.

When Alu Like first undertook the Big Island ho'oponopono program, Sonny Kinney heard reports of skepticism from Hawaiians and non-Hawaiians alike. They thought he and the elders were "talking voodoo." The program's success stories changed that attitude, and Sonny was confident the program would become a permanent resource on the Big Island.

"The outstanding part of ho'oponopono is the spiritual quality we give it," Sonny said. He related several stories about Hawaiians who had been healed. One couple was hooked on cocaine and alcohol. As an elder opened the ho'oponopono with a prayer, the couple broke down and cried like children. Having sensed the kupuna's integrity, warmth, and aloha, the couple spoke freely about their problems—how they had begun and how they were affecting themselves and their 'ohana. "We don't talk about drug abuse," Sonny said. "We talk about how they are going to settle the harm done to family and each other, and how to ask for forgiveness. In the process, they learn why they should stop drugs."

Young Hawaiian observers at the Hāna gathering and other meetings have been moved by the elders' words and have decided to promote and help revive traditional healing practices through apprenticeships and associations that will quantify healing standards for a certification program. Many of them believe that a certification program will make the healers "legitimate" by Western standards and thus more accessible to Hawaiians.

After the Hāna meeting, these new groups of young Hawaiians held more gatherings where expert healers could share their knowledge. At most places, people were not allowed to take notes or tape record the sessions; they were expected to absorb the information as their ancestors had, so the healing wisdom would become part of their spirit and be more than just words.

In November 1993, the Kūpuna Lāʻau Lapaʻau o Hawaiʻi association held an ʻūniki (graduation) for twelve elders at Lapakahi State Park on the Big Island, the site of a Hawaiian village six hundred years ago. The kūpuna's kākoʻo (assistants) and haumana (apprentices) also attended. "Papa" Henry Auwae, the eighty-five-year-old leader of the association, said the purpose of the ceremony was to recognize that each elder was prepared to teach other people and their own families. In an interview with *Ka Wai Ola o OHA,* Papa Auwae said, "In medicine we have rules to follow. You don't do it any old way you feel it should be done. They have to do it perfect. This is no fly-by-night healing."

Bill Kahuʻena did not make it to Lapakahi. Two and a half years earlier, on June 30, 1991, he died in Kaiser Medical Center, at the age of seventy-one. Bill had smoked for most of his life, giving up cigarettes only after marrying Alapaʻi. But the damage had been done. After two radiation treatments, Bill returned to his lāʻau. Three months later he passed away. Much of his wisdom and knowledge lives on through the people he shared with.

Bill helped Alapaʻi teach children about the old Hawaiian ways. Once a month he taught Windward Oʻahu kūpuna about different lāʻau. One morning back then six women met together in a backyard in Kailua to learn from Bill about koali, the blue morning glory.

Koali is so common in Hawaiʻi that most people think of it as a weed. But when a handful of freshly picked leaves from the blue variety is pounded into a pulp (along with five fingers of Hawaiian salt) and applied in a ti-leaf compress to a broken bone, morning and evening, the break is said to heal within five days. "When get through, get down on your hands and knees and pray to the Man in heaven and thank him for healing you," Bill told the ladies. "That's what a lot of people forget."

One of the women asked Bill about other varieties of koali and their healing properties, and why salt is used (it kills bacteria and helps medicine penetrate the skin), and whether they could substitute a noni leaf for ti. Another woman wondered why, if noni leaves help remove tumors, her mother's infected leg burned for thirty minutes after it was wrapped in noni (because her blood was clogged, Bill said). A young mother wanted to know where she could get clean salt water to flush toxins out of her body. "Cannot get it from here," Bill said. "Have to go outer islands. It's pitiful. Our island [Oʻahu] water is so polluted."

The elders talked some more, and Bill let people prepare the koali themselves so they would get the feel of holding the grinding stone with one hand while they cupped the leaves in the other and pounded against the wooden mortar. He wanted the group to start off with simple cures and then move on to more complicated remedies.

Afterward, Bill passed out photocopied summaries of the koali healing method. He encouraged his friends to take notes and ask questions. He wanted them to keep a record for personal use in case there was an emergency and they were unable to reach him. "When I give it to you, it's up to you and the Man in heaven. You have to have faith."

NATIVE HAWAIIAN IN PRISON

As a boy in Nuʻuanu
He heard the Ancients whisper.
His mother, who did not hear them,
Made sure he placed the maile
By their marble crypts.
Red ginger, lauaʻe,   *Composed by*
Carried in heavy buckets,   *Mahealani Kamauu*
Sloshing through underground chambers,
Paths of light going up,
Dark paths going down.

He swam at Kapena,
A young boy's reward.
At these times his heart sang
For the high waterfall,
The Ancients in his ear,
The slippery climb up,
The arcing dive down.

He tended the fires of peace:
He saw the Lord on Sunday,
A whipping on Monday.
On other days he saw other things—

When the Ancients whisper,
Who can know the heart of a boy?
In time he was sent away
To better love the Lord.
He was sent
To not where
Sweet hallelujah
Was a needle's high
And glory glory
A spreading thigh.

The Ancients came again.
This time they baptized him
In their own way—
At Napoʻopoʻo
His heart was a drum:
He danced with ʻIolani
The white sacred bird.
The next time they whispered
He swam with manō.
His heart sang
For this boy's reward:
The green world below,
The blue light above.

Prison is a place
Where the Ancients are silenced,
And Earth's song
Cannot be heard.
It is a crypt
Beyond breathing
Flowerless, without life's fragrance.

The boy sits in a cell
Far from the white bird's cry
With the incandescent hum
Of blue light from above.

9 MAHEALANI KAMAUU

Pono & Righteousness

*Mahealani Kamauu is executive director of the Native Hawaiian Legal Corporation,
a nonprofit law firm. The organization has represented two thousand native clients and has
recovered lands valued at more than $16 million. Mahealani also works with pro-sovereignty
groups, urging them to resolve their differences. "My vision of sovereignty is one that our people
create together, that enables them to restore to themselves as a people a measure of dignity."*

*Preceding page: Sovereignty demonstrators placed a "Justice for Hawaiians" message beside
a statue of Queen Liliʻuokalani, the last monarch to reign over Hawaiʻi. ʻIolani Palace, in
the background, is where the queen was imprisoned following her overthrow by pro-American
businessmen in 1893. Afterward, the palace was used as headquarters for the new government.*

T ODAY *I would like to tell you about a place where Hawaiians lived.*

This was not a beautiful place of loʻi kalo shrouded by mists and rainbows of the Koʻolaus, or any place like it.

This place was downtown, and you got to it by going upstairs from a pool hall. When you got to the top, what you found was fifty-two Hawaiian families packed into fifty-two rooms intended for fifty-two single men.

It was a place where hundreds of Hawaiian kids and adults took turns at two toilets and three kerosene stoves. It was a place where the landlord inspected to make sure additional babies were charged accordingly.

This place was always crawling with cops. In this place, walls and floors collapsed because of termite damage. Sammy the wino told everybody, "Fuck you!" and Aunty Lillian was too drunk to close the door when she had sex.

Graffiti all over the walls was explicit, and mostly of women with their legs spread apart. Downstairs on the sidewalk, boyfriends stomped the shit out of their women, for what I never knew. Upstairs, kids got the shit kicked out of them. For what they never knew.

This was a place where neighbors carried a stillborn baby out in a bucket. This was a place where Hawaiians lived. This was a place I called home.

When I look back, I think of this home, and other places like it, as what many of us believed was our legacy. This was what we were born into. This was all we knew—and all our children would ever know.

Those who could tell us otherwise never did. No one told me our history. No one explained what happened—how we had been robbed.

Mahealani Kamauu wrote this as part of a speech she delivered at a Hawaiian sovereignty commemoration. It came at a time in her life when she had thoroughly studied the history of her people, when she had faced and overcome the challenges of surviving in Hawai'i as a Hawaiian, when she had begun working with other Hawaiians who wanted to learn about their past and shape their future.

A few Hawaiian activists show up routinely in the headlines, but Mahealani—articulate, committed, with a natural beauty ideal for the six o'clock news—prefers a low profile. She would rather focus on efforts to achieve Hawaiian sovereignty and continue her work overseeing the Native Hawaiian Legal Corporation, a nonprofit organization that has represented more than two thousand Hawaiian people and through legal action has recovered lands worth more than $16 million.

"Why me? Who cares?" she responded when asked to share her stories with a larger audience. "I don't deserve it." Reluctantly, she agreed to tell her story after she was persuaded it might help other Hawaiians, who are still imprisoned by the past and unable to reconcile the path of pono (righteous behavior) with wrongs committed against them. "Perhaps," she said, "it will help."

The story of how Mahealani achieved this balance within herself and how she helps other Hawaiians work to establish it is tied to the history of her family and her people. It is a story about how the United States helped take away the sovereignty of Hawai'i and with it the Hawaiian nation's freedom to cope with the changes wrought by foreigners. Hers is a story about opportunities to create a new pono for the Islands. After almost four generations, Mahealani and other Hawaiians finally recognized what was lost and began the most talked about political movement in the Islands—the revival of the Hawaiian nation.

When the Hawaiian Kingdom was snatched away, in 1893, most Hawaiians lost with it the remnants of their fifteen-hundred-year-old culture, a culture in which many people strove to live a life of pono every day. Regardless of whether their leaders were righteous or unjust, their lands hostile or bountiful, the Hawaiians of old believed that spiritual well-being was assured by living a pono life. Hawaiian scholar Rubellite K. Johnson has described it as a life characterized by duty, responsibility, justice, and righteousness. "Without pono," Professor Johnson wrote, "no good life for mankind either on earth or beyond earth develops."

By 1893, the native Hawaiian population had dropped to fifty thousand, and the survivors lost their nation to a few hundred armed Caucasians. Most Hawaiians believe the haole succeeded after several years of a conspiracy in which they plotted, with U.S. officials, to annex the Kingdom for the United

States. This "robbery," they say, took place four decades after foreign diseases had decimated the Hawaiian population, after foreign laws and manipulation had taken away most of their lands. Equally as tragic as the epidemics, the dispossession, and the overthrow were the decades of silence that followed.

Like many Hawaiians, Mahealani's great-grandmother, grandmother, and mother did not talk about the past and their Hawaiian heritage—they simply did their best to cope with changes, even when the changes brought about suppression of their language and culture, and transformation of their land.

Mahealani's great-grandmother, Alice Pa'alua Opulauoho, was born in 1883. At that time, treaties with the United States, Great Britain, France, Belgium, and Japan recognized Hawai'i as an independent kingdom. But on the home front, King Kalākaua found his sovereignty challenged by the sons of island missionaries and foreign-born immigrants. Their newspapers attacked the king, calling him corrupt, an incompetent spendthrift, and racist for his promotion of Hawaiian culture. Some haole openly endorsed an action to assassinate the monarch and seize his government. Others favored immediate overthrow and American annexation. But the more deliberate majority, a solid group of prominent businessmen, used threats and a private militia to force the king to sign and accept a new constitution in 1887.

The "Bayonet Constitution" vested governing power with representatives of the Islands' four thousand Caucasians and reduced Kalākaua's position to nothing more than a figurehead. Suddenly, foreigners could own land, vote, and seek political office without even becoming citizens of the Kingdom. Most of the native population were disenfranchised, and sixty thousand Asian immigrants, who had been hired to work the plantations, could not vote.

Alice Pa'alua Opulauoho was living on the Big Island at that time, but later she moved to Pālama, a working-class neighborhood in Honolulu. It was close to Iwilei, where James Dole erected the Hawaiian Pineapple Company cannery. Thousands of Hawaiians, including Alice's daughter, would find jobs there and in other factories to earn money for their families.

When Kalākaua died, in 1891, his sister Lili'uokalani succeeded to the throne. Lili'uokalani was determined to write a new constitution and restore power to the Hawaiian people, to reinstate the monarch in a position of real authority. Pro-American businessmen in Honolulu were horrified. They formed the Annexation Club, whose goal to become part of the United States—according to many accounts—had the backing of President Benjamin Harrison, two members of his Cabinet, the Secretary of State and Secretary of the Navy, and the U.S. Minister to the Kingdom of Hawai'i. They began plotting.

An American warship was anchored off Honolulu when Liliʻuokalani formally proposed a new constitution on January 14, 1883, thereby giving the conspirators an excuse for action. Within two days, the American Minister to the Kingdom ordered the ship's captain to land 160 U.S. troops to protect "American life and property in Honolulu." The Marines carried Gatling guns past ʻIolani Palace and bivouacked nearby. The troops' presence intimidated the Hawaiians; a civilian haole militia seized the royal armory. Annexationist leaders then occupied the main government building, abrogated the monarchy, and declared themselves the "Provisional government until terms of union with the U.S."

Queen Liliuʻokalani was confident that when the American government learned what had taken place, it would surely reverse the actions of its minister and reestablish the rightful government of Hawaiʻi. America did not. Two years later, in skirmishes between royalists and the soldiers, government troops killed several royalists, including the first husband of Mahealani's great-grandmother. They arrested the former queen and more than two hundred royalists. Fearing for her supporters' lives, Liliʻuokalani formally abdicated and renounced all claim to her throne. By 1898, the United States had annexed the Islands and made them a territory.

Mahealani's great-grandparents lived in Pālama as American citizens. They were fluent Hawaiian speakers, but the territorial government had outlawed the speaking of Hawaiian in schools. Mahealani's maternal great-grandfather, William Akana, was employed by the County of Honolulu as a refuse collector. His daughter Elizabeth, Mahealani's grandmother, was studying to become a teacher when she contracted a mild case of Hansen's Disease, which left her homebound.

By the 1920s, social and economic conditions among dispirited and demoralized Hawaiians had deteriorated to the point where Hawaiian advocates were demanding that something had to be done. The congressional delegate from Hawaiʻi, Prince Jonah Kūhiō Kalanianaʻole, and other Hawaiian leaders of the time, promoted a homesteading program that offered Hawaiians an alternative to the urban poverty in which so many of them were trapped. If some federally held land was opened up, Hawaiian people could once again work the land in the tradition of their ancestors. But that tradition had been nothing more than a memory for generations; those ancestors had depended on the ahupuaʻa system, where many families worked together within large mountain-to-the-sea land districts to provide for their collective needs. At a time in American history when Indian reservations were being carved up into checkerboard allotments, Congress decided the "modern" Hawaiian would prosper if he similarly cultivated his farm as an individual, the way most Americans did.

The Hawaiian Homestead program might have succeeded, but the predominately Caucasian oligarchy ruling Hawai'i saw to it that much of the approximately 200,000 acres designated in the federal Hawaiian Homes Commission Act of 1920 were the least desirable agricultural lands, too arid and rocky for farming without intense labor and costly irrigation. Further, they insisted that the lands could be used only by the twenty thousand remaining pure-blooded Hawaiians. The Hawaiians disagreed. Their advocates proposed a one-thirty-second Hawaiian blood quantum requirement. A compromise was struck: Individuals with at least 50 percent Hawaiian blood would be eligible to receive a homestead.

Mahealani's grandparents were eligible for the ninety-nine-year leases made available at one dollar per year, but like thousands of other Hawaiians, they never got any land. Today, only about 40,400 acres out of the 190,299 set aside for Hawaiians have been awarded, and they have been distributed among only 6,000 homesteaders. The territorial governors of Hawai'i under federal stewardship were responsible for the illegal transfer of some 29,000 acres of the best Hawaiian homestead lands to government agencies for use as parks, airports, schools, and forest reserves—all in violation of the law and without compensation to the Department of Hawaiian Home Lands. Department officials have leased an additional 93,445 acres to nonbeneficiaries for commercial, industrial, and other uses. These leases, which produced $5.4 million in rents during 1994–1995, do not cover the department's administrative expenses. To this day, those expenses remain severely underfunded.

Mahealani's mother, Alicia Kuʻuleimomi "Pearl" Amina, was born in 1921, a time when most Hawaiians accepted the American way of life as best for their survival. It was typical of them to bury their Hawaiian past, and their silence bespoke a sense of shame in being Hawaiian. Some mothers put clothespins on their children's broad noses, hoping they might somehow grow up looking less Hawaiian, more Caucasian. For many, being Hawaiian meant being lower class, but this was not true for Mahealani's mother.

Pearl grew up in the rain-drenched town of Hilo on the Big Island of Hawai'i, where her family managed to perpetuate the Hawaiian culture that had all but disappeared in Honolulu. They owned land in and around Hilo and Waiākea-Uka, land that had been passed on to them by their parents. Pearl's family and other Hawaiian families in that area were healthy and vigorous. Her father, Daniel Amina, was a proud craftsman who made harnesses and saddles for horses at the Parker Ranch and elsewhere. During Daniel's free time he built furniture, and he was also a talented musician, adept at playing the banjo, guitar, ʻukulele, harmonica, and piano. He serenaded plantation workers, family and friends, and tourists at Christmas and New Year's parties.

To Pearl, her father lived as a Hawaiian. As a child, he had been given the name Kealanuionaʻahiʻenaʻena (the path of fiery embers), which traced his ancestry to Pele, the volcano goddess. When he grew to be an adult, he carried hoʻokupu, or offerings, to Halemaʻumaʻu once a month to pay homage to his kupuna Pele. He was also a traditional healer, a kahuna lāʻau lapaʻau, who knew about the medicinal properties of plants and could promote healing of a broken bone by applying the appropriate poultice. He knew prayers for use against a variety of illnesses, Hawaiian words that cured. He followed the phases of the moon and marked the traditional time for planting kalo. When Daniel went fishing, he let Pearl ride on the back of sea turtles in the ocean.

Pearl's father struck a balance between the old Hawaiʻi and the new, and her life was continually guided and shaped by his. Her mother became sick and died at the age of thirty-three, and her father died soon thereafter. In 1938, Pearl was fourteen and found she had become "mother" to her younger siblings. Pearl and the children had to move to Honolulu to live with their grandparents, exchanging the lush greenery of Hilo for dry, dusty city streets. Pearl went to work in the same Iwilei pineapple cannery that had once employed her mother, and after Japan attacked Pearl Harbor, in 1941, she helped the Army Signal Corps. Then Pearl fell in love, got married, and moved to Kauaʻi.

Antonio Perez was a Spaniard, the youngest of nine children whose parents left Spain to seek a better life. They found it in Kōloa, Kauaʻi, laboring for the Kōloa Sugar Plantation. The work was hard, but Pearl and her new in-laws found time for horses, hunting, and feasting; for all-day sausage making and holy sacraments; and for celebrations full of "katchi-katchi," Puerto Rican salsa music. Antonio and Pearl began their own family.

As a young child, Mahealani was free to run down to the ginger-choked banks of the Lāwaʻi Valley stream; she raced through orchards of mango, banana, avocado, and mountain apple; she picked flowers and Hawaiian medicinal plants in her mother's garden.

"It seems a child's life in Lāwaʻi was an idyll of dreams," Mahealani wrote later in an essay about her childhood, "hours spent catching crayfish with guava branches and string; hours sitting on topmost branches of trees; exploring every trail, every fence, every footbridge; knowing special rocks and secret places—we passed our time this way. We learned about family and kinship, and from the earth, we learned our place."

Just as life in paradise had ended for Mahealani's mother when she had to leave Hilo for Honolulu, so it ended in 1956 for Mahealani and her four brothers and sisters. Antonio and Pearl separated that year, and the children moved to Honolulu with their mother and ended up in a graffiti-riddled downtown tenement. Pearl meted out severe punishments if her children swore, stole, or smoked, and somehow, with much hard work, she held her family together.

"She had confidence that our situation would not be a barrier to living full, wholesome lives," Mahealani said. "Later, as an adult, I talked to friends who had encountered problems with relationships, some with children, and they would be absolutely trembling at the thought of going it alone. I had a hard time understanding this. When I grew up, my mother was fearless. I'm kind of the same way. I have no doubt that I can handle. I was a single parent for many years, but it never occurred to me that I couldn't be self-reliant and take care of my family. I always believed everything would work out somehow, and it has. I went where I thought I should be, and things fell into place." The same could not be said for other Hawaiians.

When the Hawaiian Islands became the fiftieth state, in 1959, the federal government transferred to state control almost 1.35 million acres of land that had been taken from the Kingdom by haole businessmen and ceded to the United States in 1898. As a condition for its return, Congress required that state revenues from those lands be used to establish a ceded lands trust that would support five public purposes, one of which was to better the conditions of Hawaiians. Despite this stipulation in the Admissions Act, despite subsequent court rulings, well-intentioned laws, and a state constitutional amendment, the leaders of the State of Hawai'i failed to provide Hawaiians with their full, legislatively mandated share of ceded lands revenues. Almost thirty years later, in 1992, a partial settlement for the sum of $111.8 million was finally negotiated.

By then the average life span of Hawaiians was still almost seven years less than that of other ethnic groups in the state. About 15 percent of all Hawaiian families were living below the poverty level, compared to 8 percent of all families in the state. Nearly 46 percent of all adults in state prisons were Hawaiians (though they represented 19 percent of the population), and Hawaiians in the state work force were employed in mostly entry-level positions.

Mahealani Perez Kamauu is an anomaly. She manages a legal staff of twenty as executive director of the Native Hawaiian Legal Corporation (NHLC), a nonprofit law firm that asserts, protects, and defends Hawaiian land and traditional rights on behalf of native Hawaiians. While an undergraduate at the University of Hawai'i, Mahealani had learned about Hawaiians who were losing their lands to large corporations. Hawaiians could not afford lawyers to represent them in court against the companies that laid claim to their ancestral lands. With major funding from the state Office of Hawaiian Affairs, representation of Hawaiians in "quiet title" actions became a major part of NHLC's work, along with other cases involving Hawaiian Homes, ceded lands, and related traditional rights.

Mahealani is slender and serene, with an exotic face that reveals her mixed Spanish, Hawaiian, and Chinese blood. When she talks about the struggles of the Hawaiian people—the legal wranglings, the protests, the arrests, the anger—she remains calm. A balanced spirit distances even the most important issues from her psyche, as though she cannot take anything, including her writing (she won the 1993 Elliott Cades Award for Literature), too seriously.

When she was only ten years old, growing up in the tenements near Chinatown, Mahealani had known that "something was really wrong about conditions—not only my family's, but what other families confronted every day. Something inside of me wanted to make a difference, to change the conditions. I never questioned this feeling. It really was a very strong desire to work for change. I still feel this way."

After graduation from Kamehameha Schools, Mahealani married and moved to Texas, where she worked for an insurance company and attended junior college, earning an associate degree in accounting. In 1970, she and her husband divorced, and Mahealani returned to O'ahu with two babies.

In Honolulu she worked as a secretary to support herself and her children. One day at a coffeehouse near the University of Hawai'i, she overheard two Hawaiian students, graduates of her high school, talking about a private estate that threatened to evict some local pig farmers in order to build a white-collar suburb on its lands in Kalama, the last undeveloped valley in east O'ahu. Mahealani joined in the organized protest, which came to be recognized as a pivotal action that mobilized an entire generation of Hawaiian activists. Although the organizers did not win this particular battle, they learned the rudiments of how to develop strategies to oppose similar evictions in the windward O'ahu valleys of Waiāhole and Waikāne; they learned how to protest abuses by the Hawaiian Homes trust; they established the Office of Hawaiian Affairs, a state agency with the specific mandate of serving Hawaiians; and they gained access to Kaho'olawe, an island used by the U.S. Navy for bombing practice, and eventually stopped the Navy bombing and saw Kaho'olawe returned to the state.

Mahealani continued to learn about community organizing. She enrolled in classes at the university and in 1976 earned a bachelor's degree in political science. She supported her two children with part-time secretarial and research work at various firms, including the Honolulu Legal Aid office. She entered law school at the University of Hawai'i and would have graduated if not for the hardship of an unexpected pregnancy in her second year. "After six years, it was too much of a struggle. I could not put my children through more years of privation."

She dropped out of school to care for her baby girl, again as a single mother, and on top of her part-time jobs, Mahealani worked as a volunteer for the reorganized Native Hawaiian Legal Corporation. Within two years she had written enough grant proposals and raised enough money to keep NHLC stable and effective, and they hired her for a full-time staff position. In 1986, after eight years at the legal corporation and graduate work in accounting and public administration, Mahealani was named executive director of NHLC. She also served on the boards of a dozen Hawaiian organizations and the Native American Rights Fund. In 1990, the Young Lawyers division of the Hawaii State Bar Association recognized Mahealani for her "significant contributions in a law-related field."

To Mahealani, the award was not as important as the opportunity to tell bar members about the movement to establish a sovereign Hawaiian nation. Although the sovereignty concept has become politically safe and is endorsed by many politicians, most of the state's million residents, including the 139,000 people with Hawaiian blood, do not understand what sovereignty could mean, both for the native Hawaiian people and the Islands.

In an essay for *The Price of Paradise,* Mahealani and Hawaiian attorney H. K. Bruss Keppeler grouped sovereignty activists into three categories: (1) those propounding complete separation from the United States and a return to the status of being an independent, internationally recognized Hawaiian nation; (2) those advocating nation-within-a-nation status, with federal recognition as a new Native American nation; and (3) those desirous of maintaining the political status quo while pressing for redress, reparations, and full control of Hawaiian trust assets by Hawaiians.

Mahealani and Bruss described separatists as those who work toward an independent nation, whose "citizenship is available to those [Hawaiian and non-Hawaiian] who pledge their allegiance to Hawai'i and to no other nation."

The Hawaiian nation would lessen its foreign dependence by increasing the number and diversity of its trade partners. As a nation it would be able to do what the State of Hawai'i could never do: place limitations on immigration. . . .

The form of government would be a matter for its citizens to decide. As with any nation, Hawai'i would control its own international relations, establish diplomatic posts around the world, and join regional and international forums. U.S. control of military bases in Hawai'i would end.

The territory of the re-emerged Hawaiian nation would include all the lands and waters that form the present state, plus Kalama (Johnston), Midway, and Palmyra Islands. . . .

The oldest group espousing the "nation-within-a-nation" model of Hawaiian sovereignty is Ka Lāhui Hawai'i . . . [which] "seeks inclusion of the Hawaiian People in the existing U.S. federal policy which affords all Native Americans the right to self-government and provides access to federal courts for judicial review." . . . Under its model, Hawaiians will generally continue to live, work, and worship as they do today. Jobs, social security, retirement, or pensions from the United States or the State of Hawai'i would not be affected. The primary change would be that Hawaiian lands and assets would be managed and controlled by laws passed by a Hawaiian legislature.

Two hundred fifty delegates established Ka Lāhui at a 1987 convention. They devised four branches of government: legislative, executive, and judicial branches and an ali'i nui (chiefs) branch responsible for culture, traditions, and protocol. By 1995 the group claimed more than twenty-five thousand citizens who sought federal recognition of their nation.

There are other advocates for a Hawaiian nation-within-a-nation. Some members of Ka Lāhui also belong to the State Council of Hawaiian Homesteaders, which is 30,000 strong and has an interest in maintaining sovereignty over the lands that Congress set aside for Hawaiian homesteaders. Many of these homesteaders are among the 75,000 registered voters who make up the Office of Hawaiian Affairs (OHA), a semi-autonomous state agency set up in 1980 to develop and administer programs for the Hawaiian people and serve as their advocate within the state bureaucracy. OHA voters elect nine trustees, whose unity is like that of any legislative body—sometimes divided, either by allegiances to Ka Lāhui, the homestead association, other Hawaiian groups, or as Mahealani and Bruss wrote, the "many Hawaiians [who] are reasonably happy with the existing forms of government but irate over past wrongs."

In their essay, Mahealani and Bruss cite this group of Hawaiians who "stand forthright behind initiatives that would give Hawaiians as a class the right to sue the United States for reparations and redress. They believe it's high time that a formal and official apology be given by the U.S. government to the Hawaiian people for the wrongs committed."

> *These Hawaiians are keenly aware of the loss of water rights, the erosion of Hawaiian private trust assets, and the alarming statistics on the health and social status of Hawaiians. They want something done about it—now. But they enjoy federal, state, and county services. They receive federal, state, or county paychecks or pension checks. They are intrigued by all the talk and commotion and proud that Hawaiians are speaking out. But, when the chips are down, they can't see themselves taking that final step to sovereignty.*

Mahealani has already taken that step. "Liberty is assured when a nation's citizens are courageous. Liberty is assured when a nation's citizens conform their behavior to that which is pono and righteous. . . .

Many of these Office of Hawaiian Affairs trustees have left office since this photograph was taken in 1990, but the official meetings still resemble those of other elected officials who gather around large tables to discuss and vote on stacks of bills, minutes, reports, and resolutions. A portrait of Queen Lili'uokalani hangs on the back wall.

Kawaiahaʻo Church in Honolulu has witnessed a century and a half of baptisms, weddings, and funerals for Hawaiian royalty. In 1990, members of chiefly societies attended the blessing of newly elected trustees for the Office of Hawaiian Affairs.

"I'm big on courage, as opposed to bravado, grandstanding, and demagoguery," she said. "My mother is a woman of courage, and it's the way I've tried to live my life. If you want pono in your life, you have to live your life with integrity. In order to do that, you must have courage. There are times when you are at a crossroads, where you can choose to do that which is less courageous but which will be comfortable and safe. I've tried not to take the easy path. I believe, as a result, no matter how destitute, no matter what my immediate circumstances were, I've usually been satisfied that I've done the right thing. It's very important to me."

As a result, Mahealani tries to work with all groups devoted to achieving sovereignty, regardless of their differences. Members of her staff helped draft the Office of Hawaiian Affairs blueprint for entitlements, which proposed to facilitate the native Hawaiian community's efforts to seek reparations and lands from the United States and establish a sovereign nation of its own choosing.

She wrote a federal grant for Ka Lāhui Hawaiʻi that challenged the ability of OHA, the state agency, to represent Hawaiian people fairly. She worked long hours with Ka Pākaukau, an association of pro-sovereignty groups that believed that neither OHA's blueprint nor the plan from Ka Lāhui Hawai'i for self-governance within the American system would allow kānaka maoli true sovereignty. And she was there on the cliffs of Makapu'u when the Ka'awa family and others (who would establish the Nation of Hawai'i group), occupied the rocky eastern point of O'ahu to assert an ancestral claim to 18,630 acres stretching from Makapu'u across to the suburbs of Waimānalo and Kailua.

Mahealani was appointed to the state Hawaiian Sovereignty Elections Council, and she became a member of Hui Na'auao, a coalition of forty native groups and entities that has received federal money for sovereignty education. The council and the coalition seek to promote consensus in decision making and even-handedness among all Hawaiian groups, so members will have a safe place to disagree and work on identifying common ground.

Kaua'i had been that kind of safe place for Mahealani while she was growing up. There, in the Lāwa'i gardens of her mother, aunties, and uncles, she had the freedom to become almost anyone. And even though plantation work was difficult, Mahealani's family always made time to enjoy music and family celebrations, just as she would later free herself from obligations to make time for poetry, creative writing, and family and friends.

Mahealani recalled that freedom as she prepared her speech for the annual celebration of Ka Lā Ho'iho'i Ea (Restoration Day), which commemorates the day in July 1843 when a British admiral restored King Kamehameha III to sovereignty after the Hawaiian government had been surrendered for six months to an English lord and his terrorizing warship.

"I stand before you a person utterly committed to freedom for our people. Freedom not to coerce others into believing the way I do, but freedom that our people may make their own choice—to be free and self-determining.

"I will never exhort you to hate or condemn your brothers and sisters. For when you hate or condemn your brothers and sisters, you invite hate and condemnation upon yourself.

"Understand your humble place as a being in this great universe—you are one with all things in it. If you send hate, it will return to eat you. You know this. It was taught by our kūpuna.

"Instead, let us choose life-affirming love for our people. . . . We commit every ounce of our spiritual, intellectual, and physical energy to make this world work for us."

Two hundreds years of epidemics, dispossession, and oppression have left many Hawaiians distrustful, not only of those whom they consider oppressors, but of one another as well. Although factionalism and infighting have hindered most struggles for independence and self-governance, including the colonial American struggle in the eighteenth century, outsiders and some Hawaiians expect unity. Mahealani ignores such expectations.

"Sovereignty is greater than the sum of all our parts," Mahealani said, speaking as someone who has worked with many different factions. "I am very idealistic. I see sovereignty as an ideal, and it is a vision that we should work toward together. We have to. You talk about nationhood. My nation includes all of us. It is not exclusive. So, therefore, I think it's appropriate for me to work with all people who share the vision. Obviously they have their differences, but I can't allow these differences to become an impediment. I refuse.

"My preference is full, sovereign, international status, but my overriding concern is that the decision reflect our collective will, and I am willing to accede to that, whatever it may be.

"We have to be very vigilant," Mahealani continued. "There are overwhelming pressures to make compromises. . . . We will make progress [toward sovereignty], but that progress will be incremental. There will be proposals made and proposals accepted and there will be times when many of us who are very, very concerned will be outsiders to that process. We may not figure as major players. We may not be invited to the negotiating table. But we can be very vigilant about making sure that our options are left open so that the changes and compromises made do not compromise our children's future. I would never accept that deal which forecloses future options for negotiation. I wouldn't stand for that. I couldn't.

"I wrote a poem which describes how beautiful our land is, how sacred it is, the fact that it has suffered but still sings. I too have hope. I have a lot of faith that the right thing will happen. . . . The spirit of our people will ultimately prevail and cannot be suppressed.

"It seems arrogant for us to presume that we are going to make that big a difference, because in the grander scheme of things the earth, mother earth, prevails. We have been taught that we are custodians and our stay here is temporary. It's good to be alive, part of the human comedy, drama, or tragedy, whatever it is, but our time here passes very quickly."

KEAUHOU   *Song of Renewal*

This earth is sweet,
Its spirits full of providence.
Mountains shake torrential skies,
Cloud and leaf scatter
Before their winds.
Each far shore is a vision
Of colors hovering, disappearing,
Circles of light encircling rain.

This place is sacred,
A sacrament of blood,
*   earth, shell and bone.*
Wraith spirits dance,
Teeming gossamer,
Transparent wing and gill,
While Night Marchers keep
Their ancient sojourn.

This land knows the dark incision
Of steel, granite, glass;
Gray boneyards of iron,
Chilling slabs of highrise,
Concrete vaults, embalming places
For four million souls
By the Coroner of Commerce.
This land still sings:
Grass, flower, gulls,
Surge of ocean, thunder,
The wind's lullaby,
All a chorus of renewal,
A mighty chorus
Of earth's eternal song.

MELE O KAHO‘OLAWE
Song of Kaho‘olawe

Aloha ku‘u moku ‘o Kaho‘olawe

Composed by

Love my island Kaho‘olawe

Harry Kunihi Mitchell, Sr.

Mai kinohi kou inoa ‘o Kanaloa

From the beginning your name was Kanaloa

Kohemalamalama lau kanaka ‘ole

You are the southern beacon barren and without population

Hiki mai nā pua e ho‘omalu mai

Until you were invaded by nine young men and they granted you peace

Alu like kākou Lāhui Hawai‘i

Let us band together the Hawaiian kingdom

Mai ka lā hiki mai i ka lā kau a‘e

From sunup to sundown

Kū pa‘a a hahai hō‘ikaika nā kānaka

Stand together and follow, be strong young people

Kau li‘i mākou nui ke aloha no ka ‘āina

We are but a few in number but our love for the land is unlimited

Hanohano nā pua o Hawai‘i nei

Popular are the young people of Hawai‘i nei

No ke kaua kauholo me ka aupuni

For the civil strife they caused against the government

Pa‘a pū ka mana‘o no ka pono o ka ‘āina

Together in one thought to bring prosperity to the land

Imua nā pua lanakila Kaho‘olawe

Forward young people and bring salvation to Kaho‘olawe

10 CRAIG NEFF

Hoʻomana & Religion

Craig Neff is a moʻo Lono, a priest devoted to worship of the Hawaiian god Lono. He travels regularly to the island of Kahoʻolawe, where he joins others in religious ceremonies and works to restore native use of the island. On Oʻahu and Hawaiʻi, Craig is better known as an artist and designer of his own clothing line.

Preceding page: An altar of lama wood, used to honor the god Lono, stands on the Kahoʻolawe summit of Puʻu Moaʻula Iki. Worshipers believe their Makahiki ceremonies helped bring an end to fifty years of Navy bombing practice on the island. The federal government has promised funds to help clean up the ordnance that limits access on Kahoʻolawe.

The journey to the island of Kahoʻolawe begins seven miles across ʻAlalā-keiki Channel at a small cove on the island of Maui. In the predawn darkness, a dozen men and women stand on the beach and hold hands in a circle beside their outrigger canoes. Their breath warms the air with a pule (prayer), followed by a chant to their ancestors, to the people who crossed to Kahoʻolawe before them, and to the pantheon of their gods—Kū, Lono, Kāne, and Kanaloa. As they invoke guidance and strength, their words weave a cloak of spiritual protection to guard them in what could be a four-hour pull across the channel.

The name ʻAlalākeiki means the child's wail, the sound even adults cry in the channel when high winds rush down the mountain slopes of Maui's Haleakalā and churn the dark waters into a nightmare. In years past, two friends of the assembled group have perished in the channel, but no one at the cove is fearful this morning. The paddlers draw on each word offered to their ancestors—their ʻaumākua—and reaffirm their confidence in weathering any storm.

Unless you go by helicopter, the passage across ʻAlalākeiki Channel is the primary way to reach Kahoʻolawe, a 28,000-acre island the U.S. Navy used for fifty years for bombing practice. The federal government stopped shelling it in 1990 and four years later returned the island to the State of Hawaiʻi. By then the upper third of the island had been devastated by the bombardment and by animals that had overgrazed the land before the bombing began. Unexploded ordnance made the rest of the island—already a parched desert—too dangerous to cross on foot. Nonetheless, many Hawaiians considered it a blessing when the island was returned. For almost twenty years they had prayed and protested and negotiated to end the bombing.

During those two decades, Kahoʻolawe was more than a symbol of Western abuse of the lands that had once sustained the people of the Hawaiian nation. During monthly "accesses" coordinated with the Navy, Kahoʻolawe became a sanctuary, a place where Hawaiians could be Hawaiian and revive and practice their religion far from judgmental eyes. Today, state law has decreed that the island shall be reserved for traditional Hawaiian uses, with no commercial activity.

When Craig Neff first landed on the island, in 1983, two years after the Navy began to allow Hawaiians access, he thought he knew what it meant to be Hawaiian. "When I was growing up, I was always locked into being Hawaiian. That was one thing I liked and I felt strong about. . . . I was listening to Hawaiian music. I tried to see things Hawaiian. . . . I thought walking around with your Hawaiian T-shirt, having one Hawaiian flag on the back of your car, paddling, whatever, was making you Hawaiian. But when I went over to the island, it really hit me what being Hawaiian was.

"When you're off [Kahoʻolawe], you don't have to like the guy walking on the street because you don't know him. But on the island, anybody walk by, you tell 'em 'howzit' or something like that. It's a different feeling because you're dependent on this person. If you get hurt, he has to do something to take care of you. It's a different way of thinking."

The first time Craig visited Kahoʻolawe, the sun and stars shone in clear skies for three days. But on the last night, after he had taken part in a ceremonial walk across the island, after prayers and offerings to the god Lono, clouds moved over the island, and it rained and rained—live-giving rain for the thirsty land. "That's what we were asking for, hoping for," Craig remembered, "and we stayed up the whole night talking story 'cause it was just too wet to even sleep. And the next day it was a nice, beautiful day. . . . As we left the island . . . we had to swim out and jump on this big catamaran, and I looked back and I just started to cry, and I told the person who went over with me, 'What I went through, that was one for the Hawaiians.'"

Afterward, Craig decided Kahoʻolawe was the place to be. "This is the key to get into what I was looking for. It wasn't going around beating up people, or yelling at people . . . that's not the goal of being Hawaiian. . . . [It was] going over [to Kahoʻolawe and helping to restore the island] and learning. . . . When I came back and seen Oʻahu, the streets and everything paved . . . [for the first time] I could feel the ground under the asphalt just suffocating. It's a living thing, and if you put concrete or asphalt over it, you're killing, you're suffocating it. I could feel that when I was driving on the road. . . . [Kahoʻolawe] and its people really changed the way I thought."

Craig attended Kalani High School in east Honolulu during the 1970s, when the Navy bombardment of Kahoʻolawe was becoming a political and cultural issue. In 1976, Hawaiians formed an association, the Protect Kahoʻolawe 'Ohana, to try and stop the bombing; protesters landed on Kahoʻolawe, and the military arrested them for trespassing. During the next four years, the

Top: Members and friends of the Protect Kahoʻolawe ʻOhana built this pā, a hula platform, at Hakioawa, where hula groups gather to share their dances. Sickles and machetes are stored on the island to use for cutting grasses that grow tall after the winter rains.

Bottom: Few old-growth trees remain on Kahoʻolawe. The Navy has used explosives to blast holes in the hardpan to plant a new forest of drought-resistant tamarisk trees.

ʻOhana persevered through repeated landings and arrests, protests, negotiations, and a court case. George Helm, the charismatic ʻOhana leader, and his friend Kimo Mitchell disappeared in the rough seas of ʻAlalākeiki Channel while paddling from Kahoʻolawe to Maui. In 1980, the Navy granted the ʻOhana a four-day monthly access to the island ten times a year—forty days all together—for religious, educational, and scientific activities; during an "access," the military would suspend bombing.

The ʻOhana wanted to perform religious ceremonies on Kahoʻolawe. Their elders advised them to go to the island, believe their ʻaumākua and gods, and call on the deities for help in restoring the island. At first, it was a self-conscious effort. The ʻOhana had to find teachers, kūpuna who had living experiences healing the land; then they had to research, learn, and practice the rites for the annual Makahiki rituals, seeking to reenact the ceremonies as closely as contemporary realities allowed. Makahiki is the ancient four-month celebration of Lono, the god of fertility and agriculture. Traditionally, the season began in November; when Makaliʻi, the Pleiades constellation, appeared in the night sky with the new moon, it was time for the chiefs to suspend war, collect tributes, and hold festivals with hula and physical competitions. For the ʻOhana, the Makahiki became a time to rest and remember the past, plan for the future, and ask Lono's help in restoring the island of Kahoʻolawe. But the consequences of the public ceremonies—the first in more than a century—extended beyond Kahoʻolawe. The courage of the ʻOhana led other Hawaiians to ignore criticism and incorporate religious rites from past generations into modern ceremonies. Their efforts reminded Hawaiʻi that the ʻāina, the land, has a spiritual life force; it has cultural value that is perpetuated through love, respect, responsibility, and proper cultivation of food and medicinal plants.

Craig Neff's first visit to Kahoʻolawe was during a Makahiki access. "I just went over there to take pictures, hang out in the back, and I ended up in a malo in a ceremony." The ceremony marked the beginning of Craig's development as a religious person. Although his parents sent him to an Episcopal grammar school, they never forced Christianity on him, nor on his older brother and sister. Their Hawaiian father, Aaron, a former star athlete at Kamehameha Schools, worked as a supervisor for the city Parks Department, as did their mother, Hester, whose ancestors are Chinese. Craig grew up living at the back of Wailupe Valley in ʻĀina Haina. He graduated from Kalani High School in 1977, a large, tough teenager with a talent for art who also played football and basketball, and beat up a few haole along the way. "I don't know if it was jealousy or what, but when you're a small kid you just don't like them.

I guess every local kid at that time was brought up in the same situation: You didn't like the tourist. Even the local haole, if he didn't stand for what you thought was right, you just didn't like them. That was just how I thought in those days. . . . A lot of people felt that way, still do, especially even now."

Craig shared these thoughts while sitting on a lau hala mat that covered the floor of a one-bedroom unit that he and his wife shared in a Mānoa rooming house before moving to Hilo in 1995. Craig and Luana kept the tiny living room comfortable with minimal furniture: a backless pūneʻe couch and low brick-and-board shelves for books, photographs, television, a miniature stereo, and their stones. Canoe paddles stood against the walls, which were decorated with Craig's framed sketches, including one of his wife. He parked his old white Volkswagen van alongside the building with the other tenants' cars.

At first, Craig spoke reluctantly; as a local boy, he'd rather "sit in the back, cross [his] arms, and listen." Craig does not trust reporters, and when he heard at an ʻOhana meeting that yet another writer wanted to visit Kahoʻolawe during a Makahiki ceremony, his eyes burned a warning that required no words.

"Reporters, photographers, videotape—it's an evil. It's a swear word," Craig said with a laugh. "A lot of people come over [to Kahoʻolawe] and they tell you a good story. 'Okay, we're gonna help you. We're with you. We like the Hawaiians.' And then you open up, you show 'em something. Boom— next day, you see it [in the newspapers. We tell them,] 'You're not supposed to take those pictures; you're not supposed to use that video.' It's misquoted. It's used to further their capital gains, their money, their greed."

After high school Craig took his passion about being Hawaiian to the University of Hawaiʻi, eventually earning a degree in art while working full-time at night. There were few native students on campus during the 1980s, and he was one of only two in the art department. "I figured if I was going to [college] for that many years . . . I might as well do something I liked and had a talent for. . . . All my artwork was focused on Hawaiian. That's how I learned a lot about my culture—doing a lot of research."

Returning to Kahoʻolawe again and again was a different kind of education for Craig. "You can't learn being a Hawaiian from a book. Yeah, a lot of people try, but being a Hawaiian is the way you think. Books aren't reliable. They can't actually show you or [give you] the feeling or explain it the same way. You have to live it."

His involvement with the ʻOhana evolved with each visit to Kahoʻolawe. He met a small group of men who had made a five-year commitment to being the moʻo Lono, the priests responsible for religious protocol on the island. "Every time that I went I learned something, and I am sure they were just learning. It wasn't like they were brought up in a system that taught this."

One mo'o Lono was ready to move on to other responsibilities after five years, and his friends approached Craig about taking his place. "It was a pretty big honor for me. . . . I didn't ask any questions on how long I should do this commitment or what is the protocol on being a mo'o Lono—what are the rules and regs on that. It ended up that I became a mo'o Lono and kept going. We don't want to exclude anybody. We're there to teach people. If they want to learn, we really encourage that."

"When you're on island and you're a mo'o Lono, it doesn't separate you from anybody. It's just you're the last link between you and Lono. You're the one who has taken responsibility for the ceremony, the preparation for the ceremonies, . . . continuing the ceremony, and learning what you're supposed to learn."

The 'Ohana conducts the opening and closing Makahiki ceremonies during two of its monthly accesses to Kaho'olawe, in November and January. Generally, the accesses last four days; they begin Wednesday evening or in the early morning hours on Thursday. The 'Ohana and up to eighty people leave Maui from Mā'alaea Harbor or Mākena in fishing boats, outrigger canoes, or tourist catamarans and cross 'Alalākeiki Channel to Hakioawa Bay on Kaho'olawe. They double-wrap their gear in trash bags sealed with duct tape. After the crossing, the boats anchor offshore and everyone transfers in small groups to a Zodiac to motor closer to the shorebreak. Then people jump into the surf and join a human chain passing bags and people to the beach. The ocean is cold in the darkness, and it sometimes breaks with a ferocity that reminds newcomers they could easily drown without the help of others, without confidence in themselves, without an understanding of the ocean and the island.

For the next three nights, people camp near the beach, within an area the Navy has cleared of bombs. During most accesses, the 'Ohana and its friends spend their days working on trails, erosion control, or projects such as building a pā—a hula platform. During the entire Makahiki season, the 'Ohana focuses on honoring Lono. They trust him to provide gentle rains for the island to help turn it green again within their lifetimes.

Erosion is a major problem on Kaho'olawe. Rainstorms continually wash exposed dirt into ravines and gullies, flushing thirty tons of island soil into the ocean every year. The 'Ohana once blamed the Navy's bombing and military exercises for accelerating the island's erosion. But the condition dates back to 1864 when the Kingdom of Hawai'i stopped using the island as a penal colony

Haleakalā, a 10,023-foot dormant volcano summit on Maui, blocks most rainclouds headed for Kahoʻolawe.
During the early 1900s, goats, sheep, and cattle denuded much of the island when it was used as a ranch.
The federal government in 1994 gave the island back to the state, which intends to turn Kahoʻolawe over
to a government to be established by Hawaiians.

and leased it as a cattle, sheep, and goat ranch. The goats had completely denuded the top third of the island by 1917. With minimal rainfall (less than twenty-five inches annually), the sun burned the exposed dirt into tough hardpan. When the Navy began an erosion control project in the 1980s, men used explosive charges to blast holes in the ground for planting trees. The Navy and the ʻOhana have made progress planting the island with drought-resistant tamarisks and native plant species, and a desalinating unit provides fresh water for drinking and plants at the main camp. But every furrow in the raw earth is subject to winter rains, which erode the smallest groove into a gully, which becomes a gulch, and eventually a canyon. Except for areas cleared or approved by demolition squads, the Navy considers Kahoʻolawe unsafe because military planes and ships (and those of visiting allies) dropped live bombs all over the island during three decades of maneuvers and target practice. Many of the bombs fell onto the island without exploding and became obscured. As part of its agreement to return the island to the state, the federal government has promised $400 million to clear Kahoʻolawe of live shells and the many inert bombs subsequently dropped by the Navy.

The Navy had silenced its guns and jets around Kahoʻolawe by November 1989, when the ʻOhana began its annual Makahiki access. About sixty people visited that November, including two dozen university students who had been encouraged by their professors to visit the island; a video crew documenting the work of the ʻOhana; three Sierra Club people interested in seeing the island; and three Native Americans from the Seventh Generation Fund, a California-based organization that grants money to projects benefiting Native Americans. Since 1980, about five thousand people have visited the island as guests. The Protect Kahoʻolawe ʻOhana requires that, in addition to personal gear, everyone provides a five-gallon jug of water for drinking and cooking.

The water shortage and stories about bombing and erosion perpetuate the impression that Kahoʻolawe is a rock devoid of life. But after the midnight landing of the November 1989 contingent, sunrise revealed Hakioawa green with kiawe trees and grasses waist-high after the autumn rains. But at the same time the rain watered the island plants, it also bled topsoil down Hakioawa's two gulches and into the shorebreak, which was red weeks after the rain clouds had passed.

At dawn on Thursday morning, there wasn't time to linger in a sleeping bag, enjoying the fragrance of the island as the birds chirped good morning. Another boat had arrived, and folks needed help getting ashore. People pitched in to lug water containers and gear about five hundred yards from the beach to the main camp. Then the leaders called everyone together for break-

A nighttime landing at Hakioawa Bay in heavy surf can become a nightmare. Even small surf during daylight hours makes the offshore landings difficult, so Protect Kahoʻolawe ʻOhana members ask visitors to double-bag their gear for protection. During the Makahiki season, the ʻOhana holds a purification ceremony in the shorebreak, which often runs red with soil eroded off the island.

fast and a review of the rules: Because of unexploded ordnance, no one could leave Hakioawa; volunteers were needed for cooking and cleanup; and attendance and participation in evening discussion groups were mandatory. The first day, people set up camp. On Friday, they used rakes and machetes to clear brush and kiawe from the trails leading to a shrine and heiau at Hakioawa. On Saturday, the religious processions to the heiau would begin.

Ranching and restricted access ensured that some of the ancient sites on Kahoʻolawe were preserved long after urbanization had destroyed most of them on the other islands. The Navy allocated $500,000 and spent four years

The stones of a Hale o Papa heiau are barely visible on this kiawe-covered slope, which ʻOhana women are working to stabilize. Although many archaeologists believe such sites should be closed and reserved for research purposes, the ʻOhana believes in making full use of the sites, where they offer Makahiki prayers.

(between bombings) mapping 544 sites and 2,300 archaeological features. In 1981, the island was placed on the National Register of Historic Places. Archaeologists believe Hawaiians used Hakioawa as the political and religious center on the island. Here, directly across from Maui, where canoes can beach easily, people of past generations built the largest number of sites, including a Hale o Papa heiau, now hidden among kiawe trees on the eroding north slope. On the opposite side, a fishing shrine fifty feet wide and terraced with stone walls climbs one hundred feet up a hillside. A single stone is situated on the middle terrace of Hale Mua, surrounded by pebbles and bits of coral. Many 'Ohana members believe the stone represents the god who, when properly fed and supplicated by worshipers, attracts fish—today as in times past. From the top terrace you can look out over Hakioawa Bay and across the channel to Haleakalā and the West Maui Mountains, the slopes green until they touch the coastline, which is crowded with hotels and condominiums.

The 'Ohana allows both men and women to prepare the heiau and shrine for the Makahiki ceremonies. But only the mo'o Lono, the men who devote themselves to the god Lono, conduct the formal ceremonies to the god. Women participate in the Lono rituals and, in addition, perform their own rites.

Efforts to restore the Hawaiian religion and the shrines of old have been difficult during the past fifteen years. The Navy accused the 'Ohana of revitalizing the Hawaiian religion on Kaho'olawe as a means of securing legal access to the island. Some Hawaiians, like Craig Neff's parents, could not understand what the young people were trying to do. Others dismissed the 'Ohana as crazy activists and said kūpuna would keep secret the traditional rituals in order to protect their children from the consequences of awakening old kapu. But a few elders—Harry Kunihi Mitchell, Emma DeFries, and Mary Lee—encouraged the 'Ohana. Edith K. Kanaka'ole, a Big Island kumu hula who had grown up with the Hawaiian language and culture, urged 'Ohana members to go to Kaho'olawe during the Makahiki and perform the Lono rituals so the island would become green again. After she passed on, Aunty Edith's daughters helped teach the 'Ohana the traditional chants. Other people offered additional information. They gleaned what they could from books. All this, the 'Ohana said, was an intermediate step while more Hawaiians learned to speak the language and live the culture. "We are not schooled in it," an 'Ohana leader told the students who had come to Kaho'olawe for the first time. "We have had fifteen years of experience. We are learning as we are doing it. We do the best we can."

In ancient times, at the beginning of Makahiki the Hawaiians resurrected an image of Lono from a place of refuge and carried it in procession clockwise

Attempts by the military to control erosion with old tires failed. Tamarisk trees, however, are taking hold and turning large areas of Kaho'olawe, like the hilltop in the distance, from brown hardpan into green forest.

Opposite: To stem erosion, the 'Ohana has built rock dams in gullies and has planted native plant species in the checked soil. Rain catchment systems provide water, a rare commodity on Kaho'olawe.

around an island, stopping at every district boundary. Each community presented offerings to representatives of the high chief. The people were then free to celebrate the remainder of the festival season with competitions and games. This is difficult in the twentieth century, because work schedules and logistical problems in traveling around Kaho'olawe force the 'Ohana to modify its rituals. During the closing ceremony, in January, Lono's image is carried across the middle of the island to the westernmost point, Laeokealaikahiki, the place where long-ago voyages to Kahiki, the ancestral homeland, began. At sunset the 'Ohana launches the Lono image in a ceremonial canoe filled with offerings. These will accompany the god on the journey to Kahiki until fall, when he returns. The 'Ohana then hikes back to Hakioawa for two days of Makahiki games, discussion, and personal reflection before returning to their lives across the channel.

Since the 'Ohana revived Makahiki on Kaho'olawe in 1981, vegetation on the island has increased. The Navy has exterminated the goats, and the water table has risen. "When I was [first] going," Craig said, "people were laughing at us. 'No way they gonna stop the island bombing. No way you gonna get that island back.' But look—the bombing has stopped; [the island has returned]. . . . From when I started to where it is now, we've added to our

[religious] procession, to our protocol. We've added chants, and along with us growing, we can see the island growing. . . . The island is far from being what it's supposed to be, but you can see small changes that are occurring; certain areas are greener. Just the repetition of doing [the Makahiki] every year, of doing that pule, of doing that commitment and the island seeing it; it's gotta have something to do with what's happening there."

The day before the November Makahiki ceremony, Craig Neff and the other men cleaned and cleared Hale Mua, the fishing shrine, using machetes, sickles, and a chain saw. Their vigor would have horrified archaeologists concerned about disturbing anything at the shrine, including the offerings of 'opihi shells and coral branches scattered across the terrace tops. But to the mo'o Lono, Hale Mua lives and requires caretaking the same way holy people prepare churches for Easter and temples for Yom Kippur. The chain saw cut through a kiawe limb hanging over a wall, and the limb fell, knocking down some stones. The men hauled away the branch and repaired the wall. Higher up, others cleared kiawe and grass from the upper terrace, where a retaining wall had collapsed. The mo'o Lono decided to use the scattered stones to rebuild the wall and level the terrace for the lele, an altar they made from poles of lama wood. The men carried the lele up from a lower terrace where previous Makahiki offerings had been made. "Gotta keep moving up," Craig said as he secured the altar.

The men perspired in the heat of the sun, sweat dripping into their eyes as they hauled away the kiawe and tried to avoid the thorns, which scratched their bodies and poked through their rubber slippers. Most of the men finished the work as they had begun it—quietly and thoroughly. As they left, Hale Mua absorbed the afternoon sun falling full upon the stones, and the cool dry November air blew uninterrupted across the terraces.

After clearing the shrine and the pathway to it, most of the newcomers drifted off to rest at their various camps set up along the beach and among the trees at Hakioawa. Clearing kiawe and fighting erosion is hard work. The 'Ohana hopes the young people will become committed to protecting Kaho'olawe as a Hawaiian sanctuary for future generations. "The people that are committed are the people who come back," Craig said. "You gotta make an effort. If you have a job, if you have a family, you have to make time and get over there, and that's the commitment. It's hard. Sometimes it's real hard. It's life threatening just to get on the island. You gotta be willing to go through that and . . . you have to take care of yourself there and be responsible for people who are being on access at that time."

Before each Makahiki officially begins, the 'Ohana asks everyone on-island to participate in an ocean purification ceremony, called hi'uwai. The ceremony usually takes place before dawn, but the 'Ohana decided to hold the November 1989 hi'uwai after dinner Friday night. The purification began with the sounding of the pū, a conch-shell trumpet, in the darkness. It signals kapu, and silence must be maintained. By the light of the moon and stars, people silently crossed the sand and lined up on the beach to receive from a mo'o Lono a sip of water mixed with limu kalawai, a freshwater algae symbolizing forgiveness, and 'ōlena, a ginger root, for cleansing. Then, wearing swimsuits or nothing at all, they waded into the cold shorebreak and immersed in the sea.

The next time the pū sounded, ending the kapu, the people would celebrate by shouting the name of the god, "Lono-i-ka-Makahiki." Until then, many arms and legs tensed and curled up for warmth against the ocean chill, as people waited for their minds to relax and their bodies to float in rhythm with the sea. The water washes away ill and negative feelings, the sins and wrongs known as hewa. And with purification comes peace. It was a peace too brief for some; the pū sounded and people cheered "Lono-i-ka-Makahiki" as they splashed through the water, hugging one another. A bonfire was lit on the beach, and people huddled close to warm themselves and watch sparks float up to the stars. In the blazing firelight, their eyes glowed with happiness.

Purified by the ocean and warmed by the fire, everyone went to their camps to dress. They returned to the beach when the pū announced it was time for the procession to place offerings to Lono in the imu, an underground oven. Earlier, 'Ohana members had prepared ti-leaf bundles of fish, pig, 'awa, kalo, breadfruit, banana, coconut, and sweet potato—all sacred to the god. For this Makahiki, the 'Ohana had selected ten men and ten women to carry the offerings. After cooking the ti-leaf bundles in the imu Friday night, they would remove the offerings and rewrap them in fresh ti leaves before Saturday's predawn Makahiki ceremonies at the Hale o Papa heiau and Hale Mua, the fishing shrine. Then, after an arduous hike to the top of the island, the 'Ohana would present a third set of offerings to Lono at another lele at Pu'u Moa'ulaiki.

For the imu procession, the 'Ohana dressed the ten men and ten women in simple unbleached muslin. The men wore malo and stood in a column to the left; the women were in kīkepa on the right. Two spearsmen, also barefoot and in malo, separated them from the crowd. The mo'o Lono stood before the presenters, their bodies bare except for the muslin malo that covered their loins. One of them carried the image of Lono, which was raised high above the procession on a tall, wooden pole, its crosspiece festooned with kapa, feathers, and ferns. The men selected to blow pū preceded Lono's image, the sound of their conch shells trumpeting through the darkness, announcing the god's return to Kaho'olawe.

The procession moved slowly beneath the full moon. It crossed the beach and the dry streambed, moved up the slope through the main camp and beneath the kiawe grove, past Ka'ie'ie, the pā for hula, to the imu. Each presenter silently handed an uncooked ti-leaf bundle to a mo'o Lono, who passed it to another, then to another, until the last one placed it among the roasting stones in the imu. When all the offerings rested inside, the mo'o Lono covered the imu with burlap and dirt, and the cooking began.

The people returned to the main camp, where 'Ohana leaders reminded everyone to remove jewelry and watches before the early morning procession, and urged them to wear only a kīkepa or malo. The ceremonies would begin at the beach, and together the people would walk to Hale o Papa and then on to Hale Mua, the shrine on the other side of Hakioawa.

The sound of the pū echoed through the camp before sunrise, and soon the procession set out as it had the night before, in silence. The awakening birds sang, and a young man beat cadence on a pūniu, a small drum made from a fish-skin-wrapped coconut shell. People picked up the rhythm of the pūniu as they walked barefoot over the fine, dry soil of Hakioawa.

The procession reached the edge of Hale o Papa, and the spear bearers separated the ʻOhana from the ten men and ten women carrying the offerings. One by one, pairs of presenters—a man and a woman—approached the first moʻo Lono and handed him their bundles of food. As before, he passed the offerings to the next moʻo Lono in line, who passed them to another, and so on until the offerings reached the top level and were placed on the lele. The moʻo Lono had built this altar with lama, an endemic wood whose name suggests enlightenment. They had adorned the platform with long green ti leaves, a plant sacred to Lono; the leaves hung motionless in the still, morning air. Peering through the kiawe, the assembly watched as the offerings were passed upward from hand to hand. Then everyone intoned a chant they had practiced the day before:

> *E hō mai ka ʻike mai luna mai e*
> *I nā mea huna noʻeau o nā mele e*
> *E hō mai—e hō mai—e hō mai.*

The people repeated the verse, gaining confidence, giving the message strength as the sound of their voices rose into the trees. By the third and final recitation, all of Hakioawa rang with the petition, which asked for the wisdom and secrets of the deities.

The moʻo Lono completed the offering with another chant, "Kihapai o Lono," written for them by Nalani Kanakaole. This chant is translated only for those who attend the Makahiki rituals.

> *E ke akua*
> *E ke akua ao loa*
> *E ke akua ao poko*
> *E ke akua i ka wai ola a Kāne*
> *I ke kai ola o Kanaloa*
> *I ke ao ʻekaʻeka o Lono*

Kūkulu ka ipu ʻekaʻeka o Lono
Hō mai ka ipu lau makani o Lono
Ia hiki mai ka ua o Lono
Hoʻoulu ke ea
Hoʻoulu ke kupu
Hoʻoulu ka wai nape i ke kama o Hoʻohōkūkalani
Ia hiki mai ke ala a Makaliʻi i kahikina

Eia ka ʻawa i lani
ʻAwa i Ku, ʻawa i Hina
Eia ke kupu puaʻa
Eia ke kalo o Lono
Eia ke kupu ʻāweoweo
Eia ke kupu kinolau

Ko hānai ia ke akua mai ka lani nui a Wākea
Ko hānai ia nā akua o kona hanauna hope
Hoʻoulu mai ke kupu o ka ʻāina
A ua noa—a ua noa—a ua noa.

The assembled group stepped back to allow the Lono image, his priests, and those who had borne the god's offerings to lead the procession back down the path toward the streambed. In the predawn shadows, the rhythm of the pūniu guided them across Hakioawa to the fishing shrine.

As the sun rose above the horizon, the group repeated their ceremony. The moʻo Lono passed the second set of offerings from hand to hand up the terraces to the top, where they were placed on the altar. When the assembly and moʻo Lono finished chanting, the morning kapu ended, and the people cheered the god's name, "Lono-i-ka-Makahiki," over and over again, until it became a greeting as they embraced one another. The first two ceremonies had gone well; it was time to prepare for the final one.

Most people changed into hiking clothes and filled their day packs with water bottles and lunch, preparing for a three-hour trek in the sun. The ʻOhana intended to hold the final opening rite for Makahiki at noon on the island summit called Moaʻulaiki, which is nearly fifteen hundred feet above sea level. Navy officials had cleared ordnance from the path up the mountain, and although many people had walked it since, the military insisted that four Navy demolition experts follow the procession, "just in case." The Lono image preceded the group, a reminder that the journey is a religious procession, but laughter and conversations distracted the newcomers from the steep ascent. It was too steep for several elderly visitors, who returned to the main camp exhausted after ten minutes of hiking. Sun and exertion drained the rest. Sweaty and fatigued, many of them stopped periodically for water and to ease their straining hearts and lungs, weakened by life beyond Kahoʻolawe. The only shade came from Lono's pole; the earth along the way had been baked into a red shell as hard as concrete, too tough for any trees to grow in.

As the procession pushed on, past the few plants that manage to survive in pockets of soil here and there, the people participating for the first time received another message from Kahoʻolawe: You may come here, the island seemed to say, and you may help me, but remember as you gasp for breath and water that you must also care for yourself and one another; like the handful of plants that endure on this slope, only strong Hawaiians will survive the erosion taking place beyond my shores. Only the strongest will have the strength to make my slopes bloom again. "It's a life and death situation," Craig said. "If someone gets hurt, you can't just call up 911 and the ambulance is gonna pick you up. You're really dependent on everyone there to take care of each other."

The group reached the plateau, from which people expected to see Molokaʻi, Lānaʻi, Hawaiʻi, and Maui in the distance. But a volcanic fog, or vog, drifting north and west from an eruption in Puna on the Big Island had floated across the channel. It had draped a cloak around all the islands, even Molokini, a tiny islet only three miles away. Some people look for supernatural signs when they go to Kahoʻolawe: Is a rock going to float? Will the whales come in? Was the vog Pele's way of kissing the island with her breath to obscure Kahoʻolawe and protect the Makahiki from the outside world? Craig did not remember the vog afterward. "Some people overreact, but you know that's fine. . . . You get more in tune with what you're thinking about, what you're seeing [when you're on island]. . . . It's real simple things. It's just really going [with] what your gut feeling is. That's a real hard thing to do for some people. It's your logic against your feeling of what should you do. But if you go with your feeling always, you're always gonna be right up there."

Near the mountain summit the naval escort retreated, the presenters changed into their malo and kīkepa, and the procession reformed. Craig and a group of moʻo Lono advanced up Moaʻulaiki to prepare the lele for offerings. While waiting for the pū to sound and announce kapu for this, the final ascent, the young Hawaiians visiting the island for the first time joked and laughed among themselves. Then the pū signaled that Lono was returning to another place of honor, and the procession, silent except for the beat of the

One-third of Kahoʻolawe is hardpan, which must be cleared of old Navy bombs (many of them unexploded) before revegetation attempts can begin.

pūniu, moved up to the second highest point on Kahoʻolawe. The summit is home to a bell stone, which people rang in centuries past to call the island's inhabitants together. A heiau set in place generations ago still stands, and Hawaiians gather here, as their ancestors did, to learn celestial navigation.

From the top, newcomers in the group looked down for the first time onto another plateau below them, a site formerly used by the Navy for bombing practice. They saw twelve acres of hardpan, which the Navy is trying to restore to healthy grasslands, and a nearby forest; a stand of fifty-three thousand drought-resistant tamarisk trees has been planted nearby. The ʻOhana has built rain catchments to water indigenous plants on the hillsides and gulches below. Gradually, efforts to take advantage of the life-giving gift of rain and to minimize its destructive erosion are taking effect.

As the noon sun poured through a break in the vog and a breeze stirred the dry grass and cooled the group, the twenty men and women repeated their ritual offerings. During the few peaceful moments before the chants and cries of "Lono-i-ka-Makahiki," it seemed that the climb to Moaʻulaiki had enabled some of these people to truly feel and see the island as their ancestors had known it and, in doing so, had made them one with Kahoʻolawe.

Afterward, men and women who had journeyed to Kahoʻolawe before pointed out landmarks to the newcomers, calling the bays, coves, hills, beaches, and valleys by name: Puʻumōiwi—the hilltop where people in centuries past quarried stone for adzes; Kealaikahiki—where the ʻOhana holds ceremonies in January to mark the end of Makahiki; Honokoa cove, Honokanaea beach, Ahupū gulch; and the island's original name, Kohemalamalama o Kanaloa—the shining refuge of the ocean god Kanaloa. Young Hawaiians learned how these places got their names. They heard the history of the island. These people who had never before set foot on Kahoʻolawe added knowledge to their feelings and began to understand the life that existed before the island became a ranch, then a U.S. Naval Reservation.

After the procession returned to Hakioawa, the moʻo Lono and ʻOhana leaders sat on the beach to hold private discussions. Different people have different opinions about the ceremonies taking place on Kahoʻolawe. In the past, protocol has changed to meet the limitations of a specific access. Purification ceremonies in the ocean have taken place at varying times—before dawn, before midnight, or in the early evening. Some people want to see traditional ceremonial conduct more strictly enforced. Others want to see women in the role of moʻo Lono. As with all religions, the worshipers here have differing perceptions of their gods. One woman believes if she does not worship and feed her gods every day, they will consume her. Another believes that all gods, including Lono, lead to one supreme deity who watches over everyone, regardless of whether people use the name Akua, God, Allah, or Jehovah.

"For us who are in today's society, we don't have all the [ceremonial] answers," Craig said. "We cannot go to somebody and ask them what the correct way is. We have to research. We have to ask a lot of people. Everybody has a different opinion of what went on, and our ceremony is not exactly as it would be in our ancestors' days, because of the circumstances that we are under. . . . Half of the people are gonna agree with you and half might not. You can't worry about the roadblock, you just gotta keep moving forward."

The last night on the island, everyone sat in a circle and shared his or her impressions and feelings about the trip to Kahoʻolawe. Participation in this kūkākūkā is mandatory, and newcomers usually talk about their changed perception of the island. On this particular night, some ʻOhana members were angry. They had been videotaped during Friday night's purification ceremony and the dawn procession on Saturday. They believe videotaping violates the kapu. They want people to experience the island firsthand. Sitting in a room on another island and watching a tape, they say, dulls the Kahoʻolawe experience and the goals of the ʻOhana.

The ʻOhana had granted permission for a documentary to be produced about the island. The person with the video camera, a Hawaiian, said he felt compelled to tape the rituals so more people could see the Hawaiian religion being practiced. That, he said, was more important than the objections of a few people who regarded it as an invasion of privacy.

The ʻOhana later decided to exclude the controversial scenes from the documentary, but disagreement about the taping is just one of several conflicts that surface in discussions about religion. Some Hawaiians oppose worship of the old gods, and others—including orthodox traditionalists—are critical of certain aspects of the ʻOhana protocol that they consider too "Christian."

During the kūkākūkā, Chris Peters listened to the arguments and thought about disagreements and conflict being an inherent part of religion. Chris was one of three Native Americans visiting Kahoʻolawe from the Seventh Generation Fund. He graduated from Stanford University with a master's degree and made a commitment to help indigenous people foster their traditional customs. But he ran into opposition. The U.S. Supreme Court denied his tribe's petition to prevent the construction of a logging road through pristine forest where members of the tribe went for purification ceremonies. Tribal elders questioned Chris and other young people about their reasons for reviving ceremonies no one had practiced in fifty years. Why, some elders asked, did the young people want to go back to the Stone Age?

Chris said Christianity has not helped all Native Americans cope with the abuse they suffer nor with modern American life in general. Many people need the old rituals to revive and restore their spirits. Although more tribes are performing the old ceremonies, people attack the reconstructed rituals—as in Hawaiʻi with the ʻOhana—for not being true to the past. Chris believes they are true for those who participate in them. If the rituals are stopped, "You stop their believing. You kill them. . . . In some places, it is just a memory. It is past. It is no longer practiced. This," Chris said, gesturing toward the Hakioawa base camp where people laughed together as they prepared dinner, "is life."

A prominent Hawaiian scholar dismisses the ʻOhana as a minority of a minority—weekend Lono worshipers who put on malo and kīkepa and chant memorized lines because they think that is what their ancestors did. The scholar sees Hawaiians becoming true to their culture only when they conduct themselves with a Hawaiian consciousness every moment of their lives, particularly when they cope with the westernized Hawai'i that awaits them beyond Kaho'olawe. And that, he said, requires a commitment few people are capable of making.

Craig has formulated his own ideas about Hawaiian worship. "The island knows who [we] are, and the island knows what [our] intent is in being there, and when you talk on that island, it hears you and it knows what you're about . . . not just the island, the kūpuna who are there, your ancestors if they're there, your 'aumākua if they're there. They know it's not something you turn off and on. Nowadays, you say 'aloha 'āina,' it's a buzz word. . . . For me aloha 'āina is just caring for not only the land but for everything around you. It's the ocean. It's the trees. It's the air. It's everything, and treating it as if it's a living thing. It's not dirt. It's not a rock. . . . It's another form of life. It lives. It grows. It dies. Just like you. And if you take care of it, it's gonna take care of you. . . . I don't care what religion you are, you don't have to believe in what I believe. It's a different road . . . but the concept of aloha 'āina, or caring for the land, is a real simple thing. When you go back to your own home, that's the only thing you have to practice."

This is the philosophy that guides Craig as one of two 'Ohana representatives on the Kaho'olawe Island Reserve Commission. The commission is responsible for overseeing the ten-year cleanup project for Kaho'olawe, for which the federal government has appropriated $400 million. The Navy shares access control with the commission, and the state has agreed eventually to transfer responsibility for the island to a sovereign Hawaiian entity.

The responsibility is enormous. Although state law reserves Kaho'olawe for traditional Hawaiian uses and outlaws any commercial activity there, Maui fishermen are already challenging the law by fishing the island's waters and harvesting valuable 'opihi (limpets) from the shoreline. Other people see possibilities for profit in retreat centers and wilderness excursions. Preserving the island as a wahi pana (special place) and pu'uhonua (sanctuary) where traditional and contemporary Hawaiian culture can be practiced in safety is a challenge. "One thing I learned," Craig said. "Whatever you do, if you don't do it right, it will come back to [haunt] you."

Making repeated journeys to Kaho'olawe helped Craig decide to give up his job at the Ala Wai Golf Course. He now focuses full-time on custom silkscreening for others and designing Hawaiian images for clothing printed under his logo, The Hawaiian Force. "Everybody said, 'Don't quit; you'll regret it.' Especially my mom. For her, you work for the city, you put in your thirty [years], you got your benefits, you got everything. But for me, I thought about it a lot, and I prayed on it, and I'm just going with my feelings."

Whenever Craig Neff gets a chance, he goes to Kahoʻolawe to refocus. "When you go there, you're not influenced by the car going by, by the radio; you can really concentrate on what's around you," Craig said. "You just look around and you can actually see a stone that was put there by a Hawaiian, by your ancestors, many years ago, a long time back, and it hasn't been moved. It hasn't been destroyed. It hasn't been influenced or tainted by anything. . . . You can feel the mana around you in that area, what it was used for. If it was bad mana, you feel bad mana. If it was used for something good, you feel good mana.

"You can't learn being a Hawaiian from a book," repeated Craig. "A lot of people try, but being a Hawaiian is the way you think. . . . It's your values and what you do every day. . . . See, Hawaiians didn't have a real word for religion because it wasn't something that you turned off and you turned on, and you did on Sunday and you turned it off and you went home. It was a lifestyle. It's every day you live. It's everything you do. That's your religion. That's your life."

MOKULUA

Kau aku ka manaʻo iā Mokulua,

Set is the mind on Mokulua

Punihei i ke ʻala—ʻaʻalapapa.

Tangled in fragrance, reef fragrance.

Papaʻa kai ka pua lei ʻilima,

Salt-spray coated, the ʻilima lei flower,

Ka ʻilima lei ʻāpiki, kū kahakai.

The ʻilima, mischief lei, beach-growing.

Maikaʻi ka ʻiniki a ka ʻehu kai,

Pleasant is the sting of the sea spray,

Pā mai ka makani welo-kīhei.

Gusts this way the wind "streaming shawl."

Kiʻei, halo iho i ke kumupali,

Peeping, peering down into the cliff base,

Ka ʻuaʻu-kani, kani ka puō.

The ʻuaʻu-kani bird making muffled moans.

*Composed by
Kīhei deSilva*

Pu'ō wela, pā'ū-o-Hi'iaka,

Blooming in the heat blooming, skirt-of-Hi'iaka vine,

A walea i ka nehe o ka 'ili'ili.

Then taking ease in the rustling of beach pebbles.

Huli aku nānā iā pūnāwai,

Turn back to gaze at Pūnāwai,

Ālai 'ia e ke kua o ka nalu.

Obscured by the wave's back.

Hea aku mākou, ō mai 'oe,

We call, you respond,

Kau aku ka mana'o iā Mokulua,

Thought rests at Mokulua.

'O ka nalu o ke awa—a'e emi iho,

The wave of the channel will subside,

Ke aloha a ka ipo—mea pau'ole.

The love of the sweetheart—a thing never ending.

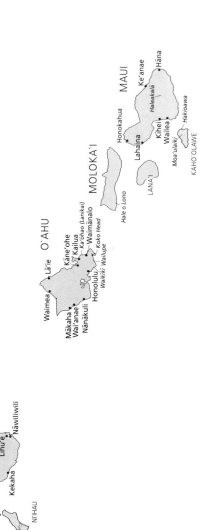
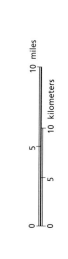
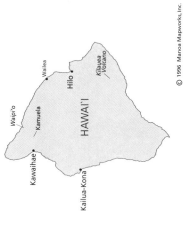

THE ISLANDS OF HAWAI'I

© 1996 Manoa Mapworks, Inc.

KAUA'I

Nāpali · Wai'oli · Hanalei · Nāwiliwili · Līhu'e · Kekaha

NI'IHAU

O'AHU

Waimea · Lā'ie · Kāne'ohe · Kailua · Ka'ōhao (Lanikai) · Waimānalo · Koko Head · Mākaha · Wai'anae · Nānākuli · Honolulu · Waikīkī · Wailupe

MOLOKA'I

Hale o Lono

LANA'I

MAUI

Honokahua · Ke'anae · Hāna · Lahaina · Haleakalā · Hakioawa · Kīhei · Wailea · Moa'ula iki

KAHO'OLAWE

HAWAI'I

Kawaihae · Waipi'o · Kamuela · Wailea · Hilo · Kīlauea Volcano · Kailua-Kona

0 ——— 5 ——— 10 miles

0 ——— 5 ——— 10 kilometers

N
W · E
S

Glossary

Sources include Mary Kawena Pukui and Samuel H. Elbert's *Hawaiian Dictionary* (1986) and *Place Names of Hawaii,* by Mary Kawena Pukui, Samuel H. Elbert, and Esther T. Mookini (1981). Most Hawaiian words have more than one meaning; the definitions given here correspond to the meanings in this book.

ahupua'a Land division, usually extending from the uplands to the sea, so-called because the boundary was marked by a heap (ahu) of stones surmounted by an image of a pig (pua'a).

'āina Land, earth.

'ākia Endemic shrub and tree used for making kapa. Also used as a narcotic for poisoning, and thus catching, fish.

akua God, goddess.

ali'i Chief, chiefess, ruler.

aloha Love, affection, compassion, mercy, pity, kindness, charity; greeting, salutation, regards.

'auana The "modern" style of hula, usually accompanied by Western musical instruments.

'aumākua Family or personal gods; deified ancestors.

'awa Kava, a plant whose root is the source of a narcotic drink.

hālau hula Hula school.

haole White person; formerly, any foreigner.

hapa haole Part white and part Hawaiian, as an individual or phenomenon.

hau A type of tree.

haumana Apprentice.

Hawai'i The island and the group of islands. Meaning unknown.

hewa Wrong, offense.

hinahina A type of plant.

hi'uwai Ritual water purification ceremony.

hō'ike Display, show, exhibit.

hōlua Sled, especially the ancient sled used on grassy slopes.

ho'okupu Ceremonial tribute, gift.

ho'olaule'a Celebration.

ho'omana Religion.

ho'oponopono To correct. The old Hawaiian method of clearing a sick person's mind by means of family discussion, examination, and prayer.

hukilau To fish with a seine. Literally, pull ropes (lau).

hula Native Hawaiian dance.

huli Taro top, as used for planting.

i'a Fish.

'iako Outrigger canoe boom.

'ili'ili Pebble or small stone, as used in hula.

'ilima Small to large native shrub bearing yellow, orange, greenish or dull-red flowers. Regarded as the flower of O'ahu.

imu Underground oven.

'iolani Royal hawk, a symbol of royalty because of its flight high in the heavens.

ipu Gourd; when used as a drum to accompany hula, it consists of a single gourd or two large gourds of unequal size joined together.

'iwa A type of bird.

kahakō Macron.

Kahiki Ancestral home for Polynesians; Tahiti.

kahiko The pre-contact style of hula, usually performed to a chant; sometimes accompanied by traditional percussive implements.

kahu Pastor of a church.

kahuna Expert in any profession; priest.

kāko'o To uphold, support, assist, as with a student or apprentice.

kalo Taro, a plant cultivated in Hawai'i since ancient times for food.

kama'āina Hawai'i born.

kamani A type of tree.

kānaka maoli Native Hawaiian person. This reference is preferred by those who consider the word Hawaiian a foreign label.

kāne Male, husband, man.

kaona Hidden meaning, as in Hawaiian poetry; concealed reference, as to a person, place, or thing.

kapa Tapa, bark cloth.

kapu Taboo, prohibition.

kāpulu Careless, slovenly, unclean, gross, slipshod.

kauila A type of tree.

keiki Child.

kī Ti plant.

kiawe A type of tree.

kīhei Cape, shawl.

kīkepa Kapa or sarong worn by women.

kō Sugarcane plant.

koa Largest of the native Hawaiian forest trees.

koali Morning-glory plant.

Kona Leeward; also, a district on the Big Island of Hawai'i.

ko'oko'olau A type of herb.

kūkākūkā Discussion.

kukui Candlenut tree, a large tree bearing nuts used medicinally and for making dyes.

kuleana province

kumu hula Hula teacher.

kupuna Grandparent; ancestor; relative of the grandparent's generation.

lāʻau Tree, plant; medicine.

lāʻau kāhea A type of faith healing for broken or crushed bones.

lāʻau lapaʻau Medicine.

lama Endemic hardwood used in medicine and placed on altars because its name suggests enlightenment.

lānai Porch, veranda, terrace.

lanakila Victory, triumph.

lapaʻau Medical practice; to treat with medicine.

lau hala Pandanus leaf used in plaiting.

lauaʻe A type of fragrant fern.

laukahi Broad-leafed plantain; used externally to ripen and heal boils and taken internally for diabetes and other ailments.

lehua Flower of the ʻōhiʻa tree. Also, a variety of kalo.

lehua mamo A form of ʻōhiʻa lehua tree with yellow flowers.

lei Garland, wreath; necklace of flowers, leaves, shells, ivory, feathers, or paper.

lele Altar or stand for offerings.

lilikoʻi A type of plant, and its fruit.

limu Seaweed; a general name for all kinds of plants living underwater.

limu kala Common long, brown seaweed.

loʻi kalo Irrigated terrace for growing kalo.

lōkahi Unity, accord, harmony.

lole wāwae Trousers, pants.

lomi To massage, rub.

lūʻau Hawaiian feast named for the taro tops served at one.

lūʻau leaf Taro leaf used in wrapping food to be cooked for a lūʻau.

māhele Portion, section. In a land division in 1848 known as the Great Māhele, Kamehameha III divided all Hawaiian lands among the king, chiefs, and commoners.

maile A native twining shrub with shiny, fragrant leaves, used for decoration and lei. Laka, goddess of the hula, was invoked as the goddess of maile, which was one of five standard plants used on her altar.

makaloa Sedge valued for making fine Niʻihau-style mats.

malo Loincloth worn by males.

māmaki Small native tree used in making kapa.

mamo The Hawaiian honeycreeper, an extinct bird; also, descendant.

mana Supernatural or divine power.

mele Song, chant of any kind, poem.

mokihana A native tree found only on Kaua'i, which produces small, anise-scented fruits that are strung into lei.

monkeypod A type of tree.

mo'o Lono Priests of Lono, devoted to the worship of the god Lono.

mu'umu'u A woman's loose gown.

noni Indian mulberry plant.

'ohana Family or association.

'ōhi'a lehua The 'ōhia tree and its flower.

'okina Glottal stop.

'ōlelo no'eau Wise saying, proverb.

'ōlelo Hawai'i The Hawaiian language.

'ōlena A kind of ginger widely used as a spice and dye in foods, to color cloth and kapa, and for medicinal purposes.

oli Chant.

'onaulu loa A wave of great length and endurance.

'opihi Limpet.

pā hula Place reserved for hula.

pa'a Firm, solid, solidified.

pahu Drum.

palapalai A native fern.

papa'a Cook Island Maori word for Caucasian.

paua Clam.

pili A type of grass used for thatching.

pilikia Trouble of any kind, great or small.

poi A food that was once the staple of the Hawaiian diet; made from cooked kalo corms, pounded and thinned with water.

pono Moral qualities of goodness and righteousness; well-being, prosperity.

pōpolo A type of herb.

pū Large triton conch shell used as a horn or trumpet.

pū'ili Bamboo rattles, as used for dancing.

pulapula Seedlings, sprouts.

pule Prayer.

pūne'e Movable couch.

pūniu Small knee drum made from a coconut shell.

pu'u Hill.

pu'uhonua Place of sanctuary, refuge.

tapa Kapa, bark cloth.

taro See kalo.

ti Kī, a woody plant. The leaves are put to many uses by Hawaiians, as for food wrappers and hula skirts.

Tumu Nu Cook Island Maori phrase that literally means trunk of the coconut tree, which is used to prepare and hold swipe. Also refers to the place where the swipe is drunk and to the group of men who drink it while singing or discussing village matters.

tūtū Grandparent.

'uhaloa A type of plant.

'ukulele Nickname given to musical instrument brought to Hawai'i by the Portuguese in 1879. Literally, leaping flea.

'ulī'ulī Gourd rattle, as used in hula.

'ulu Breadfruit tree.

ulua A type of fish.

'ūniki Graduation exercises, as for hula.

wa'a Canoe.

wahi pana Legendary or special place.

wahine Woman, lady, wife.

wana Sea urchin.

wauke Paper mulberry tree; its bark is used to make kapa.

Notes on Mele and Oli

He Mele Inoa no Aikanaka   II

Better known today as "Auʻa ʻIa," this chant may have been written two years after the arrival of Captain James Cook in 1778. Although several versions of it exist, the one reprinted here comes from the program for King Kalākaua's birthday celebration in 1886. His sister Liliʻuokalani, who reigned as queen of the Hawaiian Islands from 1891 until she was deposed in 1893, translated the chant about 1895. Liliʻuokalani was a prolific song writer and translator. She credited composition of the chant to historian and prophet Keaulumoku for the birth of Aikanaka, her grandfather. According to historian Abraham Fornander, Aikanaka was born in 1780. Three versions of "Auʻa ʻIa" can be heard on Smithsonian Folkways 1989 album *Hawaiian Drum Dance Chants: Sounds of Power in Time.*

Kumulipo   XII

Hawaiian scholar Rubellite Kawena Kinney Johnson traces "Kumulipo" to about 1700, when it was composed for the chief Ka ʻIi Mamao. The chant, in 2,102 lines, describes the genealogy of the Hawaiian people. Only the first part, conveying the beginnings of the universe, is reprinted here from Professor Johnson's *Kumulipo: The Hawaiian Hymn of Creation.* Professor Johnson is a direct descendent of the first Kamehameha. She taught Hawaiian language at the University of Hawaiʻi at Mānoa and is the author of several books. Professor Johnson is regarded as the foremost scholar on ancient Hawaiian cosmology.

Kāhea o Keale   17

The mele "Kāhea o Keale" was written by Louis Robert Kauakahi, a founding member of the musical group now called Mākaha Sons. The song can be heard on two of their albums, *Keala* (1978) and *Kahea o Keale* (1978), both produced by Poki Records.

Kāwika   38

The author of "Kāwika" is unknown, but he or she wrote the mele inoa (name song) on the occasion of King Kalākaua's return to Hawaiʻi from his 1881 world tour. The mele describes the places he visited, and his lineage. The late Mary Kawena Pukui, noted scholar of the native Hawaiian culture, translated the mele.

Mele Noi Naʻauao   64

Kalena Silva is a Hawaiian-language and chant professor at the University of Hawaiʻi at Hilo. He wrote "Mele Noi Naʻauao" for children enrolled in the state Department of Education's Hawaiian-language immersion program. According to Kalena, many references to light are in his poem because light in Hawaiian culture symbolizes wisdom, knowledge, and enlightenment. In addition to judging chant and hula competitions, Kalena is co-author of *The Hawaiian Language: Its Spelling and Pronunciation.*

Kihapai o Lono 210

Nalani Kanakaole, author of "Kihapai o Lono," shares kumu hula responsibilities for Hālau o Kekuhi, a hula school based on the Big Island.

Mokulua 218

Kīhei deSilva composed "Mokulua" in September 1988. It describes two islands about a mile off Ka'ōhao Beach near Kailua, O'ahu. "Mokulua" gives life to the old place names of an area better known as Lanikai. Kawai Cockett performs the song on his album *'O Ka'ōhao Ku'u 'Āina Nani* (1993). Kīhei assists his wife, Māpuana deSilva, in managing their hālau hula, Hālau Mōhala 'Ilima.

E Mau ana ka Ha'aheo 235

S. Haunani Apoliona is president and chief executive officer of Alu Like, a nonprofit, statewide agency that administers $9 million annually "to assist Hawaiian natives in their efforts to achieve social and economic excellence." Haunani is an award-winning musician and songwriter. She composed "E Mau ana ka Ha'aheo" for a 1991 album by the same name, which she recorded with the group Olomana.

Suggested Reading

Readers interested in finding more information about the topics and issues addressed in this book are encouraged to consult the following sources. Many of them provided valuable information used in the preparation of this book.

Ambrose, Greg. *Surfer's Guide to Hawaii*. Honolulu: Bess Press, 1991.

Barrère, Dorothy B., Mary Kawena Pukui, and Marion Kelly. *Hula: Historical Perspectives*. Pacific Anthropological Records 30. Honolulu: Bernice P. Bishop Museum, Department of Anthropology, 1980.

Beckwith, Martha. *Hawaiian Mythology*. Honolulu: University Press of Hawaii, 1970.

Begley, Bryan W. *Taro in Hawaii*. Honolulu: Oriental Publishing, 1979.

Blaisdell, Kekuni. "Historical and Cultural Aspects of Native Hawaiian Health," *Social Process in Hawaii* 32 (1989): 1–21 (special issue, *The Health of Native Hawaiians: A Selective Report on Health Status and Health Care in the 1980s*).

Charlot, John. *Chanting the Universe: Hawaiian Religious Culture*. Hong Kong: Emphasis International, 1983.

Daws, Gavan. *Shoal of Time: A History of the Hawaiian Islands*. New York: Macmillan, 1968.

Hammond, Joyce D. *Tīfaifai and Quilts of Polynesia*. Honolulu: University of Hawaii Press, 1986.

Handy, E. S. Craighill, and Elizabeth Green Handy (with Mary Kawena Pukui, collaborator). *Native Planters in Old Hawaii: Their Life, Lore, and Environment*. Bulletin 233. Honolulu: Bishop Museum Press, 1972.

Holmes, Tommy. *The Hawaiian Canoe*. Hanalei, Hawai'i: Editions Limited, 1981.

Holt, John Dominis. *On Being Hawaiian*. Honolulu: Star-Bulletin Printing, 1964.

Hopkins, Jerry. *The Hula*. Hong Kong: Apa Productions, 1982.

Johnson, Rubellite Kawena. *Kumulipo: Hawaiian Hymn of Creation*. Vol. 1. Honolulu: Topgallant Publishing, 1981.

Kaho'olawe Island: Restoring a Cultural Treasure. Final Report of the Kaho'olawe Island Conveyance Commission to the Congress of the United States. March 31, 1993. Washington, D.C.

Kamakau, Samuel Manaiakalani. *Ka Po'e Kahiko: The People of Old*. Special Publication 51. Honolulu: Bishop Museum Press, 1964.

Kame'eleihiwa, Lilikalā. *Native Land and Foreign Desires: Ko Hawai'i 'Āina a me Nā Koi Pu'umake a ka Po'e Haole*. Honolulu: Bishop Museum Press, 1992.

Kanahele, George S., ed. *Hawaiian Music and Musicians*. Honolulu: University Press of Hawaii, 1979.

Kautai, Ngatupuna, et al. *Atiu: An Island Community*. Suva, Fiji: Institute of Pacific Studies of the University of the South Pacific, in association with the Cook Islands Ministry of Education and the Atiu Island Trust, 1984.

Kirch, Patrick Vinton. *Feathered Gods and Fishhooks: An Introduction to Hawaiian Archaeology and Prehistory.* Honolulu: University of Hawaii Press, 1985.

Lawhead, Terry, ed. *Year of the Hawaiian.* Alto, N.M.: C. F. Boone Publishing, 1987.

Liliuokalani. *Hawaii's Story by Hawaii's Queen, Liliuokalani.* Rutland, Vt.: Charles E. Tuttle, 1964.

Lueras, Leonard. *Surfing: The Ultimate Pleasure.* Hong Kong: Emphasis International, 1984.

MacKenzie, Melody Kapilialoha, ed. *Native Hawaiian Rights Handbook.* Honolulu: Native Hawaiian Legal Corporation and the Office of Hawaiian Affairs, 1991.

Malo, David. *Hawaiian Antiquities.* 2nd ed. Honolulu: Bishop Museum Press, 1971.

Mitchell, Donald D. Kilolani. *Resource Units in Hawaiian Culture.* Honolulu: The Kamehameha Schools Press, 1982.

Morales, Rodney, ed. *Ho'iho'i Hou: A Tribute to George Helm and Kimo Mitchell.* Honolulu: Bamboo Ridge Press, 1984.

Pukui, Mary Kawena. *'Ōlelo No'eau.* Special Publication 71. Honolulu: Bishop Museum Press, 1983.

Pukui, Mary Kawena, E. W. Haertig, and Catherine A. Lee. *Nānā I Ke Kumu (Look to the Source).* Vol. 1 and 2. Honolulu: Hui Hānai, The Queen Lili'uokalani Children's Center, 1972 and 1979.

Reeve, Rowland B. ed., *Kaho'olawe, Nā Leo o Kanaloa.* Honolulu: 'Ai Pōhaku Press, 1995.

Report on the Culture, Needs and Concerns of Native Hawaiians, Pursuant to Public Law 96–565, Title III. Vol. 1. Prepared by Native Hawaiians Study Commission. Washington, D.C.: U.S. Department of the Interior, June 23, 1983.

Sahlins, Marshall. *Historical Metaphors and Mythical Realities: Structure in the Early History of the Sandwich Islands Kingdom.* Ann Arbor: University of Michigan Press, 1981.

Shintani, Terry, and Claire Hughes, eds. *The Wai'anae Book of Hawaiian Health.* Wai'anae, Hawai'i: The Waianae Coast Comprehensive Health Center, 1991.

Silva, Wendell, and Alan Suemori, eds. Shuzo Uemoto, photographer. *Nānā I Na Loea Hula: Look to the Hula Resources.* Honolulu: Kalihi-Palama Culture and Arts Society, 1984.

Titcomb, Margaret. *The Ancient Hawaiians: How They Clothed Themselves.* Honolulu: Hogarth Press, 1983.

Valeri, Valerio. *Kingship and Sacrifice: Ritual and Society in Ancient Hawaii.* Chicago: University of Chicago Press, 1985.

Wai'anae Coast Culture and Arts Society. *Ka Po'e Kahiko o Wai'anae.* Honolulu: Wai'anae Coast Culture and Arts Society and Topgallant Publishing, 1986.

Acknowledgments

Many people helped make this book possible. They include my late father and my mother, Dickson J. Hartwell and Patricia L. Hartwell, who by their example taught their four sons how to work hard and brought us to Hawai'i in 1970. Rick Schutte and Arthur Perkins introduced me to Hawaiian people and to places that were unfamiliar to me even after ten years in the Islands.

Many Hawaiians, among them Skippy Kamakawiwo'ole, Aloha Dalire, and Kekuni Blaisdell, encouraged me to learn and share more about the Hawaiian people, and my editors at *The Honolulu Advertiser,* Gerry Keir and Thomas J. Brislin, allowed me to tell those stories.

Penn Kimball and William Merwin urged me leave my job at the newspaper in order to pursue research for this book, and the late Peter Keolahou Perkins introduced me to Abigail Kinoike Kekaulike Kawānanakoa, whose Kawānanakoa Foundation helped support me and my family during the first two years of research and writing. The Estate of James Campbell supplied assistance for Anne Landgraf's photography. Lindsey N. Pollock and Hawaiian Airlines provided air transportation for our travels, and Ellen Blomquist, with funding from the Office of Hawaiian Affairs, shared the money necessary to publish Anne's photographs.

Without Stewart Fern, my mother, and my in-laws, Dudley and Carol Seto, work on *Nā Mamo* would have stopped more than once—they, along with Intercontinental Medical Services, Inc., made it possible for me to feed my family and continue writing. Gary Gill gave me a job at City Hall when I needed one and repeatedly allowed me time off to complete the book.

Dave Kemble from the Bishop Museum Exhibits Department believed in Anne Landgraf's photographs and helped obtain grants from the State Foundation on Culture and the Arts and the University of Hawai'i Committee for the Preservation and Study of Hawaiian Language, Art, and Culture for an exhibition of her photographs. Ruth Horie checked the Hawaiian orthography for accuracy. (I apologize for any missing kahakō or 'okina. We did not add diacritical marks to material that did not originally include them, and some families do not use them.) Joy Kitamori served as final proofreader. Editors Susan Essoyan, Curt Sanburn, and Jane Taylor taught me that writing takes time and lots and lots of work. From the beginning, in 1988, Nelson Foster, Maile Meyer, and Barbara Pope of 'Ai Pōhaku Press judged this project worthwhile, and their patience, guidance, and insistence on high quality sustained me.

Anne Kapulani Landgraf spent more than two years making the photographs for this book. She also shared insights that helped me see life from a Hawaiian perspective. I am grateful for her thoughtfulness, professionalism, and the eyes that make this book come alive.

Eight years is a long time to pursue a dream. When I became lost amid the words and deadlines, it was my wife, Cindy, and children, Chloe and Thomas, who reminded me that family and love should always come first. My special thanks to them.

ACKNOWLEDGMENTS

In addition to the people who allowed me to share their stories, mele, and chants, hundreds of other people spoke with me and helped me learn about Hawaiian culture. Besides those named in the text, the following people and organizations supported my efforts in one way or another. The appearance of anyone's name in this book should not be construed as that person's endorsement for the book or its contents.

Keahi Allen; Hannie Anderson; Clyde Aikau; James Bartels; Haunani Bernardino; Warren Bolster; Elizabeth Buck; Mitsue Cook Carlson; John Charlot; Ululani Chock; Malcolm Naea Chun; Theresia C. Cortez; Mark Cunningham; Sara Curlee; Lani Custino; Lynn Davis; Marsha Erickson; Keoni Fairbanks; Hailama Farden; Arma Fonseca; Heather Giugni; Hamilton Library Pacific Collection, University of Hawai'i at Mānoa; Hawai'i Newspaper Agency Library; Hawai'i and Pacific Room, Hawai'i State Library; Denny Hennings; Ha'alilio Heyer; Carol Hogan, Ocean Promotions; Tommy Holmes; Renée Heyum; Jay Junker; Sissy Kaio; Eddie and Myrna Kamae; Saichi Kawahara and the Kapaliko Hawaiian Band; Beatrice Kaya; Robert and Denise Koenig; Koke'e Natural History Museum; Mary Kovich; Ehulani Lum; Kepa Maly; Iosefa Maiava; Elizabeth Pa Martin; Davianna McGregor; Kalani Meinecke; Paula Dunaway Merwin; Elmer Miller; Frank and Iwalani Minton; Nalani Minton; Bennet Moffat; Linda Paik Moriarty; Barry Morrison; Boone and Tamara Wong Morrison; Momi Naughton; Nathan Napoka; Rena Kalehua Nelson; Puakea Nogelmeier; Keone Nunes; Katherine Perkins; Ilima Piianaia; Rona Rodenhurst; Ronn Ronck; O. K. Stender; John and Betty Stickney; Velina Sugiyama; Ed Tanji; Jan TenBruggencate; Earl Pa Mai Tenn; Dorothy S. Thompson; Shirley Tom, Quadrant Components; Douglas and Kellie Tolentino; Brian Tottori; JoAnn Tsark; Ab Valencia; Joana and Male Varawa; Analika Nahulu; Keoni Wagner; Iris Wiley; Pila Wilson; Norma Wong; Wong Audio-Visual Center, Sinclair Library, University of Hawai'i at Mānoa; Bob Worthington; Alan Yoshioka; and Wally Zimmerman, KITV.

Permissions

Grateful acknowledgment is made to the following for permission to use material copyrighted or controlled by them:

"Auʻa ʻIa" ("He Mele Inoa no Aikanaka") by Keaulumoku and translated by Liliʻuokalani, in liner notes to *Hawaiian Drum Dance Chants: Sounds of Power in Time.* Copyright © 1989 by Smithsonian Folkways Records. Reprinted by permission of the Queen Liliʻuokalani Children's Trust and the publisher.

"E Kū, e Nānā i nā Kai ʻĒ" (Arise and Look to the Faraway Seas) by K. Kalani Akana in *Pleiades, The Journal of the University of Hawaiʻi Community Colleges.* Copyright © 1988 by University of Hawaiʻi. Reprinted by permission of the author and the publisher.

"E Mau ana ka Haʻaheo" by S. Haunani Apoliona. Copyright © 1991 by S. Haunani Apoliona. Printed by permission of the author.

"Haʻaheo o Lapakahi" by Kupuna Katherine Kamalukukui Maunakea in *Ka Wai Ola o OHA,* January 1994. Reprinted by permission of the author and the newspaper. All rights reserved.

"Hāna by the Sea" by Aima Aluli McManus, in liner notes to *Nā Lei Hulu Makua, Nā Wahine Hawaiʻi.* Reprinted by permission of the author. All rights reserved.

"Ka Nalu" by Larry Lindsey Kimura in *Surfing, The Ultimate Pleasure.* Copyright © 1984 by Emphasis International Ltd. Reprinted by permission of the author and the publisher.

"Kahea o Keale" by Louis Robert Kauakahi. ℗ 1977, 1978 by Poki Records of Honolulu. Printed by permission of the author and Poki Records. All rights reserved.

"Kamaki Kanahele" by Kamaki Kanahele in *Nānā I Na Loea Hula (Look to the Hula Resources).* Copyright © 1984 by Kalihi-Palama Culture and Arts Society, Inc., of Honolulu. Reprinted by permission of the publisher.

"Kanaʻe o ka Pua" by Tony K. Conjugacion. Copyright © and ℗ 1984 by CEE Music. Printed by permission of the author and CEE Music.

"Ke Alaula" liner notes by Louis Robert Kauakahi. Copyright © and ℗ 1994 by Tropical Music, Inc. Reprinted by permission of the author and Tropical Music, Inc. All rights reserved.

"Keauhou" (Song of Renewal) by Mahealani Kamauu. "Aloha ʻĀina: The Native Hawaiian Issue" in *Hawaiʻi Review.* Copyright © 1989 by Board of Publications, University of Hawaiʻi at Mānoa. Reprinted by permission of the author and the publisher.

E MAU ANA KA HA'AHEO

[HUI]
E mau ana ka ha'aheo, ka ha'aheo o ka nohona
E ola kamaēhu o ka lāhui, o ka lāhui Hawai'i
E mau ana ka ha'aheo, ka ha'aheo o ka nohona
Ka lāhui pono'ī o nā kai, o nā kai 'ewalu.

Me nā mea 'oi loa mai nā wā mamua, o holomua kākou i keia au
Ua hiki mai ka wana'ao no ka ho'ōla a me ka ho'āla hou.

[HUI]
E mau ana ka ha'aheo, ka ha'aheo o ka nohona
E ola kamaēhu o ka lāhui, o ka lāhui Hawai'i
E mau ana ka ha'aheo, ka ha'aheo o ka nohona
Ka lāhui pono'ī o nā kai, o nā kai 'ewalu.

Composed by
S. Haunani Apoliona

E hō'ā kākou i ka lama kūpono no nā hulu Hawai'i
E kūkulu a'e kākou no ke ea o ka 'āina me ke aloha a me ke ahonui.

[HUI]
E mau ana ka ha'aheo, ka ha'aheo o ka nohona
E ola kamaēhu o ka lāhui, o ka lāhui Hawai'i
E mau ana ka ha'aheo, ka ha'aheo o ka nohona
Ka lāhui pono'ī o nā kai, o nā kai 'ewalu.

The Pride Endures

[CHORUS]
   The pride endures, the pride in our lifestyle and values.
   The lifestyle that is firm in resolution and fixed in purpose.
   The pride endures, the pride in our lifestyle and values.
   The lifestyle that has been nurtured by Hawaiians of all the islands.

Let us move forward to the future carrying with us the best from the past.
The time has arrived for the revitalizing and reawakening of our community.

[CHORUS]
   The pride endures, the pride in our lifestyle and values.
   The lifestyle that is firm in resolution and fixed in purpose.
   The pride endures, the pride in our lifestyle and values.
   The lifestyle that has been nurtured by Hawaiians of all the islands.

Let us set aglow the light of justice and positive improvement for
      all our Hawaiians.
Let us build the forward momentum for the good of our land and
      people moving as one in the spirit of love and patience.

[CHORUS]
   The pride endures, the pride in our lifestyle and values.
   The lifestyle that is firm in resolution and fixed in purpose.
   The pride endures, the pride in our lifestyle and values.
   The lifestyle that has been nurtured by Hawaiians of all the islands.